DIGITAL EVIDENCE
AND COMPUTER
CRIME

DIGITAL EVIDENCE AND COMPUTER CRIME

FORENSIC SCIENCE, COMPUTERS AND THE INTERNET

Eoghan Casey

ACADEMIC PRESS

San Diego   San Francisco   New York   Boston
London   Sydney   Tokyo

ACADEMIC PRESS
Harcourt Place,
32 Jamestown Road,
LONDON NW1 7BY
http://www.hbuk.co.uk/ap/

ACADEMIC PRESS
A Harcourt Science and Technology Company
525 B Street, Suite 1900, San Diego,
California 92101–4495, USA
http://www.apnet.com

ISBN 0–12–162885–X
CD 0–12–162886–8

A catalogue record for this book is available from the British Library

Typeset by Selwood Systems Typesetting, Bath
Printed in Great Britain by Cambridge University Press, Cambridge

00 01 02 03 04 05 CUP 9 8 7 6 5 4 3 2 1

CONTENTS

From our present vantage point, perched at the end of a century filled with innovation and invention, it is clear to most of us that one of that century's most significant and influential inventions was the computer. Surprisingly, that idea might have seemed absurd even as recently as 20 years ago.

The story of computers and computing has been one of evolution of purpose. The stories of other major inventions of this century, such as the automobile, the telephone, the electric light, or the elevator have been tales of success at achieving intended purposes. The automobile transports us more quickly and efficiently than the horse and buggy; the telephone permits us easier, faster communication; the electric light does just that; the elevator facilitated the vertical development of cities. Except for various improvements in efficiency these inventions have remained largely unchanged in purpose and use since their creation. The primary role of today's computers, however, is certainly not what its early inventors envisioned. It has metamorphosed from a giant calculating machine like the thirty-ton ENIAC, to a stand-alone personal tool for performing assorted routine tasks like word-processing and bookkeeping, to today's networked device permitting virtually instantaneous and global personal, corporate, and governmental interaction. The calculating machine has become the portal to a new world of human activity, a world different in so many essential ways from our everyday world that we have dubbed this new place 'cyberspace.'

Yet, cyberspace is, in the end, a place populated by humans, or perhaps more correctly, by human minds, since it is our intellects that reside and meet one another there. It should come as no surprise, then, that many of the problems of the 'real' world carry over into this new realm. Crime is one of them.

The Internet (a term which once referred to a specific set of networked computers but which has now increasingly come to mean the global network of computers) is growing so quickly that it is impossible to know at any given moment the actual number of computers connected to it. It is even less possible to determine the number of people with access to it. But use of the

Internet is clearly growing very, very quickly, and so is computer crime and the need to control it.

Some cyberspace crimes, such as unauthorized access to a computer, are new and specific to the online world. Others, such as fraud or theft of valuables, are familiar from the real world. In either case, the disembodied, often anonymous nature of activity in cyberspace creates problems in enforcing laws. Evidence, of course, is the foundation for identifying, catching, and prosecuting criminals. Forensic Science has developed well-understood techniques for dealing with real-world evidence, but how can these methods be applied in cyberspace? What must investigators do to collect, preserve, and authenticate digital evidence? How can legal admissibility of digital evidence be assured? How can digital evidence be used to reconstruct crimes and generate leads?

Many, perhaps most, of the police, lawyers, programmers or systems administrators, and forensic scientists involved in the investigation or prosecution of computer-related crimes do not know the answer to these questions. This book will tell them. It should, of course, be equally interesting to lawyers with the task of defending alleged computer criminals, since it provides a detailed guide to possible procedural weaknesses in the prosecution's evidence.

In this book, Eoghan Casey has provided a much needed 'nuts and bolts' guide to dealing with digital evidence, with step-by-step instructions for dealing with an assortment of evidentiary problems. However, and to my mind at least as importantly, Casey illustrates how these details fit within the broader contexts of forensic science, crime, and society in general, never omitting mention of the potential downsides of detection and detectability. So, for example, the difficult balancing act between a secure computing environment and individual privacy is made clear.

Nor does Casey ever lose sight of the counter-intuitive importance of the human element in a world of intangible activity, and of the ways in which the nature of digital evidence and activity in cyberspace may alter or augment the rules of real-world behavioral analysis. For example, in any crime, the victim, and the choice of that victim, can provide important clues regarding the identity or a profile of the criminal. Investigators therefore devote considerable energy to analyzing a victim's habits and activities. In cases of cyberstalking or computer harassment, the need to examine digital evidence related to the victim's activities is clear. But Casey reminds us here that digital evidence can play an important role in assessing a victim's behavioral pattern when investigating real-world crime as well, particularly if the victim is a frequent visitor to cyberspace. The unaware investigator may overlook the fact that people's cyberspace personalities are sometimes extraordinarily different than those presented to the real world. The anonymity possible in cyberspace provides a tempting opportunity to assume other identities, to play out other lives and fantasies. When these alter egos are of a particular 'high-risk' nature and spill over into the real world, the consequences can be tragic, as is illustrated by one case study presented here.

The investigation of computer crime requires a team effort of police, forensic scientists, lawyers, and programmers or systems administrators. No single individual is likely to have the requisite skill sets. Police can generally be expected to know how to oversee an investigation, but may not know much about computers and computing and thus not know what evidence to look for. Programmers and systems administrators may know a great deal about computers, networks, and how they work, but nothing about legal procedural requirements regarding the collection and preservation of evidence. Forensic scientists may know how to deal with evidence but, like the police, may not know what to look for when dealing with digital evidence or how to apply real-world forensic science methods to it. Lawyers may know about the law of evidence but not much else. Together, however, this team can know how to conduct an investigation of a computer crime, what evidence to look for, how to find it, and how to treat it so as to preserve its admissibility once it is found.

The danger in dealing with digital evidence is that the absence or ignorance of one or more members of this hypothetical investigatory team will lead to evidence being overlooked or rendered legally useless. This book addresses that danger by making police, forensic scientists, lawyers, and programmers aware of what they do not know. It is an important contribution and should be required reading for anyone involved either in criminal investigation or computer administration.

Robert L. Dunne, J.D.
Co-Director, The Center for Internet Studies
Lecturer, Department of Computer Science
Yale University

In the past thirty years, there has been a dramatic shift in the way computers are used. Previously, computer technology was seen simply as a tool, used selectively for a specific purpose. Now, however, the very infrastructure of society relies on computers and there is only a vague awareness of their prevalence and multifarious functions. Financial networks, communication systems, power stations, medical facilities, modern automobiles and appliances all depend on computers, and these computers can record withdrawals, deposits, purchases, telephone calls, usage of electricity, medical treatments, driving patterns, the time an individual awakes, and much more. In addition to the computers that form our infrastructure, individuals use personal computers regularly for convenience, education and entertainment – typing letters, managing personal finances, exploring educational CD-ROMs and playing computer games. Furthermore, personal computers are connected to networks to take advantage of a wide range of network services including e-mail and the World Wide Web. Computer networks extend the reach and control of the individuals, giving them great freedom and power to be creative – and destructive.

It should come as no surprise that computer technology is involved in a growing number of crimes. In addition to being used as a tool to perpetrate crimes (e.g. computer intrusion, stalking, harassment, and fraud), computers can contain evidence related to any crime, including homicide and rape. It is no longer sufficient to have a few experts familiar with evidence stored on and transmitted using computers. Any investigation can involve computers or networks and everyone involved in a criminal investigation or prosecution can benefit from knowledge of the associated technical, legal and evidentiary issues related to this technology.

This text is written for the computer security professionals, law enforcement officers, attorneys and forensic scientists who are making efforts to become more familiar with the technical, legal, evidentiary and behavioral aspects of investigating computer-related crime. Although these professional groups have similar goals, there is a large amount of distrust and conflict between them. Computer security professionals who are employed to minimize the impact that an investigation has on an organization often come into conflict with law enforcement officers who are responsible for exploring every lead and examining every detail. Computer security professionals view law enforcement officers as heavy-handed and law enforcement officers see computer security professionals as unhelpful and even resistant. Also, computer security professionals who are already familiar with the particular system often perceive law enforcement officers, attorneys and forensic scientists who do not have a clear understanding of computer technology as technically inept. There are many other sources of conflict between these groups that can interfere with an investigation.

The expertise of each group is required for the successful investigation and prosecution of computer-related crime. Law enforcement officers, attorneys and forensic scientists depend on computer security professionals to help them collect and interpret evidence in technically challenging situations. Computer security professionals, attorneys and forensic scientists depend on law enforcement officers to coordinate investigations. Attorneys provide legal guidance and forensic scientists provide tools and techniques for getting the most out of available evidence. Therefore, it is important for these professional groups to gain a better understanding of each other and to work in collaboration. If these groups do not collaborate, criminals will continue to escape capture and prosecution and will feel justifiably safe using computers and networks to facilitate their criminal activities.

Although computer security professionals are primarily responsible for protecting information that is stored on their computer systems, they are often responsible for investigating and resolving criminal activity on their networks with minimum disruption to the users of the system. In the past, collecting evidence was not a priority for computer security professionals. However, victims of computer-related crime are becoming more interested in pressing charges and there is an increasing pressure on computer security professionals to collect evidence to be accepted in court. When computer security professionals are compelled to collect evidence from their networks, it is important that they abide by applicable privacy laws and rules of evidence. If computer security professionals collect evidence illegally, they can be sued. If they do not collect evidence in a way that meets the legal requirements, the evidence might not be accepted in court and their efforts will be wasted.

Law enforcement officers are responsible for responding to complaints, looking for evidence, determining if a crime has been committed and obtaining authorization to gather and examine evidence. In some cases, law enforcement officers rely on computer security professionals to collect evidence from computers and networks but in certain situations the officers are required to search for and collect evidence themselves. Law enforcement officers encounter personal computers at crime scenes that contain a large amount of evidence. Additionally, the Internet often contains information about suspects, victims and even the crime itself.

Whether at a crime scene or in a corporate environment, law enforcement officers must adjust quickly to an unfamiliar computing environment. A solid understanding of the technical, legal and evidentiary aspects of computers and networks is required to adjust to these unfamiliar settings, locate sources of evidence quickly, obtain necessary assistance or authorization to search for and seize evidence, and collect evidence in a way that will be accepted in court.

Both defense and prosecuting attorneys are responsible for protecting their clients' interests. Since computers are almost as common as file cabinets and can be involved in any case, it is not sufficient to have a few attorneys familiar with computer technology. All attorneys should be comfortable dealing with evidence stored on and transmitted using computers. Defense attorneys need to recognize and make use of exculpatory evidence and prosecuting attorneys need to recognize and make use of incriminating evidence. Also, defense and prosecuting attorneys will be at a loss if they are not acquainted with the common arguments regarding evidence obtained from computers.

As computer security professionals, law enforcement officers and attorneys become more familiar with computers and networks as a source of evidence, the expectations regarding its collection and processing are increasing. Attorneys are becoming more adept at challenging evidence so the individuals who collect and process evidence are becoming more circumspect. Already, the demand for improved tools and techniques for processing computer-related evidence is increasing. Forensic scientists are in a position to meet this demand.

This text is written with the hope that this diverse audience can learn to tolerate each other and cooperate sufficiently to address the mounting problems of computer-related crime effectively. To emphasize this common goal, the term *investigator* is used throughout this text to refer to members of the computer security, law enforcement, legal and forensic science communities who investigate computer-related crime.

This text grew out of my work with Knowledge Solutions. I owe special thanks to Brent Turvey and Barbara Troyer-Turvey for their continued assistance and friendship. Without them, this work would not have been possible. Thank you, Brent, for demonstrating that you can investigate heinous crimes and be subjected to defamation and unprofessional criticism without becoming cynical and callous. Admirably, you have used your understanding of diabolical human behavior to improve yourself. Thank you, Barbara, for your kindness and tireless exertions in support of my teaching and writing. You are the calm at the eye of the storm.

This work spent its formative years in New York University. I would like to thank Paul Henry, Donald Payne and Francine Shuchat-Shaw for their insights and guidance. My deep appreciation goes out to my good friend Hon-Chih Chen for his assistance developing the CD-ROM. Also, I would like to thank Gene DeLibero and Tim O'Connor for their willingness to share their extensive knowledge and experience.

I am continually grateful to Yale University for providing me with the opportunity to exercise and refine my interests and skills. It is a joy to work with a knowledgeable and supportive group of people and I am particularly thankful to H. Morrow Long for his unfathomable perspicacity and regular tutelage. I am also beholden to Robert Dunne for expanding my view of cybercrime, deepening my knowledge of the law, and repeatedly assisting me at pivotal points in my career.

I would like to thank the folks at Academic Press for their encouragement, continuing support, and tireless efforts to complete and disseminate this work. In particular, I would like to thank Nick Fallon for initiating this adventure and for sticking by us through all of the rough patches.

I am indebted to Kathy Baken for her stunning design on the cover of this book – may your creative well never run dry. I am also indebted to Jim Casey and Irena Herskowicz for their contributions without which the CD-ROM might not have come to fruition.

My mother Ita O'Connor deserves special mention for her initial critique of this work and her enduring encouragement. Thank you for making reconstructive surgery seem like a walk in the park. Finally, I give my endless gratitude and love to my wife Genevieve for her patience, kindness and stability. I expect to have the opportunity to return the favors during your upcoming projects.

## CHAPTER 1

INTRODUCTION TO DIGITAL EVIDENCE

The term *digital evidence* encompasses any and all digital data that can establish that a crime has been committed or can provide a link between a crime and its victim or a crime and its perpetrator[1]. Digital data is essentially a combination of numbers that represent information of various kinds, including text, images, audio and video. With the increasing use of computers, digital evidence is becoming more common and more important to investigative efforts. Sometimes information stored on a computer is the only clue in an investigation. In one case, e-mail messages were the only investigative link between a murderer and his victim.

[1] This definition is adapted from the definition of physical evidence in (Saferstein 1998).

CASE EXAMPLE

In October 1996, a Maryland woman named Sharon Lopatka told her husband that she was leaving to visit friends. However, she left a chilling note that caused her husband to inform police that she was missing. During their investigation, the police found hundreds of e-mail messages between Lopatka and a man named Robert Glass about their torture and death fantasies. The contents of the e-mail led investigators to Glass's trailer in North Carolina and they found Lopatka's shallow grave nearby. Her hands and feet had been tied and she had been strangled. Glass pleaded guilty, claiming that he killed Lopatka accidentally during sex.

There are large amounts of digital evidence all around us. A hard drive can store a small library, digital cameras can store hundreds of high-resolution photographs, and a computer network can contain a vast amount of information about people and their behavior (Casey 1999). At any given moment, private telephone conversations, financial transactions, confidential documents, and many other kinds of information are moving around us, through the surrounding air and wires in digital form – all potential sources of digital evidence. However, few investigators are well versed in the evidentiary, technical, and legal issues related to digital evidence and as a result, digital evidence is often overlooked, collected incorrectly, or analyzed ineffectively. The goal of this text is to equip you, the reader, with the necessary knowledge and skills to effectively use digital evidence in any kind of investigation.

OVERVIEW OF THIS WORK

The ultimate aim of this text is to demonstrate how digital evidence can be used to identify suspects, prosecute the guilty, defend the innocent, and understand criminal behavior and motivation. To reach this end, three fields are drawn from: computer science, forensic science, and behavioral evidence analysis (Turvey 1999). Computer science provides the technical details that are necessary to understand specific aspects of digital evidence. Forensic science provides a general approach to analyzing any form of digital evidence. Behavioral evidence analysis provides a systematized method of synthesizing the specific technical knowledge and general scientific methods to gain a better understanding of criminal behavior and motivation (Chapter 9).

This text begins by introducing basic forensic science concepts in the context of a single computer. Learning how to deal with individual computers is crucial because even when networks are involved, it is usually necessary to collect digital evidence stored on computers. Several scenarios and a general set of guidelines are provided to help transfer the knowledge out of this text and apply it to investigations.

The remainder of the text covers computer networks, focusing on the Internet specifically. A top-down approach is used to describe computer networks, starting with a general overview and progressively going into more detail. The "top" of a computer network is comprised of the software that people use, like e-mail and the Web. This upper region hides the underlying complexity of computer networks and is, therefore, an excellent place to start learning about computer networks as a source of digital evidence. The underlying complexity of computer networks is gradually explored until you reach the "bottom" – the physical media (e.g. copper and fiber optic cables) that carry data between computers.

The basic forensic science concepts that are described early on in relation to a single computer are carried through to each layer of the Internet to give you an understanding of digital evidence on computer networks. Seeing concepts from forensic science applied in a variety of contexts will help you generalize the systematic approach to processing and analyzing digital evidence. Once generalized, this systematic approach can be applied to situations not specifically discussed in this text.

As well as providing a practical understanding of how computer networks function and how they can be used as evidence of a crime, this text presents relevant legal issues and behavioral evidence analysis, a systematic approach to focusing investigations and understanding criminal motivation. Understanding criminal motivation and behavior is key to assessing risks (will criminal activity escalate?), developing and interviewing suspects (who to look for and what to say to them), and focusing investigations (where to look and what to look for).

Case examples are interspersed throughout to emphasize important points and demonstrate the usefulness of digital evidence. Also, scenarios provide a practical understanding of digital evidence. The hope is that, after reading this text, you will have a solid comprehension and a basic working knowledge of digital evidence.

FORENSIC SCIENCE

Forensic science is a core component of this text, providing principles and techniques that facilitate the investigation and prosecution of criminal offenses. Generally speaking, forensic science is the application of science to law – any scientific principle or technique that can be applied to identifying, recovering, reconstructing, or analyzing evidence during a criminal investigation is part of forensic science. The scientific principles behind evidence processing are well established and are used in such procedures as:

- detecting, processing and examining fingerprints and DNA;
- ascertaining the authenticity and source of a questioned document or examining charred documents for evidence of a crime;
- determining a firearm's unique characteristics;
- recovering damaged or deleted documents from a computer hard drive;
- making an exact copy of digital evidence – ensuring that no information is lost during collection;
- collecting digitized data that is being transmitted through networks in a way that preserves its integrity and authenticity;
- using a message digest algorithm to verify that digital evidence has not been modified;
- signing digital evidence digitally to affirm that it is authentic and to preserve chain of evidence;
- determining the unique characteristics of a piece of digital evidence (e.g. documents, programs, transmissions).

In addition to using scientific techniques and theories to process individual pieces of digital evidence, forensic scientists use their training to help investigators reconstruct crimes and generate leads. Applying the scientific method, forensic scientists analyze available evidence, create hypotheses about what occurred to create the evidence, and perform tests to confirm or contradict their hypotheses. Through this process, forensic scientists can generate strong possibilities about what occurred[2].

One of the fundamental principles in forensic science that is extremely useful for crime reconstruction and linking an offender to a crime is Locard's Exchange Principle, depicted in Figure 1.1. According to this principle, anyone, or anything, entering a crime scene takes something of the scene with them, and leaves something of themselves behind when they depart. In the physical world, an offender might inadvertently leave a hair at the scene and take a fiber from the scene. With one of these pieces of evidence, investigators can demonstrate the strong possibility that the offender was at the crime scene. With two pieces of evidence the link between the offender and crime scene becomes stronger and easier to demonstrate.

[2] In forensic science, certainty is a word that is used with great care. Forensic scientists cannot be certain of what occurred at a crime scene because they only have a limited amount of information. Therefore, they can only present possibilities based on that limited amount of information.

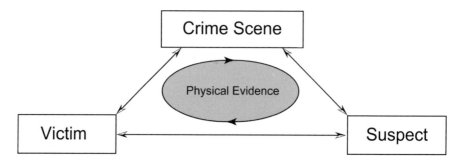

Figure 1.1
Locard's Exchange Principle.

In short, forensic science provides tools, techniques and a systematic (scientific) approach that can be used to process and analyze digital evidence and use this evidence to reconstruct what occurred during the perpetration of a crime with the ultimate purpose of linking an offender, victim and crime scene.

DIGITAL EVIDENCE VERSUS PHYSICAL EVIDENCE

Digital evidence is a type of physical evidence. Although digital evidence is less tangible than other forms of physical evidence (e.g. fingerprints, DNA, weapons, computer components), it is still physical evidence. Digital evidence is made of magnetic fields and electronic pulses that can be collected and analyzed using special tools and techniques. Furthermore, courts have held that such intangible property can be seized as evidence. Digital evidence actually has several advantages over other kinds of physical evidence:

- It can be duplicated exactly and a copy can be examined as if it were the original. It is common practice when dealing with digital evidence to examine a copy, thus avoiding the risk of damaging the original.

- With the right tools it is very easy to determine if digital evidence has been modified or tampered with by comparing it with the original.
- It is relatively difficult to destroy. Even if it is "deleted," digital evidence can be recovered from a computer disk.
- When criminals attempt to destroy digital evidence, copies can remain in places that they were not aware of.

CASE EXAMPLE
When Colonel Oliver North was under investigation during the Iran Contra affair, he was careful to shred documents and delete incriminating e-mail from his computer. However, unbeknownst to him, electronic messages sent using the IBM Professional Office System (PROFS) were being regularly backed up and were later retrieved from backup tapes.

Computers can perform millions of operations based on this digitized information in one second, and can transmit them around the world in an instant. The fact that digital evidence can be manipulated and transmitted so easily raises new challenges for investigators of crimes that involve computers. This text addresses these challenges and emphasizes the positive aspects of digital evidence.

CRIMINAL ACTIVITY AND DIGITAL EVIDENCE ON COMPUTER NETWORKS

Computer networks facilitate daily activities – including telephone calls, credit card purchases, and money withdrawals from ATMs – bringing increasing convenience to our lives. However, along with convenience comes risk and complexity. Computer networks have been involved in a wide range of crimes including child pornography, solicitation of minors, stalking, harassment, fraud, espionage, sabotage, theft, privacy violations, and defamation. Criminals are taking advantage of new technology so quickly that investigators are finding it difficult to keep up – as Carter and Katz point out:

Law enforcement has withstood many challenges over the years. Prohibition, organized crime, riots, drug trafficking, and violent crime exemplify some of the complex problems the police have faced. Now law enforcement confronts another problem that is somewhat unusual – computer-related crime.

Several factors make this type of criminality difficult to address. Lawbreakers have integrated highly technical methods with traditional crimes and developed creative new types of crime, as well. They use computers to cross state and national boundaries electronically, thus complicating investigations. Moreover, the evidence of these crimes is neither physical nor human but, if it exists, is little more than electronic impulses and programming codes.

Regrettably, the police have fallen behind in the computer age and must overcome a steep learning curve. To make matters worse, computer crime is sometimes difficult for police officials to comprehend and to accept as a major problem with a local impact, regardless of the size or location of their communities. (Carter and Katz 1996)

Carter and Katz believe that the weakest link is the lack of education and point out that the law enforcement community has devoted itself to "the high priority violent crimes, lumping computer crimes into a low priority status, yet the losses to computer crime could fund a small country." And the problem is not only economic cost. The law enforcement community's distinction between violent crimes and crimes involving computers often blinds them to hard evidence. In actuality, computers can contain evidence that is related to violent crimes; including homicide, arson, suicide, abduction, torture, and rape.

CASE EXAMPLE (Shamburg 1999)
In 1997, Oliver Jovanovic, a graduate student at Colombia University in New York, was charged with kidnapping and sexually abusing a female student he befriended over the Internet. According to the victim, Jovanovic arranged a meeting with her through e-mail, invited her back to his apartment to watch videos, overpowered and restrained her for almost 20 hours, bit her, burned her with candle wax, sexually assaulted her, and threatened to dismember her.

The Internet played a significant role in enabling the crime and e-mail messages contained quite a bit of information about Jovanovic, the victim and their relationship. However, most of the e-mail was not used during the trial. The prosecution was prevented from using Jovanovic's e-mail because it was not seized legally. The defense was prevented from using important parts of the victim's e-mail messages because the New York Rape Shield Law prohibits certain information about victims from being disclosed, including their identities and their sexual history. In her e-mails, the victim expressed some interest in snuff films and sadomasochism.

The "Cybersex trial" put the media into a reporting frenzy. It was argued that the outcome of the trial was influenced by the fact that the media publicized it so much. Although the victim contradicted herself several times and the physical evidence did not fully support her accusations, Jovanovic was sentenced to 15 years in prison. This case demonstrates how the Internet can be involved in violent crime and raises several thorny issues including the effect that media sensationalism has on the adjudication of computer-related crimes.

Given the widespread use of computers and the wide use of networks, it would be a grave error to overlook them as a source of evidence in *any* crime. Therefore, anyone who is involved with criminal investigation, prosecution, or defense work should be comfortable with personal computers and networks as a source of evidence. One of the major aims of this work is to educate students and professionals in the computer security, law enforcement, and forensic science communities about computer networks as a source of digital evidence.

WHO CAN COLLECT DIGITAL EVIDENCE?

One of the first legal questions to arise during any investigation involving computers and networks is "Who is allowed to collect and analyze the relevant digital evidence?" Only specially trained and authorized experts can process and examine most forms of physical evidence so one might assume that the same holds for digital evidence. However, investigators with limited training are often required to process and examine digital evidence.

> Seizing, preserving, and analyzing evidence stored on a computer is the greatest forensic challenge facing law enforcement in the 1990s. Although most forensic tests, such as fingerprinting and DNA testing, are performed by specially trained experts, the task of collecting and analyzing computer evidence is often assigned to untrained patrol officers and detectives. While most forensic tests are performed in the analyst's own laboratory, investigators are required to search and seize computers at unfamiliar and potentially hostile sites, such as drug labs, residences, "boiler rooms," small business offices, and warehouse-sized computer centers. (Rosenblatt 1996)

Additionally, businesses, communication service providers, and computer experts play an integral role in investigations that involve computers and are permitted to collect and disclose digital evidence under certain circumstances (discussed in Chapter 13).

The owners of private computer systems often initiate an investigation and are sometimes the only people qualified to collect and analyze digital evidence on their system. For example, victims of computer-related crime usually seek support from their employer, local communications service providers, or computer experts first, and then, if necessary, report the incident to law enforcement. A woman who is being stalked and harassed on the Internet usually contacts her employer or Internet Service Provider (ISP) first for assistance and then, if the problem persists, will file a complaint with the police. Similarly, organizations whose computers are broken into usually try to address the problem using internal computer experts and then, if the situation warrants it, they call upon law enforcement for help. Furthermore, law enforcement officers often require technical assistance and are permitted to employ an expert to assist in an investigation. So, a wide variety of individuals are permitted to collect and analyze digital evidence.

Because employers, communications service providers, computer experts, and law enforcement are regularly called upon to investigate computer-related crimes, it is important for them all to know what they are permitted to do legally. For example, if an organization inadvertently comes across digital evidence on their system during the normal course of business, they can usually divulge it to law enforcement. However, an ISP or employer is not necessarily permitted to monitor the contents of communications passing through their computers or to search through e-mail.

Monitoring and searching communications is a violation of privacy that is carefully restricted by legislation such as the Electronic Communications and Privacy Act (ECPA). Unlike the Fourth Amendment, which only applies to the government, the ECPA applies to everybody, including employers, computer experts, communication service providers, and law enforcement. The ECPA defines who can access stored communications and intercept transmitted communications under various circumstances and is discussed in general terms along with other legal issues in Chapter 13[3].

Though it is essential to involve police and attorneys in some investigations (e.g. when a search warrant or subpoena is required), it is not feasible to obtain legal counsel and inform law enforcement every time digital evidence is encountered. Many computer security professionals deal with hundreds of petty crimes each month and there is not enough time or resources to open a full investigation for each incident. Therefore, computer security professionals attempt to limit the damage and close each investigation as quickly as possible. There are two significant drawbacks to this approach. Firstly, attorneys and law enforcement officers are not given an opportunity to learn about the basics of computer-related crime and are only involved when the stakes are high and the cases are complicated. Secondly, computer security professionals develop loose evidence processing habits that can make it more difficult for law enforcement officers and attorneys to prosecute an offender. To improve this situation, computer security professionals, attorneys, and law enforcement officers must work together to investigate computer-related crime.

TERMINOLOGY

Before delving into the details of digital evidence it is necessary to become familiar with the language that is used to discuss computer-related crime. Some terms used throughout this text require clarification: cybercrime, computer crime, cybertrail, hackers and computer crackers.

CYBERCRIME

Cybercrime is used throughout this text to refer to any crime that involves computers and networks, including crimes that do not rely heavily on computers. This general term is required to cover situations where a computer network was not used to commit a crime but still contains digital evidence related to the crime. As an extreme example, take a suspect who claims that she was using the Internet at the time of a crime. Though the computer played no role in the crime, it contains digital evidence relevant to the investigation, and therefore falls within this loose definition of cybercrime[4].

[3] The general legal discussions in the text cannot substitute for expert legal advice. When in doubt about whether or not you are permitted to examine or collect digital evidence in a particular situation, seek legal counsel.

[4] Chapter 2, The Language of Cybercrime, provides language for referring to different types of cybercrime with more specificity, to avoid confusion.

It is important to note that the involvement of computers or networks does not change the crime or make it any less substantial. Stalking and harassment on a network are as terrifying for the victim as their physical world counterparts. Theft and fraud cause real losses whether a computer network is involved or not. Child abuse and distribution of child pornography over a network is little different from the international rings of pedophiles and pornographers that do not rely on computers to communicate (Henry 1984). The following case example demonstrates the scope of a serious problem; the creation and global distribution of child pornography. The Internet did not create this problem, but probably exacerbates it, and certainly makes it more visible.

CASE EXAMPLE
On 22 April 1996 in Greenfield, California, a woman contacted the local police and reported that her six-year-old daughter had been molested during a slumber party by Ronald Riva, the father of the host. Additionally, a ten-year-old girl at the party reported that Riva and his friend, Melton Myers, used a computer to record her as she posed for them. Riva and Myers led investigators into an international ring of child abusers and pornographers that convened in an Internet chat room called the Orchid Club. Sixteen men from Finland, Canada, Australia, and the United States were charged. One log of an Orchid Club chat session indicated that Riva and Myers were describing their actions to other members of the club as they abused the ten-year-old girl.

Their investigation into the Orchid Club led law enforcement to a larger group of child pornographers and pedophiles called the Wonderland Club. After more than two years of following leads, police in fourteen countries arrested over 200 members of Wonderland, in the largest coordinated effort to crack down on child exploitation and abuse to date. Evidence gathered during this latest effort suggests that there are members of the Wonderland Club in more than 40 countries, so the investigation is by no means over.

COMPUTER CRIME

Computer crime is a special type of cybercrime that deserves separate mention.

> There is no doubt among the authors and experts who have attempted to arrive at definitions of computer crime that the phenomenon exists. However, the definitions that have been produced tend to relate to the study for which they were written ... A global definition of computer crime have not been achieved; rather, functional definitions have been the norm. (United Nations 1995)

Although there is no agreed-upon definition of computer crime, the meaning of the term has become more specific over time. Computer crime mainly refers to a limited set of crimes that are specifically defined in laws such as the US Computer Fraud and Abuse Act and the UK Computer Abuse Act. These crimes include theft of computer services; unauthorized access to protected computers; software piracy and the alteration or theft of electronically stored information; extortion committed with the assistance of computers; obtaining unauthorized access to records from banks, credit card issuers, or customer reporting agencies; traffic in stolen passwords and transmission of destructive viruses or commands.

Remember that theft and fraud cause real losses whether a computer network is involved or not. According to the annual CSI/FBI Computer Crime and Security Survey, in 1998 the total financial losses for 241 organizations that could quantify them added up to $136,822,000 (CSI/FBI 1998). Despite these heavy losses, only a small percentage of computer crimes are ever reported or fully investigated. Many organizations are reluctant to report computer crimes or pursue computer criminals because of the bad publicity that it can generate with their customers and stakeholders. Also, since computer crime is so new, the terrain is uncertain and few organizations (including law enforcement agencies) are willing to spend the time and resources necessary to fully investigate a computer crime when they are uncertain of the results. Fortunately, new legislation and additional resources are emerging to assist computer crime investigators. Additionally, more computer crimes are being reported to law enforcement each year (CSI/FBI 1999).

CYBERTRAIL

In the Wild West of America, posses of deputized citizens led by sheriffs and marshals followed the trails and physical signs of passing left behind by outlaws. Modern investigators have come to understand and follow a criminal's paper trail, in the form of invoices, communications, and other records that leave behind evidence of the criminal's passing. With the advent and popularity of computer networks, investigators have a new trail to follow. Let us jump on the cyber-bandwagon and call it a *cybertrail* (Casey 1999).

Cybertrails can be rich sources of digital evidence that include, but are not limited to, Web pages, e-mail, digitized still images, digitized video, digitized audio, digital logs of synchronous chat sessions, files stored on a personal computer, and computer logs from an ISP. A cybertrail is both an extension of crime scenes in the real world, and a digital crime scene in itself. If a crime occurs in the physical world and there is a computer with network access at the crime scene, investigators should search the computer and network for related digital evidence. Similarly, if a crime is first witnessed or recorded on a network, investigators should collect all relevant digital evidence on the network and, if possible, determine the physical locations of the primary computers involved and treat those locations as crime scenes (obtain search warrants if necessary, gather physical and digital evidence, etc.). In some cases it might not be obvious that cybertrails hold key evidence, so it is best

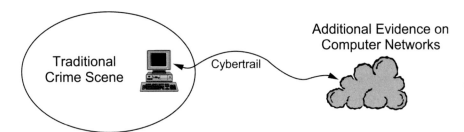

Figure 1.2
Cybertrails – networks increase the scope of an investigation.

to be safe and check. If investigators neglect to follow cybertrails, they not only risk losing valuable evidence; they also risk being held liable for their negligence. Even if investigators are not responsible for collecting evidence from a computer network in a given case, they should have a basic understanding of what digital evidence can exist so that they will be attuned to the possibility that it is missing.

HACKERS AND COMPUTER CRACKERS

The term *hacker* originally referred to talented computer programmers but the media have usurped it (with encouragement from criminals themselves) to refer to individuals who use their knowledge of computers to break the law. It has reached the point where anyone with an iota of computer savvy is called a hacker, including individuals who obtain destructive programs from the Internet and inconvenience people by bombarding computers with data until the computer stops functioning.

For the sake of clarity, the more specific term *computer cracker* (cracker for short) will be used throughout this text to refer to individuals who break into computers much like safe crackers break into safes. To avoid repetition, *intruder* and *criminal* will also be used when appropriate to refer to an individual who breaks into computers. Crackers find a computer's weak points and exploit them using specialized tools and techniques.

CASE EXAMPLE
Kevin Mitnick is the most notorious computer cracker to date. As a youth in the 1970s, Mitnick spent his spare time breaking into telephone systems in Los Angeles. He was first arrested in 1981 for destroying data over a computer network and stealing operators' manuals from a telephone company. Since then he has been in continuous trouble with the law for breaking into computers and stealing information, software, and credit card numbers. In 1989, he became the first person to be convicted under the Computer Fraud and Abuse Act for stealing software from Digital Equipment Corporation (DEC) with an estimated worth in the millions of dollars. He was sentenced to a year in prison and when he was released on probation, he disappeared and continued to commit a variety of computer crimes. He was apprehended again in 1995 after an epic chase involving the FBI and computer security expert Tsutomu Shimomura.

How skilled computer crackers gain unauthorized access to a computer and what they do once they have gained access varies considerably and investigating this type of crime is extremely challenging. Chapter 10 is devoted to investigating computer cracking.

SUMMARY

Digital evidence is all around us in large quantities just waiting for investigators to make use of it. Even crimes that were not committed with the assistance of computers can have related digital evidence.

CASE EXAMPLE (Bombshell 1999)
In April 1999, a 24-year-old sales associate put a digitized photograph on her employer's Web site. The photograph, taken at a company picnic, showed the woman wearing shorts and a bathing suit top. The woman was upset to learn that a sales manager had looked at the picture, whistled and exclaimed "Nice bazongas!" The woman later brought a sexual harassment suit against the sales manager and her employer. During the trial, it transpired that many of the company's computers contained a microphone and recording software that were used to eavesdrop on employees. The woman's attorneys were able to obtain a recording of the sales manager's comment and admit it into evidence.

Furthermore, as computers and networks become more widely used in general, they will become more widely used by criminals. Criminals will be especially eager to use computers and networks if they know that law enforcement officers, computer security professionals, attorneys, and forensic scientists are ill equipped to investigate cybercrime and deal with the subsequent digital evidence. Therefore, to address the growing problem of cybercrime and make use of digital evidence it is crucial that:

- Law enforcement officers learn to handle digital evidence, use it to generate investigative leads, and know when to call in an expert for assistance.
- Computer security professionals who handle digital evidence, use it to generate investigative leads, and know when to call in law enforcement for assistance.
- Attorneys (both prosecution and defense) learn to dig up digital evidence, defend it against common arguments, and determine whether it is admissible.
- Forensic scientists become intimately familiar with every aspect of digital evidence so that they can process it to support an investigation.

Although the same concerns exist when dealing with physical and digital evidence (to prevent further crimes and protect valuable evidence) the methods required to address these concerns are very different. Specialized knowledge and tools are required to find, collect, and make use of digital evidence. By combining general theory with practical examples, exercises, and guidelines, this text will equip you with the necessary knowledge and skills to effectively use digital evidence in any kind of investigation.

REFERENCES

"Bombshell," *PC Computing* (April 1999).

Carter, D. L. and Katz, A. J. (1996) "Computer Crime: An Emerging Challenge for Law Enforcement," *FBI Law Enforcement Bulletin* [available at http://www.fbi.gov/leb/dec961.txt].

Casey, E. (1999) "Cyberpatterns," in Turvey, B. *Criminal Profiling*, London: Academic Press, Chapter 25.

CSI/FBI (1998) *1998 CSI/FBI Computer Crime and Security Survey* [http://www.gocsi.com].

CSI/FBI (1999) *1999 CSI/FBI Computer Crime and Security Survey* [http://www.gocsi.com].

Henry, J. F. (1984) Testimony before Permanent Subcommittee on Governmental Affairs, the United States Senate, Ninety-Ninth Congress [available at http://www.igc.apc.org/nemesis/ACLU/NudistHallofShame/Henry.html].

Rosenblatt, K. S. (1999) *High-Technology Crime: Investigating Cases Involving Computers*, San Jose, CA: KSK Publications.

Saferstein, R. (1998) *Criminalistics: An Introduction to Forensic Science*, 6th edn, Upper Saddle River, NJ: Prentice Hall.

Shamburg, R. (1999) "A Tortured Case," *Net Life*, 7 April.

Shimomura, T. and Markoff, J. (1996) *Takedown: The Pursuit of Kevin Mitnick, America's Most Wanted Computer Outlaw – By the Man Who Did It*, New York, NY: Hyperion.

Turvey, B. (1999) *Criminal Profiling: An Introduction to Behavioral Evidence Analysis*, London: Academic Press.

United Nations (1995) *International Review of Criminal Policy No. 43 and 44 – United Nations Manual on the Prevention and Control of Computer-Related Crime* [available at http://www.ifs.univie.ac.at/~pr2gq1/rev4344.html#crime].

## CHAPTER 2

THE LANGUAGE OF CYBERCRIME

As described in the previous chapter, cybercrime is a general term used to refer to any crime that involves computers and networks. Additional language is required to distinguish between the different roles that computers can play in cybercrime. More specific language is crucial for developing a deeper understanding of how computers can be involved in crime and for developing more refined approaches to investigating different kinds of cybercrime.

> As computer-related crimes become more prevalent, an increasing need emerges for police personnel – particularly those who do not have expertise in computer technology – to understand how these crimes vary. An understanding of the types of computer-related crimes will assist law enforcement by providing insight for investigative strategies. (Carter 1995)

For example, investigating computer cracking requires one approach, while investigating a homicide with related digital evidence requires a completely different procedure.

The specific role that a computer plays in a crime also determines how it can be used as evidence. When a computer contains only a few pieces of digital evidence, investigators might not be authorized to collect the entire computer. However, when a computer is the key piece of evidence in an investigation and contains a large amount of digital evidence, it is often necessary to collect the entire computer and its contents. Additionally, when a computer plays a significant role in a crime, it is easier to obtain a warrant to search and seize the entire computer.

Several attempts have been made to develop a language to help investigators differentiate between distinct kinds of cybercrime. This language comes in the form of categories and it is instructive to see how these categories evolved. Three sets of categories are presented in this chapter. The first set of categories was developed in the 1970s when computer-related crime began to be recognized as a serious problem. These initial categories are useful for discussing cybercrime in a general way, but are not specific enough for focusing an investigation.

In the 1990s, another set of cybercrime categories was developed that furthered our understanding of cybercrime, and encouraged us to create procedures for dealing with specific types of crime. However, this second set of categories was not adequate, for reasons that will be discussed presently.

In 1994, the US Department of Justice (DOJ) created a more complete set of categories and an associated set of search and seizure guidelines that have yet to be improved upon (DOJ 1994). The DOJ categories and guidelines were specifically developed to help us form procedures for collecting digital evidence in varying situations, in a way that conforms to existing laws.

THE FIRST CYBERCRIME CATEGORIES

Donn Parker was one of the first individuals to perceive the development of cybercrime as a serious problem back in the 1970s. Parker studied the evolution of cybercrime for more than two decades and wrote several books on the subject (Parker 1976, 1983). He also played a major role in enacting Florida's Computer Crime Act of 1978, the first law specifically created to deal with computer crime. Though Parker is primarily concerned with computer security and has gone on to develop more specific categories for protecting digitized information (Parker 1998), his early categorization was foundational and is general enough to apply to most kinds of cybercrime. Parker proposed the following four categories. While reading through these categories, notice the lack of reference to digital evidence.

1 A computer can be the *object* of a crime. When a computer is affected by the criminal act, it is the object of the crime (e.g. when a computer is stolen or destroyed).

2 A computer can be the *subject* of a crime. When a computer is the environment in which the crime is committed, it is the subject of the crime (e.g. when a computer is infected by a virus or impaired in some other way to inconvenience the individuals who use it).

3 The computer can be used as the *tool* for conducting or planning a crime. For example, when a computer is used to forge documents or break into other computers, it is the instrument of the crime.

4 The *symbol* of the computer itself can be used to intimidate or deceive. An example given is of a stockbroker, who told his clients that he was able to make huge profits on rapid stock option trading, by using a secret computer program in a giant computer in a Wall Street brokerage firm. Although he had no such programs nor access to the computer in question, hundreds of clients were convinced enough to invest a minimum of $100,000 each.

The distinction between a computer as the object of a crime, and the tool that was used to plan or commit a crime, is a useful one. If a computer is used like a weapon in a criminal act, much like a gun or a knife, this could lead to additional charges or a heightened degree of punishment. The second and fourth categories, however, are not as useful for developing investigative strategies and procedures. When a computer is infected with a virus, it can be thought of as both the object of attack, and the tool for committing the destructive or disruptive act. The "computer as subject" does complement the "computer as object" category nicely when one thinks in terms of English grammar, but it does not serve any practical purpose when investigating cybercrime. The fourth category is also extraneous when investigating cybercrime because no actual computers are involved and, therefore, none can be collected as evidence.

The most significant omission in Parker's categories is computers as sources of digital evidence. In many cases, computers did not play a role in a crime but they do contain evidence that proves a crime occurred. For example, a revealing e-mail between US President Clinton and intern Monica Lewinsky could indicate that they had an affair, but the e-mail itself played no role in Clinton's alleged act of perjury. Similarly, a few of the millions of e-mail messages that were examined during the Microsoft anti trust case contained incriminating information, yet the e-mail messages did not play an active role in the crime – they were simply evidence of a crime.

CRIMINAL JUSTICE CYBERCRIME CATEGORIES

Professor David L. Carter, quoted at the beginning of this chapter, used his knowledge of Criminal Justice to improve upon Parker's categories. Carter proposed the following categories (Carter 1995).

1   Computer as the target (e.g. computer intrusion, data theft, techno-vandalism, techno-trespass).

2   Computer as the instrumentality of the crime (e.g. credit card fraud, telecommunications fraud, theft, or fraud)[1].

3   Computer as incidental to other crimes (e.g. drug trafficking, money laundering, child pornography).

4   Crimes associated with the prevalence of computers (e.g. copyright violation, software piracy, component theft).

[1] *An instrumentality is any tangible object designed or intended for use or which has been used as a means of committing a criminal offense.*

Instead of using the terms *object* and *tool* as Parker did, Carter used the more direct and legally oriented terms *target* and *instrumentality*, respectively. Also, when Carter referred to computers as incidental to other crimes, he mainly described scenarios in which computers were a source of digital evidence. The computer need not have an active part in the execution of the crime, but it might hold evidence that is key in prosecution or defense.

> Cases involving drug raids, money laundering seizures, and other arrests also have produced computers and electronic storage media containing incriminating information … All of these situations require unique data recovery techniques in order to gain access to the evidence. And, in every case, the crimes could have occurred without the computers; the systems merely facilitated the offense. (Carter 1995)

So, Carter discarded Parker's computer as subject and symbol categories, and corrected Parker's main omission by including a category for computers as a source of digital evidence. Carter also included one extra category to catch anything not covered by the first three. However, "Crimes associated with the prevalence of computers" is too general and vague a category to be useful for developing investigative procedures. Carter might have felt the need for a fourth, catch-all category because he did not distinguish between physical computer components and digital evidence (the contents of the computer components). Very different procedures are required when dealing with physical components and digital evidence, as described in Chapter 3.

US GUIDELINES FOR SEARCHING AND SEIZING COMPUTERS

The US Federal Guidelines for Searching and Seizing Computers (DOJ 1994) contains an excellent set of guidelines and cybercrime categories. These categories make the necessary distinction between hardware and information. In this context, *hardware* refers to all of the physical components of a computer, and *information* refers to the data and programs that are stored on and transmitted using a computer. The final three categories that refer to information all fall under the guise of *digital evidence*.

1 Hardware as contraband or fruits of crime.
2 Hardware as an instrumentality.
3 Hardware as evidence.
4 Information as contraband or fruits of crime.
5 Information as an instrumentality.
6 Information as evidence.

These categories are not intended to be mutually exclusive. A single crime can fall into more than one category. For example, when a computer is instrumental in committing a crime, it is also evidence of the offense. The details of collecting hardware and processing information as evidence (digital evidence) are introduced in Chapter 3 and developed in the context of computer networks in Chapters 4, 5, 6 and 7. Be aware that each of these categories has unique legal procedures that must be followed. In most cases, a warrant is required to search and seize evidence but there are exceptions such as consent, exigency, and evidence in plain view. However, in some situations, privacy laws might protect the evidence. Some of these issues are discussed in Chapter 13 but it is important to obtain legal counsel on these matters when investigating cybercrime and developing associated procedures.

HARDWARE AS CONTRABAND OR FRUITS OF CRIME

Contraband is property that the private citizen is not permitted to possess. For example, under certain circumstances, it is illegal for an individual in the US to possess hardware that is used to intercept electronic communications (18 USC 2512). The concern is that these devices enable individuals to obtain confidential information, violate other people's privacy, and commit a wide range of other crimes using intercepted data. Cloned cellular phones and the equipment that is used to clone them are another example of hardware as contraband.

The fruits of crime include property that was obtained by criminal activity such as computer equipment that was stolen, or purchased using stolen credit card numbers. For example, microprocessors are regularly stolen because they are very valuable, they are in high demand, and they are easy to transport.

The main reason for seizing contraband or fruits of crime is to prevent and deter future crimes. When law enforcement officers decide to seize evidence in this category, a court will examine whether the circumstances would have led a reasonably cautious agent to believe that the object was contraband or a fruit of crime.

HARDWARE AS AN INSTRUMENTALITY

When computer hardware has played a significant role in a crime, it is considered an instrumentality. The clearest example of hardware as the instrumentality of crime is a computer that is specially manufactured, equipped and/or configured to commit a specific crime. For instance, sniffers are pieces of hardware that are specifically designed to eavesdrop on a network[2]. Computer crackers often use sniffers to collect passwords that can then be used to gain unauthorized access to computers.

The primary reason for authorizing law enforcement to seize an instrumentality of crime is to prevent future crimes. When deciding whether or not a piece of hardware can be seized as an instrumentality of crime, it is important to remember that "significant" is the operative word in the definition of instrumentality. Unless a plausible argument can be made that the hardware played a significant role in the crime, it probably should not be seized as an instrumentality of the crime.

[2] A sniffer is not always a piece of hardware. With the right software, a regular computer that is connected directly to a network can be used as a sniffer, in which case the software might be considered the instrumentality of the crime. Software sniffers fall into the category of information as an instrumentality.

It is ultimately up to the courts to decide whether or not an item played a significant role in a given crime. So far, the courts have been quite liberal on this issue. For example, in a New York child pornography case the court ruled that a computer was the instrumentality of the offense because the computer hardware *might* have facilitated the sending and receiving of the images (US v. Lamb, 945 F. Supp. 441, 462 [N.D.N.Y. 1996]). Even more liberal was the Eastern District Court of Virginia decision that a computer with related accessories was an instrumentality because it contained a file that detailed the growing characteristics of marijuana plants (US v. Real Property & Premises Known as 5528 Belle Pond Drive, 783 F. Supp. 253 [E.D. Va. 1991]).

HARDWARE AS EVIDENCE

Before 1972, "mere evidence" of a crime could not be seized. However, this restriction was removed and it is now acceptable to "search for and seize any property that constitutes evidence of the commission of a criminal offense" (Federal Rule of Criminal Procedure 41(b)). This separate category of *hardware as evidence* is necessary to cover computer hardware that is neither contraband nor the instrumentality of a crime. For instance, if a scanner that is used to digitize child pornography has unique scanning characteristics that link the hardware to the digitized images, it could be seized as evidence.

INFORMATION AS CONTRABAND OR FRUITS OF CRIME

As previously mentioned, contraband information is information that the private citizen is not permitted to possess. A common form of information as contraband is encryption software. In some countries, it is illegal for an individual to possess a computer program that can encode data using strong encryption algorithms, because it gives criminals too much privacy. If a criminal is caught but all of the incriminating digital evidence is encrypted, it might not be possible to decode the evidence and prosecute the criminal. Information as fruits of crime include illegal copies of computer programs, stolen trade secrets and passwords, and any other information that was obtained by criminal means.

INFORMATION AS AN INSTRUMENTALITY

Information can be the instrumentality of a crime if it was designed or intended for use or has been used as a means of committing a criminal offense. Programs that computer crackers use to break into computer systems are the instrumentality of a crime. These programs, commonly known as *exploits*, enable computer crackers to gain unauthorized access to computers with a specific vulnerability. Also, computer programs that record people's passwords when they log into a computer can be an instrumentality, and computer programs that crack passwords often play a significant role in a crime. As with hardware, the significance of the information's role is paramount to determining if it is the instrumentality of crime. Unless a plausible argument can be made that the information played a significant role in the crime, it probably should not be seized as an instrumentality of the crime.

INFORMATION AS EVIDENCE

This is the richest category of all. Many of our daily actions leave a trail of digits. All service providers (e.g. telephone companies, ISPs, banks, credit institutions) keep some information about their customers. Though telephone companies and ISPs try to limit the amount of information that they keep on customer activities, to limit their storage and retrieval costs and their liability, law makers in some countries are starting to compel some communications service providers to keep more complete logs. For instance, the US Computer Assistance Law Enforcement Act that takes effect in 2000 compels telephone companies to keep detailed records of their customers' calls for an indefinite period of time. In Japan, there is an ongoing debate about whether ISPs should be compelled to keep more complete logs.

For fun, take a single day in a life as an example. After breakfast, Jane Doe reads and responds to her e-mail. Copies of this e-mail remain in various places so Jane takes care to encrypt private messages. However, even if her encrypted e-mail is never opened, it shows that she sent a message to a specific person at a specific time. This simple link between two people can be important in certain circumstances. Encrypted e-mail can be even more revealing in bulk. If Jane sends a large number of e-mails to a newspaper reporter just before publication of a story about a confidential case she is working on, an investigator would not have to decrypt and read the e-mails to draw some daring inferences. Similarly, if a suspect used encrypted e-mail to communicate with another individual around the time a crime was committed, this might be considered sufficient probable cause to obtain a warrant to examine the e-mail or even search the second person's computer or residence.

After checking her e-mail, Jane opens her schedule in her computerized planner. Jane's small planner contains vast amounts of information about her family, friends, acquaintances, interests, and activities. Next, on the way to the bank, Jane makes a few quick phone calls on her cellular phone, propelling her voice through the air for anyone to listen to. At the bank, she withdraws some cash, creating a record of her whereabouts at a specific time. Not only is her transaction recorded in a computer, her face is captured by the camera built into the automated teller machine.

Although she pays for her lunch in cash, Jane puts the receipt in her wallet, thus keeping a record of one of the few transactions that might have escaped the permanent record. After lunch, Jane decides to page her husband John. From her computer she accesses a Web page that allows her to send John a short message on his pager. This small act creates a cascade of digits in Jane's computer, on the Web, and ultimately on John's pager. Unfortunately, the battery on Jane's phone is low so when John tries to call, he gets Jane's voice mail and leaves a message. Then it occurs to him that Jane was probably at her computer when she sent him the short alphanumeric message, so he connects to the Internet and uses one of the many computer programs that allow live communication over the global network. These few minutes of digital tag create many records in many different places and though some of this information might dissolve in a matter of hours, some of it will linger indefinitely on backup tapes and in little-used crannies on Jane's hard drive.

As an exercise, think back on some recent days and try to imagine the trail of digits that you left on various computers (e.g. at banks, telephone companies, work, home, and on the Internet).

SUMMARY

One of the fundamental purposes for creating cybercrime categories, is to emphasize the role of computers in crime and to give guidance for dealing with computers in that role. The categories presented in this chapter can be used to develop procedures for dealing with digital evidence and cybercrime. Early categories were necessarily general because cybercrime was not well understood. As the categories were refined, guidelines were developed to help investigators deal with cybercrime and digital evidence. These guidelines are still in their early stages, especially with regard to digital evidence. More detailed guidelines for dealing with digital evidence are presented in Chapters 4, 6, 7 and 8.

The language described in this chapter both enables and limits our ability to describe and interpret digital evidence. This language is useful for talking about cybercrime and developing evidence-processing procedures but does not include other important aspects of investigating cybercrime. Concepts and techniques that are helpful for interpreting digital evidence, discerning patterns of behavior, understanding motives, generating investigative leads, linking cases, and develop trial strategies are presented in Chapters 3 and 9.

REFERENCES

Carter, D. L. (1995) "Computer Crime Categories, How Techno-Criminals Operate," *FBI Law Enforcement Bulletin,* July.

Parker, D. (1976) *Crime by Computer,* New York, NY: Charles Scribners' and Sons.

Parker, D. (1983) *Fighting Computer Crime*, New York, NY: Charles Scribners' and Sons.

Parker, D. (1998) *Fighting Computer Crime: A New Framework for Protecting Information*, New York, NY: John Wiley & Sons.

US Department of Justice (DOJ) (1994) *Federal Guidelines for Searching and Seizing Computers* [http://www.usdoj.gov/criminal/cybercrime/search_docs/toc.htm].

US Department of Justice (DOJ) (1998) *Supplement to Federal Guidelines for Searching and Seizing Computers* [http://www.usdoj.gov/criminal/cybercrime/supplement/ssgsup.htm].

## CHAPTER 3

MODUS OPERANDI, MOTIVE AND TECHNOLOGY

Brent E. Turvey, M.S.

*All our lauded technological progress – our very
civilization – is like the axe in the hand of the
pathological criminal.*

(Albert Einstein)

The purpose of this chapter is to discuss the development of computer and Internet technology as it relates to both offender *modus operandi* and offender motive. The context of this effort will be necessarily informed by a historical perspective, and by examples of how computer and Internet technologies may influence criminal behavior. It is hoped through this brief rendering that readers may come to appreciate that while technology and tools change, as does the language that describes them, the underlying psychological needs, or motives, for criminal behavior remain historically unchanged.

AXES TO PATHOLOGICAL CRIMINALS, AND OTHER UNINTENDED CONSEQUENCES

What the Internet is today was never intended or imagined by those who broke its first ground.

In 1969 the United States Department of Defense's research arm, ARPA (the Advanced Research Projects Agency) began funding what would eventually evolve to become the technological basis for the Internet[1]. Their intent was to create a mechanism for ensured communication between military installations. It was not their intent to provide for synchronous and asynchronous international person-to-person communication between private individuals, and the beginnings of a pervasive form of social-global connectedness. It was not their intent to create venues for trade and commerce in a digital-international marketplace. Nor was it their intent to place axes in the hands of pathological criminals in the form of robust and

[1] *The development of the Internet is discussed in more detail in Chapter 5.*

efficient tools for stealing information, monitoring individual activity, covert communication, and dispersing illicit material. Regardless, that technology, and every related technology subsequent to its evolution, provides for these things and much more.

The Internet began as an endeavor to help one group within the United States government to share information and communicate within its own ranks on a national level. It has evolved into a system that provides virtually any individual, who has some basic skills and materials, with the ability to share information and contact anyone else connected with that system on an international level. Without exaggeration, the Internet and its related technologies represent nothing short of historically unparalleled trans-social and trans-economic connectedness.

However, history is replete with similar examples of sweet technological success, followed by deep but unintended social consequences:

- The American businessman, Eli Whitney, invented the cotton gin in 1793, which effectively cleaned the seeds from green-seeded inland cotton, bringing economic prosperity to the South and revitalizing the dying slave trade. This added much fuel to the engines which were already driving the United States towards civil war.

- The American physician, Dr Richard J. Gatling, invented the hand crank operated rapid-fire multi-barreled Gatling gun in 1862, which he believed would decrease the number of lives lost in battle through its efficiency. This led the way for numerous generations of multi-barreled guns with increased range and extremely high rates of fire. Such weapons have been employed with efficient yet devastating results against military personnel and civilians in almost every major conflict since. The efficiency of such weapons to discharge projectiles has not been the life-saving element that Dr Gatling had hoped, but rather has significantly compounded the lethality of warfare.

- The American theoretical physicist, Robert J. Oppenheimer, director of the research laboratory in Los Alamos, New Mexico, headed the US Government's Manhattan Project in the mid-1940s with the aim of unlocking the power of the atom, which resulted in the development of the atomic bomb. The atomic bomb may have been intended to end the Second World War and prevent the loss of more soldiers in combat on both sides. However its use against the citizens of Japan in 1945 arguably signalled the official beginning of both the Cold War and the arms race between the United States and the Soviet Union, not to mention the devastation it caused directly, the impact of which is still felt today.

These simple examples do us the service of demonstrating that, historically, no matter what objective a technology is designed to achieve, and no matter what intentions or beliefs impel its initial development, technology is still subordinate to the motives and morality of those who employ it. Technology helps create more efficient tools. Any tool, no matter how much technology goes into it, is still only an extension of individual intent. And there are invariably individuals that are driven to satisfy criminal motives and intentions.

Sadly, there are those who fear technology and argue differently. They often argue that the technology itself is to blame. This is a misguided endeavor, and one that shifts the responsibility for human action away from human hands:

> "It's something I call 'technophobia,' " says Paul McMasters, First Amendment ombudsman at the Freedom Forum in Arlington, Virginia. "Cyberpanic is all about the demonization of a new form of technology, where that technology is automatically perceived as a crime or a criminal instrument." (Shamburg 1999)

But, as Meloy (1998) is well to point out, "The rather mundane reality is that every new technology can serve as a vehicle for criminal behavior." Computers and the Internet are no different. Only with this simple observation in mind may we proceed towards understanding how it is that criminals employ technology in the commission of their crimes.

MODUS OPERANDI

Modus operandi (MO) is a Latin term that means, "a method of operating." It refers to the behaviors that are committed by a criminal for the purpose of successfully completing an offense. A criminal's *modus operandi* reflects *how* they committed their crimes. It is separate from their motives, which have to do with *why* they commit their crimes (Burgess *et al.* 1997).

A criminal's *modus operandi* has traditionally been investigatively relevant for the case linkage efforts of law enforcement. However, it is also investigatively relevant because it can involve procedures or techniques that are characteristic of a particular discipline or field of knowledge. This can include behaviors that are reflective of both criminal and non-criminal expertise (Turvey 1999).

A criminal's MO is comprised of learned behaviors that can evolve and develop over time. It can be refined, as an offender becomes more experienced, sophisticated, and confident (Geberth 1996). It can also become less competent and less skillful over time, decompensating by virtue of a deteriorating mental state, or increased uses of mind-altering substances (Turvey 1999).

In either case, an offender's MO behavior is functional by its nature. It most often serves (or fails to serve) one or more of three purposes (Turvey 1999):

- protects the offender's identity;
- ensures the successful completion of the crime;
- facilitates the offender's escape.

Examples of MO behaviors related to computer and Internet crimes include, but are most certainly not limited to (Turvey 1999):

- Amount of planning before a crime, evidenced by behavior and materials (i.e. notes taken in the planning stage regarding location selection and potential victim information, found in e-mails or personal journals on a PC).
- Materials used by the offender in the commission of the specific offense (i.e. system type, connection type, software involved, etc.).
- Presurveillance of a crime scene or victim (i.e. monitoring a potential victim's posting habits on a discussion list, learning about a potential victim's lifestyle or occupation on their personal website, contacting a potential victim directly using a friendly alias or a pretense, etc.).
- Offense location selection (i.e. a threatening message sent to a Usenet newsgroup, a conversation had in an IRC chat room to groom a potential victim, a server hosting illicit materials for covert distribution, etc.).
- Use of a weapon during a crime (i.e. a harmful virus or Trojan programs sent to a victim's PC as an e-mail attachment, etc.).
- Offender precautionary acts (i.e. the use of aliases, stealing time on a private system for use as a base of operations, IP spoofing, etc.).

TECHNOLOGY AND *MODUS OPERANDI*

As already alluded to at the beginning of this chapter, technology has long shared a relationship with criminal behavior. For example, without notable exception each successive advance in communications technology (including most recently the proliferation of PCs and Internet-related technologies) has been adopted for use in criminal activity, or has acted as a vehicle for criminal behavior. Some prominent examples include, but are not limited to:

- *Spoken language* has been used to make threats of violence and engage in perjury.
- *Paper and pencil* have been used to write notes to tellers during bank robberies, to write ransom notes in kidnappings, and to falsify financial documents and records.
- *The postal system* has been used for selling non-existent property to the elderly, distributing stolen or confidential information, distributing illicit materials such as drugs and illegal pornographic images, the networking of criminal subcultures, and the delivery of lethal explosive devices to unsuspecting victims.
- *Telephones* have been used for anonymous harassment of organizations and individuals, the networking of criminal subcultures, and for credit card fraud involving phony goods or services.
- *Fax machines* have been used for the networking of criminal subcultures, distributing stolen or confidential information, and the harassment of organizations and individuals.
- *E-mail* has been used for anonymous harassment of organizations and individuals,

the networking of criminal subcultures, for credit card fraud involving phony goods or services, distributing stolen or confidential information, and distributing illicit materials such as illegal pornographic images.

- *Web sites* have also been used for anonymous harassment of organizations and individuals, the networking of criminal subcultures, and for credit card fraud involving phony goods or services, distributing stolen or confidential information, and distributing illicit materials such as illegal pornographic images.

The *proactive* aspect of this relationship has been that criminals can borrow from existing technologies to enhance their current *modus operandi* in order to achieve their desired ends, or to defeat technologies and circumstances that might make the completion of their crime more difficult. If dissatisfied with available or existing tools, and sufficiently skilled and motivated, they can also endeavor to develop new technologies.

The result is a new technological spin on an existing form of criminal behavior.

EXAMPLE 1 (Swiss 1997)

In August of 1997, a Swiss couple, John (52 years old) and Buntham (26 years old) Grabenstetter, were arrested at the Hilton in Buffalo, New York and accused of smuggling into the United States thousands of computerized pictures of children having sex.

The couple were alleged by authorities to have sold wholesale amounts of child pornography through the Internet, and carried with them thousands of electronic files of child pornography to the United States from their Swiss home. They were alleged to have agreed over the Internet to sell child pornography to US Customs agents posing as local US porn shop owners. They were alleged to have agreed to sell 250 CD-ROMs to US investigators for $10,000. According to reports, one CD-ROM had over 7000 images.

It is further alleged that their two-year-old daughter, who was traveling with them at the time of their arrest, is also a victim. Authorities claim that photographs of their daughter are on the CD-ROMs her parents were distributing.

In Example 1, an existing MO, which consisted of manufacturing and marketing child pornography to other distributors, was allegedly enhanced by digital imaging technology and the Internet. Alleged contact with international buyers was first made using Internet technologies, through which communications resulted in an agreement for sale of illicit materials. The illicit images were then alleged to have been digitized for transport, ease of storage, and ease of duplication once in the US.

EXAMPLE 2

Quoted from an article in *Wired* magazine from February 1998 (Cops 1998):

Police in four states say they're the victims of what amounts to a cybersex sting in reverse, the latest in a string of Internet pornography cases getting headlines around the United States.

The *News & Observer* of Raleigh, North Carolina, reports that the officers encountered a 17-year-old Illinois girl in chat rooms – and that their e-mail relationships quickly became sexually explicit. The girl then told her mother about the contacts with deputies in Virginia, North Carolina, Georgia, and Texas, and her mother informed authorities in those states. Discipline followed.

The chain of events – which included one North Carolina deputy sending the girl a photograph of his genitals – led an attorney for one of the officers to decry what he suggests was a setup.

"This young woman has gone around the country, as best we can determine, and made contact with a very vulnerable element of our society – police officers – and then drawn them in and alleged some type of sexual misconduct," said Troy Spencer, the attorney for one suspended Virginia officer. "She's a cyberspider."

The same teenager from the above instances, who acted under the alias "Rollerbabe," was connected to other similar incidents which were published in *The News Observer* of North Carolina in November of 1998 (Jarvis 1998):

… Earlier this year, Wake County sheriff's deputies were accused of taking advantage of a Midwestern teenager in an Internet sex scandal that eventually snared law enforcement officers in several states.

Now another officer has been caught in the Web, raising questions about who is snaring whom. A rural county sheriff in Illinois said this week that he had been enticed into a romantic e-mail correspondence with "Rollerbabe" – who claimed to be an athletic, 18-year-old blonde from suburban Chicago named Brenda Thoma. The summer relationship surfaced this month when her mother complained to county officials about it.

That pattern also emerged in Wake County and in three other states – prompting one officer's attorney to call the young woman a "*cyberspider*" – where e-mail friendships between law enforcement officers and Rollerbabe escalated into sexually explicit electronic conversations. Scandals broke out when her mother, Cathy Thoma, 44, complained to the officers' superiors. One officer whose career was ruined by the encounter, former Chesapeake, Va., police Detective Bob Lunsford, said Friday that he is convinced the young woman's mother is involved with the e-mail. No one has brought criminal charges against the pair, nor has any one claimed that the women did anything illegal.

In March, Mrs Thoma insisted her daughter was courted by the police officers whom she trusted after meeting them online. She said she wasn't troubled by her daughter's computer habits. The Thoma family – a husband and wife and several children – were living in Manhattan, Ill., until several weeks ago when they moved to Lansing, Mich. An e-mail request for comment about the incident with the sheriff brought a brief response Friday, signed by someone identifying herself as Brenda Thoma.

… Earlier this week, [Paul] Spaur, 56, a Clinton County, Ill., sheriff, acknowledged carrying on an Internet romance with Rollerbabe from his county computer this summer. When Mrs Thoma complained to county officials, Spaur said he had done nothing wrong but offered to pay $1222 for 679 hours worth of phone bills spent on the computer.

… In January, Wake County Sheriff John H. Baker Jr suspended seven deputies and demoted one of them because some of the officers had e-mail conversations with Rollerbabe while on duty; their supervisors were punished because it happened on their watch. Mrs Thoma said the deputy who was demoted had initiated the relationship and sent nude photos of himself over the Internet, but Baker said there was no way to prove who was depicted in the photos.

… Shortly afterward, it was discovered that officers in Virginia, Texas and Georgia had had similar encounters with Rollerbabe. An officer in Richland, Texas, resigned after Mrs Thoma complained about the relationship.

Lunsford, the Virginia detective, was publicly humiliated when he was suspended and a local TV station referred to the investigation as a child pornography case, because the girl was then 17. Before that he had won several commendations, including one for saving another police officer's life. In May, the Chesapeake Police Department formally cleared Lunsford, who had been on leave because of a stress-related illness; he eventually resigned. His marriage also broke apart.

In Example 2, we have the MO of what might be referred to as a female law enforcement "groupie." Arguably, she is responding to what is referred to by some in the law enforcement community as the *Blue Magnet*. This term is derived from the reality that some individuals are deeply attracted to those in uniform, and who, by extension, have positions of perceived authority. In the past, their have been cases where law enforcement groupies have obsessively made contact with those in blue through seductive letter writing, random precinct house telephone calling, the frequenting of "cop bars," and participation in law enforcement conferences or fund raisers. Now, law enforcement e-mail addresses and personal profiles can be gathered quickly and easily over the Internet on personal and department Websites, and in online chat rooms, making them more easily accessible to those attracted to the blue magnet. And the truth is that some officers provide this information, and seek out these online chat areas, with the overt intention of attracting just these types of individuals (i.e. registered IRC chat rooms such as #COPS, dedicated to "Cops Who Flirt;" AOL chat rooms such as "Cops who flirt," etc.).

It is important to keep in mind, however, that law enforcement groupies are not necessarily individuals engaged in criminal activity; that is, unless they attempt to blackmail an officer in some fashion after they get them to engage in some kind of compromising circumstance, or engage in harassment and/or stalking behavior, all of which can and does happen. The criminal activity in these instances (if there is any at all), as in the example above, can actually come from the law enforcement officers involved. This can take the form of misusing and abusing department resources and violating the public trust, including but not limited to things like inappropriate telephone charges, vehicle use, and desertion of one's assigned duties. And we are not talking about small misallocations, but rather large ones such as in the example, which are symptomatic of ongoing patterns of departmental resource misuse and abuse.

As in Example 2, criminal activity in these instances can also take on the form of the distribution of pornographic materials (an officer allegedly e-mailed a digital photograph of his genitals to the 17-year-old girl), which, depending on the circumstances, can have serious legal consequences.

In both examples, technology facilitated criminal behavior in terms of providing both the mechanisms for initial contact between the involved parties, and a means for communication and illicit materials sharing between the parties over great distances. But as we have shown, less complex and "immediate" technologies do exist which have facilitated the same type of behavior in the past.

A more *reactive* aspect of the relationship between MO and technology, from the criminal's point of view, involves the relationship between the advancement of crime detection technologies in the forensic sciences, and a criminal's knowledge of them.

Successful criminals are arguably those who avoid detection and identification, or at the very least capture. The problem for criminals is that as they incorporate new and existing technologies into their MO which make their criminal behavior or identity more difficult to detect, the forensic sciences have made advances to become more competent at crime detection. Subsequently, criminals that are looking to make a career, or even a hobby, for themselves with their illegal activity must rise to the meet that challenge. That is to say, as criminals learn about new forensic technologies and techniques being applied to their particular area of criminal behavior, they must be willing to modify their MO, if possible, in order to circumvent those efforts.

But even an extremely skillful, motivated, and flexible offender may only learn of a new forensic technology when it has been applied to one of their crimes and resulted in their identification and/or capture. While this encounter can teach them something that they may never forget in the commission of future crimes, in such cases the damage will already have been done.

This text is replete with examples of such instances, so we will not adduce specifics in this chapter.

MOTIVE AND TECHNOLOGY

The term *motive* refers to the emotional, psychological, or material need that impels, and is satisfied by, a behavior (Turvey 1999). Criminal motive is generally technology independent. That is to say, the psychological or material needs that are nurtured and satisfied by a criminal's pattern of behavior tend to be separate from the technology of the day. The same motives that exist today have arguably existed throughout recorded history, in one form or another. However, it may also be argued that existing motives (i.e. sexual fetishes) can evolve with the employment of, or association of, offense activities with specific technologies. Towards understanding these issues, this section will demonstrate how an existing behavioral motivational typology may be applied within the context of computer- and Internet-related criminal behavior.

In 1979, A. Nicholas Groth, an American clinical psychologist working with both victims and offender populations, published a study of over 500 rapists. In his study, he found that rape, like other crimes involving behaviors that satisfy emotional needs, is complex and multi-determined. That is to say, the act of rape itself serves a number of psychological needs and purposes (motives) for the offender. The purpose of his work was clinical, to understand the motivations of rapists for the purpose of the development of effective treatment plans (Groth 1979).

Eventually the Groth rapist motivational typology was taken and modified by the FBI's National Center for the Analysis of Violent Crime (NCAVC) and its affiliates (Hazelwood *et al.* 1991; Burgess and Hazelwood 1995).

This author has found, through casework, that this behaviorally based motivational classification system, with some modifications, is useful for understanding the psychological basis for most criminal behavior. The basic psychological needs, or motives, that impel human criminal behaviors remain essentially the same across different types of criminals, despite their behavioral expression, which may involve computer crimes, stalking, harassment, kidnapping, child molestation, terrorism, sexual assault, homicide, and/or arson. This is not to say that the motivational typology presented here should be considered the final word in terms of all *specific* offender motivations. But in terms of general types of psychological needs that are being satisfied by offender behavior, they are fairly inclusive, and fairly useful.

Below, the author gives a proposed behavioral motivational typology (Turvey 1999), and examples, adapted from Burgess and Hazelwood (1995), with some input from Geberth (1996). This author takes credit largely for the shift in emphasis from classifying *offenders* – to classifying *offense behaviors* (turning it from an inductive labeling system to a deductive tool). They include the following types of behaviors: *power reassurance, power assertive, anger retaliatory, sadistic, opportunistic,* and *profit oriented.* (Sections of text in this typology are taken directly from Turvey (1999).)

POWER REASSURANCE (aka COMPENSATORY)

These include criminal behaviors that are intended to restore the criminal's self-confidence or self-worth through the use of low aggression means. These behaviors suggest an underlying lack of confidence and a sense of personal inadequacy. This may manifest itself in a misguided belief that the victim desires the offense behavior, and is somehow a willing or culpable participant. It may also manifest itself in the form of self-deprecating or self-loathing behavior which is intended to garner a response of pity for sympathy from the victim.

The belief motivating this behavior is often that the victim will enjoy and eroticize the offense behavior, and may subsequently fall in love with the offender. This stems from the criminal's own fears of personal inadequacy. The offense behavior is restorative of the offender's self-doubt, and therefore emotionally reassuring. It will occur as his need for that kind of reassurance arises.

EXAMPLE
The following is a media account of the circumstances surrounding Andrew Archambeau, a Californian man who pleaded no contest to harassing a woman via e-mail and the telephone (Durfee 1996):

… Archambeau, 32, was charged with a misdemeanor almost two years ago for stalking the Farmington Hills woman.

… Archambeau met the woman through a computer dating service. He messaged her by computer and [they] talked on the phone.

The couple met in person twice. After the second meeting, the woman dumped Archambeau by e-mail.

He continued to leave phone messages and e-mail the woman [urging her to continue dating him], even after police warned him to stop.

Archambeau was charged in May 1994 under the state's stalking law, a misdemeanor.

"Times have changed. People no longer have to leave the confines and comfort of their homes to harass somebody," [Oakland County Assistant Prosecutor Neal Rockind] said.

In this example, the offender was unwilling to let go of the relationship, perceiving a connection to the victim that he was unwilling to relinquish. The content of the messages that he left was not described as violent, or threatening, merely persistent. While it is possible that this could have eventually escalated to more *retaliatory* behaviors, the behaviors did not appear to be coming from that emotion.

POWER ASSERTIVE (aka ENTITLEMENT)

These include criminal behaviors that are intended to restore the offender's self-confidence or self-worth through the use of moderate to high aggression means. These behaviors suggest an underlying lack of confidence and a sense of personal inadequacy, that are expressed through control, mastery, or humiliation of the victim, while demonstrating the offender's perceived sense of authority.

Offenders evidencing this type of behavior display little doubt about their own adequacy and masculinity. In fact, they may be using their attacks as an expression of their own virility. In their perception, they are entitled to the fruits of their attack by virtue of being a male and being physically stronger.

Offenders evidencing this type of behavior may grow more confident over time, as their egocentricity may be very high. They may begin to do things that can lead to their identification. Law enforcement may interpret this as a sign that the offender desires to be caught. What is actually true is that the offender has no respect for law enforcement, has learned that they can commit their offenses without the need to fear identification or capture, and subsequently they may not take precautions that they have learned are generally unnecessary.

This type of behavior does not indicate a desire to harm the victim, necessarily, but rather to possess them. Demonstrating power over their victims is their means of expressing mastery, strength, control, authority, and identity to themselves. The attacks are therefore intended to reinforce the offender's inflated sense of self-confidence or self-worth.

EXAMPLE
The following is taken from a media account of the circumstances surrounding the Dwayne and Debbie Tamai family of Emeryville, Ontario (High-tech 1997). This case of electronic harassment involved their 15-year-old son, Billy, who took control of all of the electronic devices in the families home, including the phone, and manipulated them to distress other family members for his own amusement. The incidents began in December of 1996, when friends of the family complained that phone calls to the Tamia home were repeatedly being waylaid and cut off:

… Police confirmed that the sabotage was an inside job, but refused to name the culprit and said nothing would be gained by filing charges against him. Dwayne and Debbie Tamai issued a statement saying that their son, Billy, had admitted to making the mysterious calls.

The interruptions included burps and babbling and claims of control over the inner workings of the Tamais' custom-built home, including what appeared to be the power to turn individual appliances on and off by remote control.

"It started off as a joke with his friends and just got so out of hand that he didn't know how to stop it and was afraid to come forward and tell us in fear of us disowning him," the Tamais said in their statement, which was sent to local news media.

On Saturday, the Tamais said they were planning to take their son to the police to defend him against persistent rumors that he was responsible. Instead, he confessed to being the intruder who called himself Sommy.

"All the crying I heard from him at night I thought was because of the pain he was suffering caused by Sommy," the letter said. "We now realize it was him crying out for help because he wanted to end all this but was afraid because of how many people were now involved."

… "We eliminated all external sources and interior sources," Babbitt said.

A two-day sweep by a team of intelligence and security experts loaded with high-tech equipment failed to locate "Sommy" on Friday. The team was brought in by two television networks.

… missed messages and strange clickings seemed minor when a disembodied voice, eerily distorted by computer, first interrupted a call to make himself known.

After burping repeatedly, the caller told a startled Mrs Tamai, "I know who you are. I stole your voice mail."

Mocking, sometimes menacing, the high-tech stalker became a constant presence, eavesdropping on family conversations, switching TV channels and shutting off the electricity.

"He would threaten me," Mrs Tamai said last week. "It was very frightening: 'I'm going to get you. I know where you live.'"

"I befriended him, because the police asked me to, and he calmed down and said he wasn't going to hurt me. The more I felt I was kissing his butt, the safer I felt."

In this case, the son repeatedly made contact with the victims (his parents), and made verbal threats in combination with the electronic harassment, all in an effort to demonstrate his power and authority over them. The victims were not physically harmed, though they were in fear and greatly inconvenienced by the fact that an unknown force appeared to have control over a great many aspects of their lives.

ANGER RETALIATORY (aka ANGER OR DISPLACED)
These include criminal behaviors that suggest a great deal of rage, either towards a specific person, group, institution, or a symbol of either. These types of behaviors are commonly evidenced in stranger-to-stranger sexual assaults, domestic homicides, work-related homicide, harassment, and cases involving terrorist activity.

Anger retaliatory behavior is just what the name suggests. The offender is acting on the basis of cumulative real or imagined wrongs from those that are in their world. The victim of the attack may be one of these people such as a relative, a girlfriend, or a coworker. Or the victim may symbolize that person to the offender in dress, occupation, and/ or physical characteristics.

The main goal of this offender behavior is to service their cumulative aggression. They are retaliating against the victim for wrongs or perceived wrongs, and their aggression can manifest itself spanning a wide range, from verbally abusive epithets to hyper-aggressed homicide with multiple collateral victims. In such cases, even sexual acts can be put into the service of anger and aggression (this is the opposite of the sadistic offender, who employs aggression in the service of sexual gratification).

It is important not to confuse retaliatory behavior with sadistic behavior. Although they can share some characteristics at first blush, the motivations are wholly separate. Just because a crime is terrible or brutal does not confirm that the offender responsible was a sadist, and tortured the victim. Reliance upon a competent reconstruction by the appropriate forensic scientists is requisite.

EXAMPLE

The following is a media account of the circumstances surrounding the homicide of Marlene Stumpf (Wife's 1997). Her husband, Raymond Stumpf, who was host and producer of a home shopping show that aired in Pottstown, Pennsylvania, allegedly stabbed her to death. He was known as "Mr Telemart," and also worked full-time as a manager at a fast-food restaurant.

A woman who received flowers from a man she corresponded with on the Internet has been slain, and her husband has been charged with murder.

The dozen roses were sent several days ago to "Brandis," the online name used by Marlene Stumpf, 47, police said. Her son found her body Monday night on the kitchen floor with three blood-covered knives nearby.

Raymond Stumpf, 54, her husband of 13 years and host of a local cable television show, was found in the dining room, bleeding from arm and stomach wounds that police consider self-inflicted.

"It was a particularly gruesome scene with a lot of blood that showed evidence of extreme violence," prosecutor Bruce Castor Jr. said Wednesday. "(Stumpf) tried to kill himself, presumably because he felt bad he had killed his wife."

Stumpf told police his wife started slapping him during an argument Monday night and he "just went wild." Police said he couldn't remember what happened.

Detectives hope Mrs Stumpf's computer and computer files will provide information about her online relationships and people who could help prosecutors with a motive, Castor said.

In this example, it is alleged that the husband killed his wife after an argument over her Internet romance, and then tried to kill himself. The fact that there is digital evidence related to this crime, and that the Internet is somehow involved, is incidental to the husband's motive for killing her. Instances of similar domestic murder-suicides involving real or perceived infidelity are nothing new in the history of human relationships, and always tragic.

The retaliatory aspect of this case comes from the description of the nature and extent of the injuries to the victim (i.e. that Mr Stumpf "just went wild," and that there was "extreme violence").

The retaliatory aspect of this case is further evidenced by circumstances that supporting the context of that retaliatory behavior, including:

- the argument;
- the use of available materials;
- the use of multiple weapons;
- the relatively short duration of the attack.

ANGER EXCITATION (aka SADISTIC)

These include criminal behaviors that evidence offender sexual gratification from victim pain and suffering. The primary motivation for the behavior is sexual, however the sexual expression for the offender is manifested in physical aggression, or torture behavior, toward the victim.

This offense behavior is perhaps the most individually complex. This type of behavior is motivated by intense, individually varying fantasies that involve inflicting brutal levels of pain on the victim solely for offender sexual pleasure. The goal of this behavior is total victim fear and submission for the purposes of feeding the offender's sexual desires. Aggression services sexual gratification. The result is that the victim must be physically or psychologically abused and humiliated for this offender to become sexually excited and subsequently gratified.

Any example of sadistic behavior must include evidence of sexual gratification that an offender achieves as a result of directly experiencing the suffering of their conscious victim. Dead or unconscious victims are incapable of suffering in the manner that gives the necessary sexual stimulation to the sadist.

PROFIT ORIENTED

These include criminal behaviors that evidence an offender motivation oriented towards material or personal gain. These can be found in all types of homicides, robberies, burglaries, muggings, arsons, bombings, kidnappings, and fraud, just to name a few.

This type of behavior is the most straightforward, as the successful completion of the offense satisfies the offender's needs. Psychological and emotional needs are not necessarily satisfied by purely profit-motivated behavior (if one wants to argue that a profit-motivated person is also motivated by a need for reassurance that one is a good provider, that would have to be followed by a host of other reassurance behaviors). Any behavior that is not purely profit motivated, which satisfies an emotional or psychological need, should be examined with the lens of the other behavior motivational types.

EXAMPLE
The following is excepted from a media account regarding the circumstances surrounding the activities of Valdimir Levin in St Petersburg, Russia (Piper 1998):

> Vladimir Levin, a computer expert from Russia's second city of St Petersburg, used his skills for ill-gotten gains. He was caught stealing from Citibank in a fraud scheme and said he used bank customer passwords and codes to transfer funds from their accounts to accounts he controlled in Finland, the Netherlands, Germany, Israel and the United States.

In this example, regardless of any other motivation that may be evident in this offender's behavioral patterns, the desire for profit is clearly primary.

REFERENCES

Burgess, A., Burgess, A., Douglas, J. and Ressler, R. (1997) *Crime Classification Manual*, San Francisco: Jossey-Bass, Inc.

Burgess, A. and Hazelwood, R. (eds) (1995) *Practical Aspects of Rape Investigation: A Multidisciplinary Approach*, 2nd edn, New York: CRC Press.

"Cops 'Lured' into Net Sex," *Wired News*, 16 February 1998.

Durfee, D. (1996) "Man pleads no contest in stalking case," *The Detroit News*, 25 January.

Geberth, V. (1996) *Practical Homicide Investigation*, 3rd edn, New York: CRC Press.

Groth, A. N., *Men Who Rape: The Psychology of the Offender* (New York: Plenum, 1979).

Hazelwood R., Reboussin R., Warren J. I. and Wright J. A. (1991) "Prediction of Rapist Type and Violence from Verbal, Physical, and Sexual Scales," *Journal of Interpersonal Violence*, 6 (1): 55–67.

"High-tech 'Stalking' of Canadian Family Linked to Teen-aged Son," *Associated Press*, 20 April 1997.

Jarvis, C. (1998) "Teen again linked to e-mail affair," *The News Observer*, North Carolina, 28 November.

Meloy, J. R. (ed.) (1998) *The Psychology of Stalking: Clinical and Forensic Perspectives*, San Diego: Academic Press.

Piper, E. (1998) "Russian cybercrime flourishes: Deteriorating economic conditions have brought pirating and cracking mainstream," *Reuters*, 30 December.

Shamburg, R. (1999) "A Tortured Case," *Net Life*, 7 April.

"Swiss couple charged in U.S. child pornography sting," *Reuters Information Service*, 22 August 1997.

Turvey, B. (1999) *Criminal Profiling: An Introduction to Behavioral Evidence Analysis*, London: Academic Press.

"Wife's Internet friendship may have led to her death," *Associated Press*, 23 January 1997.

## CHAPTER 4

APPLYING FORENSIC SCIENCE TO COMPUTERS

In an investigation, the nature and extent of the search will depend on the known circumstances of the crime. If a computer is the fruit or instrumentality of a crime, the investigators will focus on the hardware. If the crime involves contraband information, the investigators will look for anything that relates to that information, including the hardware containing it. If information on a computer is evidence and the investigators know what they are looking for, it might be possible to collect the evidence needed quite quickly. Swift searches are necessary in exigent circumstances, e.g. when there is a fear that another crime is about to be committed or a perpetrator is getting away. If the information is evidence but the investigators do not know what they are looking for, then either a lengthy search of the computers involved will be required or it might make sense to collect everything and search it later in a controlled environment.

In any case, the investigators must be able to prove the authenticity and integrity of the evidence collected, e.g. that the evidence is what it is said to be, came from where it is said to have come from, and has not been altered or contaminated in any way. This can be particularly difficult when dealing with digital evidence because it is so easily changed. The simple act of turning a computer on or off can change or destroy evidence. Therefore, it is important to be methodical, well organized, and familiar with the technology involved. This chapter describes a methodical approach for dealing with digital evidence, concentrating on a single, non-networked computer. Subsequent chapters describe how this methodical approach can be applied to digital evidence on different parts of computer networks.

It is crucial to understand how to deal with an individual computer as a source of evidence before venturing into the complicated domain of digital evidence on computer networks. Individual computers are a fundamental part of computer networks, and the majority of digital evidence on a network is either stored on or passing through individual computers. In short, this chapter provides the necessary foundations for understanding the remainder of this text, computer networks as a source of evidence.

A BRIEF HISTORY OF COMPUTERS

The evolution of the electronic computer encompasses a relatively brief period in modern history. Driven by military defense requirements for more sophisticated intelligence code-cracking and artillery trajectory prediction devices, the first electronic mathematical computation machines were constructed just after the end of World War II. In fact, the first operational Electronic Numerical Integrator and Computer (ENIAC) was switched on over 50 years ago in February of 1946. ENIAC was comprised of thousands of electric vacuum tubes, filled a 30 by 50 foot room, generated vast quantities of heat, weighed 30 tons, and possessed less computing power than today's basic hand-held calculator. It was a second technological breakthrough, however, that insured the future viability of the electronic computer; namely, the invention of the solid-state transistor one year later in 1947. (Hollinger 1997)

There have been revolutionary developments in computer technology since the 30-ton ENIAC was created. In particular, personal computers enable individuals to own and command a powerful machine that only a nation could afford 50 years ago. The personal computer became possible in 1974 when a small company named Intel started selling inexpensive computer chips called 8080 microprocessors. A single 8080 microprocessor contained all of the electronic circuits necessary to create a programmable computer. Almost immediately, a few primitive computers were developed using this microprocessor.

Figure 4.1

Photo of left side of ENIAC as installed in BRL Bldg 328. The white cabinet in the rear is the core memory, a late addition ("US Army Photo" from the archives of the ARL Technical Library).

By the early 1980s, Steve Jobs and Steve Wozniak were mass marketing Apple computers and Bill Gates was working with IBM to mass market IBM personal computers. In England, the Acorn and the Sinclair computers were being sold. The Sinclair, a small keyboard that plugged into a standard television and audio cassette player for memory storage, was revolutionary in 1985. By supplanting expensive, centralized mainframes, these small, inexpensive computers made Bill Gates' dream of putting a computer in every home a distinct possibility. Additionally, all of these computers spread around the globe making a global network of computers the next logical step.

Today, personal computers and computer networks are commonplace and advances in their use are occurring every day. Computers are being embedded in cars, phones, coffee makers, and toys. Researchers are developing miniature computers and computers that work on the quantum level. All of these computers could be a source of evidence in a crime.

COMPUTER COMPONENTS AND OPERATIONS RELEVANT TO DIGITAL EVIDENCE ANALYSIS

Each time a computer is turned on, it must familiarize itself with its internal components and the peripheral world. This start up process is called the *boot process*, because it is as if a computer has to pull itself up by its bootstraps. The boot process has three basic stages: the Central Processing Unit (CPU) reset, the *power-on self test* (POST), and the *disk boot*.

CENTRAL PROCESSING UNIT (CPU)

The CPU is the core of any computer. Everything depends on the CPU's ability to process instructions that it receives. So, the first stage in the boot process is to get the CPU started – 'reset' – with an electrical pulse. This pulse is usually generated when the power switch or button is activated. Once the CPU is reset it starts the computer's basic input and output system (BIOS).

BASIC INPUT AND OUTPUT SYSTEM (BIOS)

The basic input and output system deals with the basic movement of data around the computer. Every program that you run on your computer uses the basic input and output system to communicate with the CPU. Some BIOS programs allow an individual to set a password and until the password is

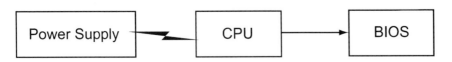

Figure 4.2

An electrical pulse resets the CPU which in turn activates the BIOS.

typed in, the BIOS will not run and the computer will not function. There are some ways to override a BIOS password but these techniques are beyond the scope of this book.

POWER-ON SELF TEST (POST)

The BIOS contains a program called the *power-on self test* (POST) that tests the fundamental components of the computer. When the CPU first activates the BIOS, the POST program is initiated. To be safe, the first test verifies the integrity of the CPU and POST program itself. The rest of the POST verifies that all of the computer's components are functioning properly, including the disk drives, monitor, RAM, and keyboard.

In many computers, the results of the POST are checked against a permanent record stored in what is called the *CMOS* microchip. If there is a problem at any stage in the power-on self test, the computer will emit a series of beeps and possibly an error message on the screen. The computer manual should explain the beep combinations for various errors. When all of the hardware tests are complete, the BIOS instructs the CPU to look for a disk containing an operating system.

OPERATING SYSTEM

An operating system extends the functions of the basic input and output system, and acts as an interface between a computer and the outside world. Without an operating system it would be very difficult to interact with the computer – basic commands would be unavailable and software would not run on the machine.

Most computers expect an operating system to be provided on a floppy disk, hard disk, or compact disk. So, when the computer is ready to load an operating system, it looks on these disks in a specific order (the order depends on the type of computer and how it is configured). The computer loads the first operating system it finds. This fact allows anyone to preempt a computer's primary operating system by providing an alternate operating system on another disk. For instance, a floppy disk containing an operating system can be inserted into a computer to prevent the operating system on the hard drive from loading. The usefulness of this option will become apparent later in this chapter.

COMPUTER DISK

When computer disks are first formatted they are divided into tracks and sectors. A combination of two or more sectors on a single track is called a cluster – the basic storage unit of a disk. Different disk formats have different cluster sizes but the concept is the same.

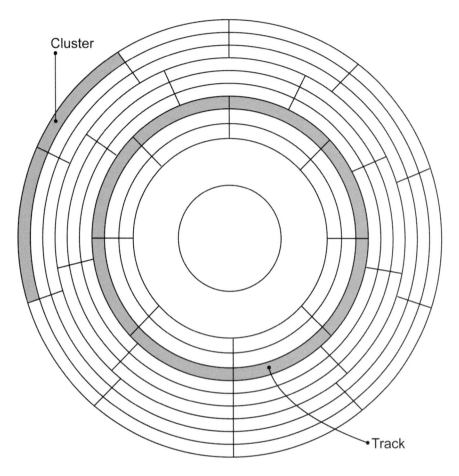

Cluster

Track

Figure 4.3

*A depiction of tracks and
clusters on a computer disk.*

When you save a file that takes up less than one cluster, other files will not use the additional space in that cluster. In short, once a cluster contains data, the entire cluster is reserved. This is similar to the situation in most restaurants. If three people are sitting at a table that seats four, the additional seat remains empty until the three people have finished using the table. The idea is that a fourth stranger might interfere with these three people's meal. Similarly, if a computer tried to squeeze extra data into the unused part of a cluster, the new data might interfere with the old. The extra space in a cluster is called slack space.

Each computer disk keeps a record of the data in each cluster. When a file is deleted, the reference to that file is removed from the record but the data is not actually deleted from the disk. Therefore, it is usually possible to retrieve a file after it has been deleted. The data will remain on the disk indefinitely. Even when a deleted file is overwritten, if the new file does not take up the entire cluster, a portion of the old file might remain in the slack space. In this case, a portion of a file can be retrieved long after it has been

Figure 4.4

When old data is overwritten with new data, some of the old data can remain.

deleted and partially overwritten. Data that has been overwritten several times can be recovered using advanced techniques. The process of recovering deleted or overwritten data from a disk is described later in this chapter.

APPLYING FORENSIC SCIENCE TO COMPUTERS

It is easy enough to claim that a bloody glove was found in a suspect's home, but it is another matter to prove it. When guilt or innocence hangs in the balance, the proof that evidence is authentic and has not been tampered with becomes essential. The US Federal Rules of Evidence, the UK Police and Criminal Evidence Act, and similar rules of evidence in other countries were established for this reason. Evidence must comply with these rules to be admissible; these rules distinguish between hearsay and direct evidence.

Digital evidence can be either hearsay or direct evidence, depending on the content, how it was created, and what it is being used to prove. Hearsay is generally inadmissible because its truthfulness cannot be verified.

> Evidence is hearsay where a statement in court repeats a statement made out of court in order to prove the truth of the content of the out of court statement. Similarly, evidence contained in a document is hearsay if the document is produced to prove that statements made in court are true. The evidence is excluded because the crucial aspect of the evidence, the truth of the out of court statement (oral or documentary), cannot be tested by cross-examination. (Hoey 1996)

However, there are some exceptions to the hearsay rule that are relevant to the discussion of digital evidence. For instance, the US Federal Rules of Evidence specify that records of regularly conducted activity are not excluded by the hearsay rule:

> A memorandum, report, record, or data compilation, in any form, or acts, events, conditions, opinions or diagnoses, made at or near the time by, or from information transmitted by a person with knowledge, if kept in the course of a regularly conducted business activity, and if it was the regular practice of that business activity to make the memorandum, report, record, or data compilation, all as shown by the testimony of the custodian or other qualified witness, unless the source of the information or the method or circumstances of preparation indicate lack of trustworthiness. The term "business" as used in this paragraph includes business, institution, association, profession, occupation, and calling of every kind, whether or not conducted for profit. (US Federal Rules of Evidence)

These forms of evidence are acceptable because they portray events quite accurately and are easier to verify than other forms of hearsay. For instance, computer log files are created routinely and contain information about acts and events made at specific times by, or from information transmitted by, a person with knowledge. In fact, some computer-generated information has been seen as so reliable that it has been accepted as direct evidence. Direct evidence is usually something tangible that is presented to prove a fact. Under certain circumstances, a computer log file might be accepted as direct evidence[1].

For both hearsay and direct evidence to be admissible, it must generally be proved that evidence is authentic and has not been modified. This is where forensic science is useful – offering carefully tested methods for ensuring that evidence is trustworthy. Concepts from forensic science can also help investigators take advantage of digital evidence in ways that would otherwise not be possible. For example, scientific techniques can be used to discern minor details that would escape the naked eye. Additionally, using the scientific method to generate and verify hypotheses can lead investigators to suspects and additional evidence.

From the forensic science perspective, there are several key aspects to processing and examining evidence (Lee 1994):

- recognition;
- preservation, collection and documentation;
- classification, comparison and individualization;
- reconstruction.

As digital evidence is found, it should be collected, documented, preserved, classified, compared with other samples, and individualized. The evidence can then be used to reconstruct the crime. Gaps in the resulting reconstruction often lead to additional evidence, at which point the cycle begins again, resulting in an increasingly clearer picture of the criminal act as a whole. Since each stage of this evidence processing cycle is key to this text, they are covered separately in more depth.

RECOGNITION OF DIGITAL EVIDENCE

Recognition of digital evidence is a two-fold process. Firstly, investigators have to recognize the hardware (e.g. computers, floppy disks, network cables) that contains digital information. Secondly, investigators have to be able to distinguish between the irrelevant information and the digital data that can establish that a crime has been committed or can provide a link between a crime and its victim or a crime and its perpetrator.

[1] *Existing rules of evidence are not entirely clear about when digital evidence is hearsay and when it is direct evidence. Therefore, the courts are ultimately responsible for deciding if evidence is admissible.*

RECOGNIZING HARDWARE

There are many computerized products that can hold digital evidence such as telephones, handheld devices, laptops, desktops, larger servers and mainframes. There are also many forms of storage media including compact disks, floppy disks, magnetic tapes, zip and jazz disks. In addition, wires, cables, and the air can carry digital evidence that, with the proper tools, can be picked out of the ether and stored for future examination.

Exposure to different kinds of computing environments is essential to develop expertise in dealing with digital evidence. Local organizations (especially local computer science departments and Internet Service Providers) may provide a tour of their facilities. Visits can be made to local computer stores, university computer labs, and Internet cafes. Whenever possible, ask people about their systems. Most system administrators are delighted to talk about their networks if asked. Also, many computer manufacturers and suppliers have Websites with detailed pictures and functional specifications of their products. Investigators can use this information to become more familiar with a variety of hardware.

RECOGNIZING DIGITAL EVIDENCE

Different cybercrimes result in different types of digital evidence. For example, cyberstalkers often use e-mail to harass their victims, computer crackers sometimes inadvertently leave evidence of their activities in log files, and child pornographers sometimes have digitized images stored on their computers. Additionally, operating systems and computer programs store digital evidence in a variety of places. Therefore, the ability to recognize digital evidence depends on an investigator's familiarity with the type of crime that was committed and the operating system(s) and computer program(s) that are involved.

COLLECTING AND PRESERVING HARDWARE AND DIGITAL EVIDENCE

Once recognized, digital evidence must be preserved in its original state. Remember that the law requires that evidence be authentic and unaltered. This is understandable when you consider the alternative of convicting someone with evidence that is like, but not the same as, the actual evidence. Having said this, a printout or duplicate of digital evidence is admissible unless a genuine question is raised as to the authenticity of the original, in which case the original has to be examined for authenticity.

A major aspect of preserving digital evidence is collecting it in a way that does not alter it. Special tools and techniques are available to preserve and collect digital evidence properly in a way that will be acceptable in a court of law. For example, it is possible to use message digests of files and disks to verify that they have not been altered. Also, it is possible to make an exact copy of data, including any data that is stored in slack space on a disk. These tools and techniques are discussed towards the end of this section.

There are two competing factors to consider when collecting digital evidence. On the one hand, to avoid leaving any evidence behind, an investigator might want to take every piece of equipment found. On the other hand, an investigator might want to take only what is essential to conserve time, effort and resources and to reduce the risk of being sued for damaging or disrupting a person's life or business more than absolutely necessary. Some computers are critical for running institutions like hospitals and taking such a computer could endanger life. Additionally, sometimes it simply is not feasible to collect hardware because of its size or quantity.

> It is simply unacceptable to suggest that any item connected to the target device is automatically seizable. In an era of increased networking, this kind of approach can lead to absurd results. In a networked environment, the computer that contains the relevant evidence may be connected to hundreds of computers in a local-area network (LAN) spread throughout a floor, building, or university campus. That LAN may also be connected to a global-area network (GAN) such as the Internet. Taken to its logical extreme, the "take it because it's connected" theory means that in any given case, thousands of machines around the world can be seized because the target machine shares the Internet. (Department of Justice 1994)

The severity of the crime and the category of cybercrime will largely determine how much digital evidence investigators collect. For example, in homicide and child pornography cases, it is often reasonable to seize everything that might contain digital evidence. In fact, during the Wonderland case described in the first chapter, US investigators seized every possession of some suspects, including their houses. Such heavy-handed methods can have adverse effects – the fear that US investigators created during the Wonderland investigation resulted in the suicides of several suspects. However, even in a homicide or child pornography investigation, the other uses of the computers should be considered. If a business depends on a computer that was collected in its entirety when only a few files were required, the investigator could be required to pay compensation for the business lost.

Table 4.1

Summarizes the considerations, advantages and disadvantges of the three evidence collecting options, each of which is discussed further in this section.

COLLECTION METHOD	RELEVANT CYBERCRIME CATEGORIES	ADVANTAGES	DISADVANTAGES
Collect hardware	■ Hardware as fruits of crime ■ Hardware as instrumentality ■ Hardware as evidence ■ Hardware contains large amount of digital evidence	■ Requires little technical expertise ■ The method is relatively simple and less open to criticism ■ Hardware can be examined later in a controlled environment	■ Risk damaging the equipment or not being able to operate it later ■ Risk liability for unnecessary disruption of business ■ Develop a bad reputation for heavy-handedness
Collect all digital evidence, leave hardware	■ Information as fruits of crime ■ Information as instrumentality ■ Information as evidence	■ Digital evidence can be examined later in a controlled evironment ■ Working with a copy prevents damage of original evidence ■ Avoids the risks and liabilities of collecting hardware	■ Requires equipment and technical expertise ■ Risk not being able to restart computer or access entire contents ■ Risk missing evidence ■ Time consuming ■ Methods are open to criticism
Only collect the digital evidence that you need	■ Information as fruits of crime ■ Information as instrumentality ■ Information as evidence	■ Allows for a range of expertise ■ Can ask for help from system admin/owner ■ Practical, quick and inexpensive ■ Avoid risks and liabilities of collecting hardware or evidence not speciified in warrant	■ Can miss or destroy evidence

Whether collecting hardware or digital evidence, one person should be designated to take charge of all evidence to reduce the risk of misplacing anything. Such coordination is especially valuable when dealing with large volumes of data that are distributed on a network.

COLLECTING AND PRESERVING HARDWARE

When dealing with hardware as contraband, instrumentality or evidence, it is usually necessary to collect computer equipment. Additionally, if a given piece of hardware contains a large amount of information relating to a case, it can be argued that it is necessary to collect the hardware. One of the most difficult decisions regarding digital evidence collection is whether to turn the computer off or leave it running. Most law enforcement training programs recommend turning all computers off immediately in all situations. Many experts insist that turning a computer off immediately is the best option because of the possibility of evidence being destroyed while the computer remains on. In fact, many investigators are trained to unplug all of the power and data cables from the back of a computer rather than use a computer's power switch just in case the switch is rigged to set off explosives. This philosophy grew out of unverifiable horror stories in which disks were reformatted while investigators stood by, or computers blew up when investigators turned the computer off[2].

Although caution often saves lives, there are many situations in which such extremes can do damage. For example, summarily turning off a large, multiple user system attached to a network could destroy evidence, disrupt many people's lives, and even damage the computer itself. Indiscriminate use of this heavy-handed method quickly gives rise to a bad reputation, as many law enforcement agencies have discovered[3]. Furthermore, if the hardware is damaged during collection, or if the computer does not work for some other reason, evidence could be lost. In many cases it makes sense to leave the computer on, save the few files that are needed, and leave. With this method, there is a reduction in the risk of damaging the computer, destroying evidence, disrupting business, and not being able to start the computer again.

If it is determined that some hardware should be collected but there is no compelling need to collect everything in sight, the most sensible approach is to employ the *independent component doctrine*. The independent component doctrine states that investigators should only collect hardware "for which they can articulate an independent basis for search or seizure (i.e. the component itself is contraband, an instrumentality, or evidence)" (Department of Justice 1994). Also, investigators should collect hardware that is necessary for the basic input and output of the computer components that are being seized. For instance, it is risky to open a computer, remove the hard drive, and collect the hard drive as an independent component. The hard drive could be damaged by such removal and it must be connected to a computer to be examined thoroughly.

If investigators decided to collect an entire computer, the collection of all of its peripheral hardware like printers and tape drives should also be considered. It is especially important to collect peripheral hardware related to the type of digital evidence one would expect to find in the computer. When looking for images, any nearby digital cameras, video cassette recorders, film digitization equipment, and graphic software disks and documentation should be collected. The reasoning behind seizing these peripherals is that it might have to be proved that the suspect created the evidence and did not just download it from the Internet. It can sometimes be demonstrated that a particular scanner was used to digitize a given image. Any software installation disks and documentation associated with the computer should also be collected. This makes it easier to deal with any problems that arise during the examination stage. For example, if documents created using a certain word processing software are collected, but the installation disks are not, it might not be possible to open the documents without that software.

[2] A quick, careful look at the internals of the computer is usually all that is required to determine if there are explosives inside.

[3] Unfortunately, many organizations distrust all law enforcement when it comes to computers because they have experienced or heard of damage as a result of this severe approach. These organizations will not involve law enforcement until they decide it is absolutely necessary – which is often too late.

Printouts and papers that could be associated with the computer should be collected. Printouts can contain information that has been changed or deleted from the computer. Notes and scraps of paper that could contain dial-up phone numbers, account information, e-mail addresses, etc. should be collected. Although it is often overlooked, the garbage often contains very useful evidence. A well-known forensic scientist once joked that whenever he returns home after his family has gone to bed, he does not bother waking his wife to learn what happened during the day, he just checks the garbage.

When a computer is to be moved, spare floppy disks should be put in the disk drives to prevent the drives from being broken in transit. Evidence tape should be put around the main components of the computer and across the floppy drives. Taping the computer will not only help to preserve the chain of evidence, it will also warn people not to use the computer. Whenever possible, investigators should write the date and their initials on each piece of evidence.

Any hardware and storage media collected must be preserved carefully. Computers and storage media are quite delicate and must be protected from dirt, fluids, humidity, impact, excessive heat and cold, strong magnetic fields, and static electricity. According to the US Federal Guidelines for Searching and Seizing Computers discussed in Chapter 2, safe ranges for most magnetic media are 50–90 degrees Fahrenheit and 20–80% humidity. There are many anecdotes about computer experts who religiously backed up important information carefully but then destroyed the backups by inadvertently exposing them to (or storing them in) unsuitable conditions. Leaving disks in a hot car, a damp warehouse, or near a strong magnetic field can result in complete loss of data, so be careful. Fortunately, there are equally many stories about recovery of digital evidence despite criminals' attempts to destroy it, so not all hope is lost when faced with damaged digital evidence.

COLLECTING AND PRESERVING DIGITAL EVIDENCE

When dealing with digital evidence (information as contraband, instrumentality or evidence) the focus is on the contents of the computer as opposed to the hardware. There are two options when collecting digital evidence from a computer: copying everything, or just copying the information needed. If there is plenty of time and uncertainty about what is being sought but a computer is suspected to contain key evidence, it makes sense to copy the entire contents of the computer and examine it carefully at leisure. However, if a quick lead is needed, as is often the case when computers are involved, or only a small portion of the digital evidence on a computer is of interest, it is more practical to search the computer immediately and just take the information required.

When collecting the entire contents of a computer, the general concept is the same in most situations:

- all related evidence should be taken out of RAM;
- the computer should be shut down;
- the computer should be booted using another operating system that bypasses the existing one and does not change data on the hard drive(s);
- a copy of the digital evidence from the hard drive(s) should be made.

When collecting the entire contents of a computer, a bitstream copy of the digital evidence is usually desirable. In short, a bitstream copy copies what is in slack space and unallocated space, whereas a regular copy does not[4] (see Figure 4.5). The importance of this becomes apparent when you remember the description of slack space earlier in the chapter.

A bitstream copy duplicates everything in a cluster, including anything that is in the slack space, whereas other methods of copying a file only duplicate the file and leave the slack space behind. Therefore, digital evidence may be lost if a bitstream copy is not made. Of course, this is only a concern if slack space or unallocated space contains important information. If a file contains evidence and the adjacent slack space is not required, a simple file copy will suffice.

There is one empirical law of digital evidence collection that should always be remembered:

> **Empirical Law of Digital Evidence Collection and Preservation**: If you only make one copy of digital evidence, that evidence will be damaged or completely lost.

Therefore, always make at least two copies of digital evidence and check to make certain that at least one of the copies was successful and can be accessed on another computer. Verifying that a backup was successful is not just a suspicious activity – computer crackers have been known to interfere with the backup process to prevent backups from occurring normally. Also, it is imperative that digital evidence is saved onto completely clean disks or write-once media like compact disks. If digital evidence is copied onto a disk

[4] Unallocated space is space on a disk that the computer is not actively using to store data. Unallocated space might have been used in the past and can contain data if the space was never reused.

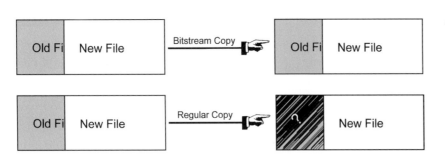

Figure 4.5

Comparing bitstream copying to regular copying.

that already has data on it, that old data could remain in the slack space, commingling with and polluting the evidence.

Whether all available digital evidence or just a portion is collected, the task is to get the evidence from the computer with the least amount of alteration. Different approaches are required in different situations[5]. The following three scenarios deal with the most common single computer situations and will also give a general sense of what to do and what to look for on other kinds of systems (e.g. VMS, OS/2). All three of these scenarios assume the entire contents of a computer are required as evidence. Though it is not always necessary to make a bitstream copy of an entire hard drive it is important to be prepared should the need arise.

If the focus of the investigation is only on a small selection of the information stored on a computer the "just take what you need approach" is an alternative to seizing all of the hardware or seizing all of the digital evidence on a computer. The approach of just taking what is needed has the advantage of being easier, faster, less expensive and less risky than shutting down a computer, rebooting it and making full bitstream copies.

SCENARIO 1: A PERSONAL COMPUTER RUNNING MICROSOFT DOS, WINDOWS OR MAC OS

If the computer is running when first encountered in an investigation, the decision must be made as to whether to pull all of the cables out of the back of the computer to cut off power and communication or to get evidence out of RAM before shutting down. For example, if investigators notice a suspect at a computer typing a warning e-mail message to an accomplice, that message might only be stored in RAM and could be lost if the computer is unplugged. To get evidence out of RAM, all open programs must be closed and if any of them prompt to save, they should be saved to a clean floppy disk. This will prevent the program from writing over existing evidence on the hard drive, leaving both the old version and the new one intact.

After the computer has been shut down, and before turning it on again to copy digital evidence from the hard drive, the computer's operating system should be bypassed to avoid corrupting evidence, and to avoid any tricks or traps that an advanced user might have set up. Personal computers store their operating system on the hard drive, and this operating system can be bypassed using a boot disk. Instructions for creating a boot disk are provided in the online help of most operating systems.

After booting the computer, digital evidence can be copied to disks or tapes that have been completely cleaned of data and viruses. Whenever possible, digital evidence should be saved on storage media that can only be written to once, like compact disks. However, it is not always possible to use

[5] To avoid modifying evidence, some experts open a computer and unplug the power cards from the hard drive(s), only reconnecting the power when they are certain they can boot the system successfully.

a writable compact disk drive so investigators should practice using different backup devices to collect digital evidence. Be aware that most tape and disk drives require specialized drivers that must be loaded in addition to the operating system so investigators should do some research and preparation before using a drive to collect evidence in an actual investigation. If there is a concern that a certain tape or disk drive will not work with a specific computer, test the device on an identical or very similar system before proceeding.

As mentioned earlier, if there is a suspicion that the slack space on a disk contains important digital evidence, a bitstream copy of the data should be made. There are a growing number of products that make the process of collecting and documenting digital evidence easier and faster (see Resources section at the end of this chapter)[6].

This scenario also applies to Windows NT machines that have FAT 32 partitions (as opposed to NTFS partitions). NTFS partitions offer additional security on a Windows NT machine by restricting access to data on the disk. The restrictions that NTFS imposes can make it more difficult to gain access to all of the data on a hard drive as described in the next scenario.

[6]Specific software recommendations are avoided because new tools are emerging regularly. The resources at the end of this chapter refer to solutions that are widely used at the moment.

SCENARIO 2: A WINDOWS NT WORKSTATION/SERVER

This scenario is similar to the previous one except that Windows NT has a higher degree of security that can make it more difficult to collect digital evidence. Windows NT enables a number of individuals to use a computer without having access to each other's files. This is achieved by creating separate password protected accounts for each individual who uses the computer. This added protection can interfere with evidence collection.

Fortunately, it is possible to bypass the restrictions that Windows NT attempts to enforce. Some investigators use a boot disk that contains an operating system called Linux to bypass Windows NT and give them access to the entire contents of the hard drive(s) on a computer. Alternately, a boot disk containing the DOS evidence collection software operating system can be used to bypass Windows NT and can be used to access the hard drive(s). However, few investigators have the time or expertise to create such disks and deal with the additional issues of loading device drivers that are necessary to connect tape or disk drives to the computer. Fortunately, some companies are developing products that makes collecting and documenting digital evidence on Windows NT machines easier (see Resources section at the end of this chapter)[7].

There is one caveat: it is possible to configure Windows NT to prevent booting from another disk – in which case more advanced methods will be needed to gain access to the digital evidence on the computer. For example,

[7]Using some utilities, an evidence collection computer can be connected to a source computer using a cable, and digital evidence can be copied directly onto the collection computer. However, not all of these utilities can make a bitstream copy.

the hard drive could be removed entirely and put into another computer. Removal of hard drives is a delicate process requiring the skills of an expert – a process beyond the scope of this text. Some organizations listed at the end of this chapter send data recovery experts to help investigators collect digital evidence and though this can be costly, it can save investigators from collecting the entire computer.

SCENARIO 3: A UNIX WORKSTATION/SERVER

Collecting digital evidence from a Unix system can be technically challenging, but the basic concept is the same: collect evidence in RAM; shutdown the computer; reboot the computer using another operating system that bypasses the existing one; make a bitstream copy of digital evidence on the hard drive(s).

Collecting evidence out of RAM on a Unix machine is not a simple matter of clicking on a save button. On a machine running Unix there is often no obvious visible sign that programs are running in RAM. Unix allows programs to run in the background so it is necessary to explicitly list all of the programs that are running. The "ps" command is used to list programs that a machine is running but one must specify that one wants to see all processes – using command options like "ps -aux" for most versions of Unix and "ps -ef" for others. The output of the ps command on a Unix system looks like this:

```
% ps -aux | more
```

USER	PID	%CPU	%MEM	SZ	RSS	TT	S	START	TIME	COMMAND
root	3	0.4	0.0	0	0	?	S	Apr 25	64:39	fsflush
root	199	0.3	0.2	4800	1488	?	S	Apr 25	2:14	/usr/sbin/syslogd
root	3085	0.2	0.2	2592	1544	?	S	14:07:12	0:00	/usr/lib/sendmail
root	1	0.1	0.1	1328	288	?	S	Apr 25	4:03	/etc/init -
root	3168	0.1	0.1	1208	816	pts/5	O	14:07:27	0:00	ps -aux
root	2704	0.1	0.2	2096	1464	?	S	14:05:37	0:00	/usr/local/etc/ssh
root	163	0.0	0.1	1776	824	?	S	Apr 25	0:19	/usr/sbin/inetd -s
root	132	0.0	0.1	2008	584	?	S	Apr 25	0:00	/usr/sbin/keyserv
root	213	0.0	0.1	1624	776	?	S	Apr 25	0:16	/usr/sbin/cron
root	239	0.0	0.1	904	384	?	S	Apr 25	0:07	/usr/lib/utmpd

If a particularly interesting program appears in this list like "sniffer" or "destroyer," an investigator might want to take a closer look. Unix allows investigators to extract key evidence from RAM. For example, some types of Unix allow one to save and view the contents of RAM that is associated with a particular program using the "gcore" command. There are also programs that provide a list of files (and sockets) that a particular program is using (e.g. LSOF). This is useful when investigators want to determine (and document) what a criminal is doing on a Unix system.

Several issues arise when it comes to rebooting Unix machines. Investigators can sync the disk, halt the system, and reboot the computer in single user mode. However, some wily computer crackers modify the sync command to destroy evidence so that, when investigators attempt to follow standard procedures, they end up destroying digital evidence. Also, booting a Unix machine from a disk is a complicated process that might not work depending on how the computer is configured. Therefore, only investigators who are very experienced with Unix should attempt to reboot the system using reliable system binaries and boot disks.

Finally, investigators can use the "dd" command to make a bitstream backup. The "dd" command has many options and parameters that investigators should become familiar with. Also, remember that it is often possible to ask the system owner to administrator for assistance. If the computer is not turned on, a system administrator can help start it up. If data is protected or encrypted, a system owner or administrator might be able to help gain access to it.

It is usually safe to allow a system administrator to operate a computer while assisting the investigator. However, a suspect must never be allowed to operate a computer. Instead, the suspect should be asked to provide the information required. If there is a warrant to seize a particular type of evidence, the suspect is usually compelled to give information necessary to collect this evidence (e.g. passwords). When there is difficulty obtaining passwords, access privileges, or other information that is needed to collect specific pieces of digital evidence, it might be necessary to make a copy of the entire drive or seize the hardware itself for future examination.

DOCUMENTING HARDWARE AND DIGITAL EVIDENCE

Documentation of evidence is essential for a number of reasons. Documentation showing evidence in its original state is regularly used to demonstrate that it is authentic and unaltered. For example, a video of a live chat can be used to verify that a digital log of the conversation has not been modified – the text in the digital log should match the text on the screen. Also, individuals who collected evidence are often called upon to verify that a specific piece of evidence is the same piece of evidence that they originally collected. Since two copies of a digital file are identical, documentation may be the only thing that an investigator can use to tell them apart. If an investigator cannot clearly demonstrate that one of the files is the original and the other is a copy, this inability can reflect badly on the investigator.

Documenting the original location of evidence can also be useful when trying to reconstruct a crime. Documentation is particularly crucial in situations where there are several identical computers with identical components. As standard procedure, everything should be documented as thoroughly as possible. For example, when collecting a computer, each cable should be labeled as it is unplugged from the computer to indicate where it came from. Most importantly, documenting who collected and handled evidence at a given time is required to maintain the chain of custody. It is not unusual for every individual who handled an important piece of evidence to be examined on the witness stand.

> Continuity of possession, or the chain of custody, must be established whenever evidence is presented in court as an exhibit … Frequently, all of the individuals involved in the collection and transportation of evidence may be requested to testify in court. Thus, to avoid confusion and to retain complete control of the evidence at all times, the chain of custody should be kept to a minimum. (Saferstein 1998)

So, make careful note of when the evidence was collected, from where, and by whom. If evidence is poorly documented, an attorney could shed doubt on the abilities of those involved and convince the court not to accept the evidence.

When documenting hardware, note the serial numbers and other details that can be used to specifically identify each item. It is prudent to document the same evidence in several ways. If one form of documentation is lost or unclear, other backup documentation can be invaluable. So, the computer and surrounding area should be photographed and/or videotaped to document evidence *in situ*. Detailed sketches and copious notes should be made that will facilitate an exact description of the crime scene and evidence as it was found. Paper printouts of important text are also used to show the original state of evidence stored on a computer.

Whenever digital evidence is copied onto a floppy disk, compact disk, tape, or any other form of storage media, an indelible felt-tipped pen should be used to label it with the following information:

- current date and time and the date/time on the computer (any discrepancy should be noted);
- the initials of the person who made the copy[a];
- the name of the operating system (e.g., Windows NT 4.0, Mac OS 8.1, SunOS 5.6);
- the program(s) and/or command(s) used to copy the files;
- the information believed to be contained in the files.

[a]*Investigators should eventually become familiar with the process of signing digital evidence digitally as described in the next section.*

Also, a complete list of all of the files and their properties (e.g. date created/last modified) should be made and the message digest of all files and disks should be computed using appropriate software.

MESSAGE DIGESTS AND DIGITAL SIGNATURES

For the purposes of this text, a message digest algorithm can be thought of as a black box, shown in Figure 4.6, that accepts a digital object (e.g. a file, program or data on a disk) and produces a number. A message digest algorithm always produces the same number for a given input. Also, a good message digest algorithm will produce a different number for different inputs. Therefore, an exact copy will have the same message digest as the original but if a file is changed even slightly it will have a different message digest from the original.

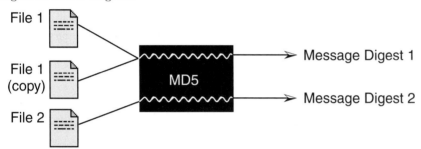

Figure 4.6

Black box concept of the message digest.

Currently, the most commonly used algorithm for calculating message digests is MD5[9]. Basically, the MD5 algorithm uses the data in a digital object to calculate a combination of 32 numbers and letters. Like human fingerprints and DNA, it is highly unlikely that two files will have the same message digest unless the files are duplicates.

> It is conjectured that the difficulty of coming up with two messages having the same message digest is on the order of 2^{64} operations, and that the difficulty of coming up with any message having a given message digest is on the order of 2^{128} operations. (RFC 1321 1992)

[9]There are other message digest algorithms such as SHA, HAVAL and SNEFRU. SHA is very similar to MD5 and is currently the US government's message digest algorithm of choice.

Message digests provide a method of near individualization and, therefore, are sometimes referred to as digital fingerprints. Message digests are also useful for determining if a piece of digital evidence has been tampered with. Even if data is slightly modified, it will have a different message digest from the original. Table 4.2 shows that changing one letter in a sentence changes the message digest of that sentence.

Table 4.2

MD5 is used to calculate the message digest of two sentences that differ by one letter. The message digest is significantly different.

DIGITAL INPUT	MD5 OUTPUT
The suspect's name is John	7e6c8f0d5e3a218a5b9387f1c764a784
The suspect's name is Joan	c48d0f4fe739b278428922597b7e07e3

Digital signatures add reliability to a message digest. Essentially, a digital signature indicates that a given (trusted) individual calculated the message digest of a certain file. In essence, the message digest speaks for the integrity of the file and the digital signing process speaks for the authenticity of the file. An excellent discussion of message digests and digital signatures can be found in *Practical Unix and Internet Security* by Garfinkel and Spafford (1996).

CLASSIFICATION, COMPARISON AND INDIVIDUALIZATION OF DIGITAL EVIDENCE

Classifying digital evidence is the process of finding characteristics that can be used to describe it in general terms and distinguish it from similar specimens.

> An item is classified when it can be placed into a class of items with similar characteristics. For example, firearms are classified according to caliber and rifling characteristics and shoes are classified according to their size and pattern. (Inman and Rudin 1997)

Most individuals are familiar with e-mail messages and will be able to say, "This is an e-mail message" the moment they see one. With training, investigators can classify e-mail even more precisely – determining what application was used to create it. Similarly, graphics created using computers are similar to each other in many ways, forming a class, and there are different types of graphics files (e.g. JPG, GIF, TIFF) making it possible to be specific when classifying them.

The importance of classifying digital evidence is often overlooked because it cannot be directly associated with a specific individual or computer. However, classifying digital evidence is useful when reconstructing a crime because it provides additional, reliable details. When combined, these details can converge, leading to additional evidence and suspects. Recall Locard's Exchange Principle from Chapter 1 – if there is a large amount of evidence linking an individual to a crime scene, the stronger the possibility that the individual was involved in the crime.

> The value of class physical evidence lies in its ability to provide corroboration of events with data that are, as nearly as possible, free of human error and bias. It is the thread that binds together other investigative findings that are more dependent on human judgements and, therefore, more prone to human failings. (Saferstein 1998)

There are many kinds of digital evidence that most individuals are unfamiliar with and will have difficulty classifying. For example, there is a class of computer programs called *scanners* that computer crackers use to probe a computer for information and vulnerabilities[10]. There are many different types of scanners and few people have seen every kind. Therefore, it is often necessary to closely examine a piece of digital evidence and compare it with other samples before one can say, "This is a scanner" with any degree of certainty and classify a scanner even more precisely (e.g. determine what type of scanner it is). Also, if digital evidence has been damaged in some way, it might not be immediately obvious whether it was a computer graphic, a program, or some other type of digital data.

Comparison is key when examining digital evidence. In addition to revealing class characteristics, comparing a piece of digital evidence with a control specimen can highlight unique aspects of the digital evidence (individualizing characteristics). Some individualizing characteristics are created at random – like a flaw in a particular piece of computer equipment that was used to digitize child pornography. Other individualizing characteristics are created purposefully for later identification (e.g. an identification number associated with a computer). These individualizing characteristics of a piece of digital evidence can be used to link cases, generate suspects and associate a crime with a specific computer.

[10]These scanner programs have no relation to the hardware scanners that are used to digitize images and documents.

CASE EXAMPLE
In 1999, a virus called Melissa hit the Internet. Melissa traveled in a Microsoft Word document that was attached to an e-mail message. This virus propagated so quickly that it overloaded many e-mail servers, and forced several large organizations to shut down their e-mail servers to prevent further damage.

Richard Smith, president of Phar Lap Software tracked down the individual who created the virus. Smith used a feature of Microsoft Office 97 to verify that the suspect's computer was used to create the virus. Any files created using Microsoft Office 97 contains a hidden line with a unique number identifying the computer that was used to create the file.

For instance, One Word 97 document created on a computer with the Ethernet address 00-10-4B-DE-FC-E9 contained the line:

_PID_GUID‰AN{2083B360-E6EF-11D2-9DC8-00104BDEFCE9}

and another document created on the same computer contained the line:
PID_GUID‰AN{CC79EA90-E6EE-11D2-9DC8-00104BDEFCE9}

Notice the unique Ethernet address at the end of each line. To see this line the document must be viewed using a program that does not interpret the word processor commands (e.g. a simple text viewer).

The Melissa virus raised hopes for investigators and concerns for privacy advocates. Investigators caught a glimpse of a hopeful future in which catching criminals was facilitated by the very tools that criminals are taking advantage of. Privacy advocates caught a glimpse of an oppressive future in which technologically savvy individuals could obtain private information about people.

Digital evidence can be classified, compared and individualized in several ways:

- Contents - investigators use the contents of an e-mail message to classify it and to determine which computer it came from. Also, swap files and slack space contain a random assortment fragments of digital data that can often be classified and individualized.
- Function - investigators examine how a program functions to classify it and sometimes individualize it. For example, a program that surreptitiously transfers valuable information from an unsuspecting computer to a remote location is classified as a Trojan horse program and is individualized by the remote location that it transmits data to.
- Characteristics - file names, message digests, and date stamps can be helpful in classifying and individualizing digital evidence.

Although the process of classifying, comparing and individualizing evidence can be tedious, it is extremely important to examine digital evidence in minute detail. The smallest clue can often have significant bearing on a case. Also, it is crucial to be able to describe accurately and completely your evidence when called upon to do so in a court of law. Any lack of understanding could damage an investigator's testimony, particularly if the minutiae turn out to be important. Although it can be tedious to study each piece of digital evidence carefully, it is far better to be bored with the evidence than to be stuck with no evidence at all.

DIGITAL EVIDENCE AND RECONSTRUCTION

There are two aspects to reconstruction and both are quite involved: (a) digital evidence that has been damaged can be reconstructed through various processes and (b) digital evidence can also be used to help reconstruct events surrounding a crime.

RECONSTRUCTING DELETED, DAMAGED, HIDDEN OR ENCRYPTED EVIDENCE

The details of recovering and reconstructing digital evidence depends on the kind of digital evidence, the type of computer involved, the operating system being run, and the configuration of the computer's hardware and software. When a file is deleted, it actually remains on a disk for a time. These deleted files can be recovered using special programs[11]. When a deleted file is partially overwritten, part of it remains in slack space. Again, specially designed software has been written to make it easier to find and read these file fragments.

It is more difficult to recover deleted data from Unix machines because

[11]The Resources section at the end of this chapter contains information about data recovery programs.

the high level of activity quickly overwrites recently deleted information. It is possible to recover some recently deleted information from a Unix system using standard commands (e.g. strings, dd). However, more sophisticated approaches are required for more effective recovery. Some Unix experts have written programs to recover data but these tools are not widely available because there is not a large demand for them.

Even when data on a disk is deleted and overwritten, part of the data might remain. This "shadow data" is a result of the minor imprecision that naturally occurs when data is being written on a disk. The arm that writes data onto a disk has to swing to the correct place, and it is never perfectly accurate. Skiing provides a good analogy. When you ski down a snowy slope, your skis make a unique set of curving tracks. When people ski down behind you, they destroy part of your tracks when they ski over them but they leave small segments.

A similar thing happens when data is overwritten on a disk – only some parts of the data are overwritten leaving other portions untouched. A disk can be examined for shadow data in a lab with advanced equipment (e.g., scanning probe microscopes, magnetic force microscopes) and the recovered fragments can be pieced together to reconstruct parts of the original digital data[12] (Gutmann, 1996).

There are also many binary files on a computer that contain a large amount of information. For example, many operating systems and computer programs use swap files to store information temporarily while it is not being used. For instance, Windows NT uses PAGEFILE.SYS, and Unix uses dedicated swap partitions (areas on a disk or entire disks) to store information temporarily[13].

Binary files cannot be read using standard word processors but there are many utilities for viewing and searching these files, some of which are available from organizations listed in the Resources section at the end of this chapter. In addition to slack space and swap space, there are other areas on a computer disk or drive where data can be hidden. New Technologies, Inc. offers a course that deals specifically with the topic of recovering hidden data from a disk.

An emerging challenge for investigators who are trying to recover digital evidence is encryption. Encryption software is becoming more commonplace, allowing criminals to scramble incriminating evidence using very secure encoding schemes, making it unreadable. Recovering encrypted data can be difficult.

A special password is required to decrypt this data. Some encryption schemes can be broken given time and the necessary tools and expertise. However, trying to break the code is impractical in most investigations.

[12]*Data can sometimes be recovered from RAM using advanced techniques but there is very little literature on this process.*

[13]*I have both Windows NT and Linux (a version of Unix) on one laptop. My Windows NT swap file is 400MB and my Linux swap partition is 36MB. This is a lot of digital data!*

Figure 4.7

The title "Digital Evidence and Computer Crime" becomes incomprehensible when encrypted using Pretty Good Privacy (PGP).

————BEGIN PGP MESSAGE————

Version: PGPfreeware 6.0 for non-commercial use <http://www.pgp.com>

qANQR1DbwU4DoU0XmZnflOEQB/9K9dEs5wkiP3AcfwrCTDS7Fce2EJ0QX93Ecq1f
z3FmlcRhA+v1r5ko/ZKkqzc2EjVPZobpJuISGgTubwKHH0KT3nDoMRVZRvWn8jMd
sdtTi/aSvswSTgdo+znZZNr82utruojbeA2cKEGz753MlqWCQbkyduywllFNV+Ei
YYdpYfHXJL/L9QES4UIDN/cZHeOmbANIXMR6REN68uGpi1zb+cFpGqdIU/VUAM6C
KRw6rEtAxpAmd62O01Tf/Q9pSvvliDdD/BYOT+0+b0SzlOPywwZSifX99Ol8lTmK
pYHMKT61bkyUxfUeUxEx6Uk5mrtnDLxZYUBJEQyfy7Ir+mHxB/0bUg0na/KNCXfS
Wgg62xDvxbsUqNfoY/jjRaDC/1fHFHJYe0O2Vsl7LjedjcEl1RfBJXhFrYVjgScL
u5YlzcUr1yJtEzEaZPv0pf1lciEDQns30qswEhXCPJeF4hl558H8hzNxES/k3YzL
J478Zygp5TGdWyScEFOkLXaeC2YdXjGMYCtVWTp7+9ut7bDaKW1RTWlfGS6RDIrE
aCp9vvnCOTuu2aKxqxNY7MrbKOxJFRDt7/Xpm1G1bFdAXBoMyC9U5mT3S5zv2jKQ
dP/Jc3Kexvw8HjY0U+L132jby8UqLRNdolklNoxCwlUTRF6eFTsRFMV09ChtzgsX
tqgidDtryYVBs454HiD8qkil3h1kaodbQ/th8Y8L6lpiMNEg8TNjVbP2D8/n2rc1
XeRdDjX8BmtyU6jGdZnt744FUmdMVUvbzsVSAvuHuEq1OtlQQv5eAPJ6efiiuu8P
Cx4bfRlDxPkpr3PlHo+f59AXUs7S8NOL81och1dOFfDgsx3u9hhWtTGS3/TO =86FB
————END PGP MESSAGE————

Additional reading on the subject of cryptography can be found in Schneider (1996) *Applied Cryptography: Protocols, Algorithms, and Source Code in C* and in the Electronic Frontier Foundation's (1998) *Cracking DES: Secrets of Encryption Research, Wiretap Politics and Chip Design.*

RECONSTRUCTING A CRIME

As was already mentioned, reconstructing a crime is a twofold process of repairing damaged evidence and using it to determine the actions surrounding a criminal act. The ultimate goal of a crime reconstruction is to establish what happened and when. It is not enough to know that someone was injured or that a computer was broken into. Reconstructing the details surrounding the injury or break-in are often essential to understanding what happened, who caused the events when, where, how, and why. Without an accurate reconstruction it is difficult to determine what the intent was, and what actually transpired. As the circumstances of a crime are reconstructed, gaps in the evidence will likely appear – and moves to address these gaps often lead to new evidence.

As the following quotation explains, evidence that is used to reconstruct crimes falls into three categories: relational, functional, and temporal.

> Most evidence is collected with the thought that it will be used for identification purposes, or its ownership property. Fingerprints, DNA, bullets, casing, drugs, fibers, and safe insulation are examples of evidence used for establishing *source* or ownership. These are the types of evidence that are brought to the laboratory for analysis to establish the identification of the object and/or its source.

> The same evidence at the crime scene may be the evidence used for reconstruction. We use the evidence to sequence events, determine locations and paths, establish direction or establish time and/or duration of the action. Some of the clues that are utilized in these determinations are *relational*, that is, where an object is in relation to the other objects or to the crime; *functional*, the way something works or how it was used or *temporal*, things based on the passage of time. (Chisum in Turvey 1999)

Temporal aspects of evidence, or when events occurred, are obviously important. Since computers often note the time of specific events, such as the time a file was created or the time a person logged on using a private password, digital evidence can be very useful for reconstructing the sequence of events. Less obviously, the position of digital evidence in relation to other objects can be very informative. For instance, the geographic location of computers in relation to suspects and victims are important, as are the locations of files or programs on a computer. Determining where a cracker hides files can help reconstruct a crime and can help investigators of similar crimes discover similar hiding places. Missing items are also important but the presence of these items must be inferred from other events. For example, if there is evidence that a certain program was used but the program cannot be found, it can be inferred that the program was removed after use. This could have significant implications in the context of a crime, since covering behavior is very revealing about a criminal, as is *what* he/she wants to hide. The functionality of a piece of digital evidence can shed light on what happened. Of course, knowing what a program does is crucial for reconstruction, but if a computer program has options that determine what it does, then the options that are selected to commit a crime are also very telling.

The concept of reconstructing a crime is fairly simple; all available evidence should be used to gain an understanding of the what, who, how, where, and why of a crime. In practice, however, this process can be time consuming, difficult, and frustrating. When there are large gaps in a timeline of events with no evidence to fill in the space, individuals try to guess. While forming hypotheses is important in any investigation, it can be dangerous because it is easy to guess wrongly, and to become entrenched in an incorrect hypothesis that cannot be supported by evidence. Therefore, it is important to be open to the possibility that a hypothesis can be wrong. As a rule, when conducting an investigation, nothing should be presumed, everything should be queried, and nothing that anyone says should be believed until it is verified.

When reconstructing a cybercrime there are two common pitfalls to be wary of. First, it is important not to become too dependent on the digital evidence – look for supporting physical evidence whenever possible. People role-play quite a bit on the Internet and much of what they say is fantasy, not reality. Therefore, if an individual on the Internet claims to have killed someone, look for supporting evidence. Even if an individual writes about killing someone, this is not a crime.

> CASE EXAMPLE
> In 1994, Jake Baker, a student at University of Michigan, submitted a fictitious story to the Internet newsgroup alt.sex.stories in which he mentioned the name of one of his female classmates, describing how he and a friend brutally tortured, raped and killed her.
>
> "C'mon, man, let's go." My friend said. So we got the gasoline and spread it all over [Jane Doe's] apartment [real name excluded to protect her identity]. We chucked it over her. It must have burned like hell when it came into contact with her open cuts, but I couldn't tell. Her face was already a mask of pain, and her body quivered fiiercely [sic.].
>
> "Goodbye, [Jane]" I said, a lit a match ...
>
> The subject in the story was understandably upset and the University of Michigan suspended Baker and reported the incident to the FBI. After a brief investigation, Baker was arrested for using interstate communications to transmit a threat and he was deemed a threat to society and denied bail. Ultimately, however, the charges were dismissed because there was no proof that Baker intended to commit the crimes that he fantasized and wrote about. One important point to note is that is it not a crime to talk or write about committing a crime.

Secondly, it is important not to be influenced by the media. Several significant cases (e.g. Mitnick, Jovanovic) have been sensationalized and misreported by the media changing the way we perceive facts and often changing the facts themselves. If investigators allow their crime reconstruction to be influenced by media reports, justice probably will not be served.

DIGITAL EVIDENCE GUIDELINES

[14]*These are only guidelines. Use your discretion and legal counsel when necessary.*

To summarize, a list of guidelines is provided here[14]. Investigators should get in the habit of following these guidelines even during routine investigations. Practice will improve an investigator's ability to process digital evidence and will increase the chance that the evidence will stand under scrutiny. If an investigator does not regularly follow a reliable procedure when collecting digital evidence, attorneys will find it much easier to cast doubt on the evidence.

It is important to remember that digital evidence does not just refer to evidence found on personal computers. Computers (in the form of microprocessors, circuits, and memory devices) are also used in watches, pagers, phones, cars, and many other modern machines. Digital evidence can originate from these computers and can be transmitted through wires and the air to other computers. The focus of these guidelines is on personal computers and computer networks, but the general concepts and considerations apply to all computerized devices.

PRELIMINARY CONSIDERATIONS

Before approaching digital evidence there are several things to consider. One should be certain that the search is not going to violate any laws or give rise to any liability. For example, there are strict privacy laws protecting certain forms of digital evidence like e-mail. If these laws are violated, the evidence could be inadmissible. As a rule, a search warrant should be obtained if there is a possibility that the evidence to be seized requires a search warrant. The effort it takes to get a search warrant is minuscule in comparison to the trouble that will be encountered if a warrant is not obtained. If there is any doubt about the law as it relates to a particular case, expert legal advice should be sought. It is also important to be aware that if the collection of evidence interrupts a business unnecessarily the investigators can be held personally responsible.

CASE EXAMPLE
On 1 March 1990 US federal agents searched the premises and computers of the Steve Jackson Games company for evidence relating to a hacker group that called itself the Legion of Doom. Steve Jackson Games designed and published role-playing games based on fictional ways of breaking into computer systems. They also ran a Bulletin Board System called Illuminati to provide support and private e-mail services to their customers. In addition to seizing computers and everything that looked like it was related to a computer, the federal agents confiscated all copies of a book that was under development at Steve Jackson Games. No charges were ever brought against Steve Jackson Games or anyone else as a result of this raid, but Steve Jackson Games did suffer significant losses. After several unsuccessful attempts to recover the seized items, Steve Jackson Games decided to sue the Secret Service and the individual agents for the wrongful raid of their business. During the trial, it was determined that Secret Service personnel/delegates had read and deleted private e-mail that had not yet been delivered to its intended recipients (the Secret Service denied this until it was proven). Steve Jackson Games dropped the charges against the individual agents to speed up the trial and the court ruled that the government had violated the Electronic Communications Privacy Act (ECPA) and the Privacy Protection Act (PPA). The court awarded Steve Jackson Games $51,040 in damages, $195,000 in attorneys' fees and $57,000 in costs.

PLANNING

Once the preliminaries about the legality of collecting digital evidence have been satisfied, the search should be planned in as much detail as possible. Attempts should be made to determine what computer equipment to expect. Without this information it is difficult to know what expertise and evidence collection tools are required for the search. In some cases the hardware will be seized while in others only specific information will be taken from a computer. If a computer is to be examined on-site, it will be necessary to know which operating system the computer is running (e.g., Mac OS, UNIX, Windows). Similarly it will be necessary to know if there is a network involved and if the cooperation of someone who is intimately familiar with the computers will be required to perform the search.

> Before the search begins, the search leader should prepare a detailed plan for documenting and preserving electronic evidence, and should take time to carefully brief the entire search team to protect both the identity and integrity of all the data. At the scene, agents must remember to collect traditional types of evidence (e.g. latent fingerprints off the keyboard) before touching anything. (DOJ 1994)

If the assistance of system administrators or other individuals who are familiar with the system to be searched is required, they should be included in a pre-search briefing. They might be able to point out oversights or common pitfalls. One person should be designated to take charge of all evidence. This person should make a complete inventory of what is found. In situations where investigators only have one chance to collect digital evidence, practice beforehand under similar conditions to become comfortable with the process.

RECOGNITION

- Look for hardware. In addition to desktop computers, look for laptops, handheld computers, external hard drives, digital cameras and any other piece of equipment that can store evidence related to the crime being investigated. If the hardware is being collected for future examination, consider collecting peripheral hardware that is attached to the computer. Also collect any peripheral hardware that needs to be examined by a forensic scientist. For example, printers, cameras and scanners might have unique characteristics that can be linked to documents or digitized images.

- Look for software. If digital evidence was created using a program that is not widely used, collecting the installation disks will make it easier to examine the evidence.

- Look for removable media. There are a wide variety of removable media that can contain digital evidence including floppy disks, zip/jazz disks, compact disks and magnetic tapes. In particular, look for backups either on-site or in a remote storage facility. Determine what hardware and software was used to make the backups. In some instances, backup tapes can only be accessed using the type of hardware and software that created them. Therefore, consider collecting the unusual backup hardware and software. It is not necessary to collect hardware and software if a common, readily available method of backup was used. Keep in mind that criminals often hide removable media that contain incriminating or valuable information.

- Look for documentation that is related to the hardware, software and removable media. Documentation can help investigators understand details about the hardware, software and backup process that are useful during an investigation and a trial.

- Look for passwords and important phone numbers on or near the computer. Individuals who have several Internet Service Providers often write down the phone numbers and passwords for their various accounts. This is especially true of computer crackers.

- Look through the garbage for printouts and other evidence related to the computer. Computer printouts can contain valuable evidence and can sometimes be compared with the digital copies of the information for discrepancies.

- Look for cybertrails as described throughout this text.

PRESERVATION, COLLECTION AND DOCUMENTATION

- Videotape and/or photograph evidence *in situ*, paying particular attention to serial numbers and wiring to help identify or reconstruct equipment later. This type of vivid documentation, showing evidence in its original state, can be useful for reconstructing a crime and demonstrating that evidence is authentic.

- Note, photograph, or videotape the contents of the computer screen. If a program is running that might be formatting the hard drive or erasing data, immediately cut off power to that computer by pulling the cables out of the rear of the computer.

- Print out as much as possible, signing and dating it immediately. Printouts can be useful if the digital version is lost or is not admitted. Also, in some situations, a hard copy will be more acceptable as evidence than the original digital file.

- Take notes that will be useful when reconstructing the scene and draw diagrams with the overall dimensions to get overview of scene and make it easier to remember and explain where things were found.

- Label, date and initial all evidence. If other people are collecting evidence, record their names and where they found the evidence. The aim is to preserve chain of evidence and document the evidence in a way that helps investigators reconstruct the crime. Not knowing where evidence came from or who collected it can render it useless.

IF YOU NEED TO COLLECT THE ENTIRE COMPUTER

- Label cables and ports. Empty ports should be labeled "unused." If there is no label on a port, it could be argued that the evidence was not properly documented or that the label fell off. Any doubts that can be shed on the evidence collection and documentation process can weaken a case.

- Put an unused disk in each floppy drive to protect the drive.

- Use evidence tape to seal the computer case and drives to protect them against tampering.

- Carefully package the hardware and do not expose it to potentially damaging conditions (e.g. dirt, fluids, humidity, impact, excessive heat and cold, strong magnetic fields, and static electricity).

IF YOU NEED ALL OF THE DIGITAL EVIDENCE ON A COMPUTER BUT DO NOT NEED THE HARDWARE

- Start the computer using a boot disk. Boot disks should be virus checked before use to avoid damaging the computer and the digital evidence that it contains.
- Note the current date and time and the date/time on the computer (note any discrepancies).
- Make two copies of all digital evidence (consider making a bitstream copy if there might be valuable evidence in slack space). Whenever possible, check each copy on another computer to ensure that the copy was successful.
- Label, date and initial all evidence. Include the type of computer (e.g. Digital Alpha, Sun Sparc2) and operating system (e.g. Windows 95, Mac OS, UNIX), what program(s) and/or command(s) you used to copy the files.
- Inventory contents of all disks, including file creation and modification dates. Calculate the message digest of all files and disks. Also, make a brief note describing the significance of the evidence to help others understand why it was collected.

IF YOU ONLY NEED A PORTION OF THE DIGITAL EVIDENCE ON A COMPUTER

- Note the current date and time and the date/time on the computer (note any discrepancies). If investigators do not realize that a computer clock is inaccurate this can skew their crime reconstruction. For instance, if the time a file was created is important, investigators should be sure that they know the actual time the file was created and not an inaccurate time set by the computer.
- Make two copies of all evidence to your own disks. Whenever possible, check each copy on another computer to ensure that the copy was successful.
- Label, date and initial all evidence. Include the name of the operating system (e.g. Windows 95, Mac OS, UNIX), what program(s) and/or command(s) you used to copy the files.
- Inventory contents of all disks, including file creation and modification dates. Calculate the message digest of all files and disks. Also, make a brief note describing the significance of the evidence to help others understand why it was collected.

CLASSIFICATION, COMPARISON AND INDIVIDUALIZATION

- Carefully examine evidence for class traits, comparing it with other samples to classify it more precisely. It might be obvious that a digital file contains a picture or a recording of a voice. However, small details are important when evidence is concerned so try to pick out as much detail from the available digital evidence as possible. Ask questions like: was the specimen created on a computer running Windows, Mac OS or Unix? What hardware and software was used to create it? How common is the hardware and software?

- Compare digital evidence with known samples to determine if they came from the same source. Also, look for any characteristics that are unique.

RECONSTRUCTION

- Make a note of every action taken during the reconstruction process. Although this is an aspect of documentation, it is worth reiterating here.

- If possible, replicate the process that created the digital evidence. Trying to replicate the process can improve investigators understanding of the evidence and the criminal.

- Recover deleted or damaged digital evidence using data recovery tools and techniques described in this chapter.

- Search slack space and search binary files (e.g. swap files) using raw disk editors or software programs specially designed for the task.

- Reconstruct relational aspects of the crime. Determine where digital evidence was in relation to the other evidence or to the crime.

- Reconstruct functional aspects of the crime. Determine the purpose of each piece of digital evidence, how it works or how it was used.

- Reconstruct temporal aspects of the crime – when events occurred.

SUMMARY

Computer technology is evolving rapidly but the fundamental components and operations are relatively static. A central processing unit starts the basic input and output system, which performs a power-on self test, and loads an operating system from a disk. Rules of evidence also remain fairly static – distinguishing between hearsay and direct evidence and requiring proof of authenticity and integrity.

This chapter presents concepts from forensic science and computer science that can be used to process and analyze digital evidence stored on a computer. The forensic science concepts described in this chapter are applicable to any investigation and are applied to computer networks in later chapters. Several scenarios are presented in this chapter to emphasize that different situations require different approaches. Although this chapter focuses on information it also provides some suggestions for dealing with hardware as contraband, fruits of crime, instrumentality and evidence.

Given the variety of computer equipment that exists and the rate at which this equipment changes, it is impossible for any one person to know everything about digital evidence. Therefore, it is important for one to know and admit one's limitations and seek help when necessary.

> CASE EXAMPLE
> A system administrator of a large organization was the key suspect in a homicide. The suspect claimed that he was at work at the time and so the police asked his employer to help them verify his alibi. Coincidentally, this organization occasionally trains law enforcement personnel to investigate computer crimes and was eager to help in the investigation. The organization worked with police to assemble an investigative team that seized the employee's computers – both from his home and his office – as well as backup tapes of a server the employee administered. All of the evidence was placed in a room to which only members of the team had access. These initial stages were reasonably well documented but the reconstruction process was a disaster. The investigators made so many omissions and mistakes that one computer expert, after reading the investigator's logs, suggested that the fundamental mistake was that the investigators locked all of the smart people out of the room. The investigators in this case were either unaware of their lack of knowledge or were unwilling to admit it.

As a result of the investigator's omissions and mistakes, the suspect's alibi could not be corroborated. Digital evidence to support the suspect's alibi was found later but not by the investigators. If the investigators had sought expert assistance to deal with the large amount of digital evidence they might have quickly confirmed the suspect's alibi rather than putting him through years of investigation and letting the murderer go free.

REFERENCES

Clark, F. and Diliberto, K. (1996) *Investigating Computer Crime*, New York, NY: CRC Press.

Electronic Frontier Foundation (1998) *Cracking DES: Secrets of Encryption Research, Wiretap Politics and Chip Design.*

Garfinkel, S. and Spafford, G. (1996) *Practical Unix and Internet Security*, 2nd edn, Cambridge, MA: O'Reilly & Associates, Inc.

Gutmann, P. (1996) Secure Deletion of Data From Magnetic and Solid-State Memory, Sixth USENIX Security Symposium Proceedings.

Hoey, A. (1996) "Analysis of The Police and Criminal Evidence Act, s.69 – Computer Generated Evidence," *Web Journal of Current Legal Issues*, in association with Blackstone Press Ltd.

Hollinger, R.C. (1997) *Crime, Deviance and the Computer*. Brookfield, VT: Dartmouth Publishing Company.

Icove, D., Seger, K. and VonStorch, W. (1995) *Computer Crime: A Crimefighter's Handbook*, Sebastopol, CA: O'Reilly & Associates.

Inman, N. and Rudin, K. (1997) *An Introduction to Forensic DNA Analysis*, 2nd edn, CRC Press.

Lee, H. C. (ed.) (1994) *Crime Scene Investigation*, Taoyuan, Taiwan, ROC; Central Police, University Press.

Rivest, R. (1992) *Request for Comments: 1321 (The MD5 Message-Digest Algorithm)*, MIT Laboratory for Computer Science and RSA Data Security, Inc.

Rosenblatt, K. S. (1995), *High-Technology Crime: Investigating Cases Involving Computers*, San Jose, CA: KSK Publications.

Saferstein, R. (1998) *Criminalistics: An Introduction to Forensic Science*, 6th edn, Upper Saddle River, NJ: Prentice Hall.

Schneider, B. (1996) *Applied Cryptography: Protocols, Algorithms, and Source Code in C*, New York, NY: John Wiley & Sons.

US Department of Justice (1994) *Federal Guidelines for Searching and Seizing Computers* [http://www.usdoj.gov/criminal/cybercrime/search_docs/toc.htm].

US Department of Justice (1998) *Federal Rules of Evidence* [http://www.usdoj.gov/].

Turvey, B. (1999) *Criminal Profiling: An Introduction to Behavioral Evidence Analysis*, London: Academic Press.

RESOURCES

Computer Forensics, Ltd. (http://www.computer-forensics.com)

Computer Forensics, Inc. (http://www.forensics.com)

Electronic Evidence Discovery (http://www.eedinc.com)

Guidance Software (http://www.guidancesoftware.com)

New Technologies (http://www.forensics-international.com)

Ontrack (http://www.ontrack.com)

Sydex (http://www.sydex.com)

Vogon (http://www.vogon.co.uk/)

GENERAL

PGP (http://www.pgpi.com) (http://www.nai.com)

Tripwire (http://www.cert.org/tools/Tripwire) (http://www.tripwiresecurity.com)

MD5 (e.g. http://www.threel.co.uk/tech/tools/md5.htm)

Sysinternals (http://www.sysinternals.com)

## CHAPTER 5

DIGITAL EVIDENCE ON COMPUTER NETWORKS

Until recently, it was sufficient to look at individual computers as isolated objects containing digital evidence. Computing was disk-centered – collecting a computer and several disks would assure collection of all of the digital evidence. Today, however, computing has become network-centered – it is not adequate to think about computers in isolation since many of them are connected together using various network technologies. Now digital evidence can be found on a small computer network or on the global Internet. It is, therefore, important to learn to follow the cybertrails and deal with digital evidence on computer networks.

When a computer network is directly or marginally involved in a crime, evidence is often distributed on many computers and it is rarely feasible to collect all of the hardware or even the entire contents of a network as evidence. Also, unlike crime in the physical world, a criminal can be several places on a network at any given time. Obviously, this distribution of evidence and criminal activity makes it difficult to isolate a crime scene. Generally the more removed an investigator is from a computer when collecting digital evidence, the more susceptible that evidence will be to criticism. For example, if an investigator is unable to access a computer directly, and can only see digital evidence over a network, it may not be possible to get a copy or message digest of the original file. This makes it difficult to verify the integrity of the digital evidence. In such situations, it is necessary to make extra efforts to collect the evidence carefully and document it thoroughly to protect the collection methods against every criticism. For instance, if a Web page or newsgroup contains important digital evidence, it would be wise to take screen shots and photographs of the evidence as well as save it to a disk. Additionally, digital evidence is often present on a network for only a split second, making it difficult to collect. Again, careful collection and documentation is called for. For example, if the activities in an Internet chat room are going to be used as evidence, consider videotaping it as well as capturing it in a log file.

At the same time, having evidence distributed on many computers can be an advantage in an investigation. The distribution of information makes it difficult to destroy digital evidence. If digital evidence is destroyed on one computer, a copy can usually be found on various computers around the network or on backup tapes. Many organizations backup their information regularly and some even store a second copy of all backups at a different location for added protection. Additionally, computer networks offer an alternative to saving evidence on a floppy disk, compact disk or other removable media as the following example demonstrates.

CASE EXAMPLE

Organizations that investigate computer intrusions on a regular basis can designate one secure computer as the repository for all digital evidence. In addition to copying digital evidence to removable disks, investigators can use an encrypted connection (using SSH or SFTP) to transfer digital evidence to the secure computer. Using an encrypted connection to the secure computer ensures that the digital evidence cannot be modified in transit, thus ensuring its integrity. Even if the digital evidence is intercepted in transit, it cannot be decrypted let alone modified. Using two methods to collect all digital evidence provides investigators with a backup copy that can be used to verify the other copy[1].

[1]Before transferring the digital evidence to the secure computers, investigators should routinely document and preserve the evidence – calculating the message digest of all the evidence (e.g. using MD5), bundling it together in a way that preserves date/time stamps (e.g. using the "tar" command) and digitally signing it (e.g. using PGP).

This chapter introduces the main concepts and challenges relating to computer networks as sources of evidence. This chapter also provides an overview of networks and goes on to describe how these different networks are joined together to form the seemingly homogeneous Internet. This chapter ends with an overview of the crimes that occur at different levels of networks. Subsequent chapters go into more detail, discussing network layers.

A BRIEF HISTORY OF COMPUTER NETWORKS

As with the ENIAC, the military spurred the creation of computer networks that have developed into the Internet. In 1969, the Advanced Research Projects Agency (ARPA), a part of the Defense Department, began funding companies and universities to develop a communications system to withstand heavy enemy attacks. The primary aim was to enable military installations around the country to communicate even if significant parts of the communications system were destroyed. However, an early memorandum noted that such a system would have additional benefits.

> While highly survivable and reliable communications systems are of primary interest to those in the military concerned with automating command and control functions, the basic notions are also of interest to communications systems planners and designers having need to transmit digital data. (Baran 1964)

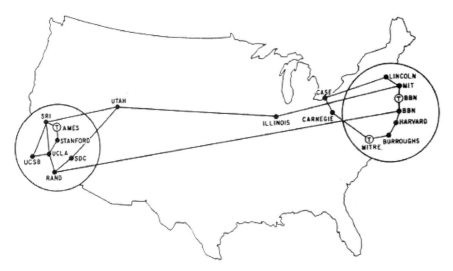

Figure 5.1

Map of ARPANET.
From P. Salus, Casting the Net,
(Figure from page 64). ©1995
Addison-Wesley Publishing
Company Inc. Reprinted by
permission of Addison-Wesley
Longman.

MAP 4   September 1971

By the end of 1969, a primitive network named the ARPANET was in place. This network was the foundation of the modern Internet (see Figure 5.1). In 1991, the World Wide Web (WWW) was released to the general public, making it easier for people to use the Internet. Since then, the Internet has been commercialized and its popularity has grown exponentially. In fact, so many people have been using the Internet that several universities decided to set up a second, higher-speed network in an effort to bypass the traffic jams on the Internet. This second network is imaginatively named Internet 2 (see Figure 5.2).

In a relatively short period, technology has advanced to the point where the lines between computers, televisions, telephones and print media have been blurred. Many experts in computing and telecommunications agree that, with this seamlessly integrated global infrastructure in place, the next five years of computing and telecommunications will bring more changes than the last twenty. Already households and neighborhoods are being connected to networks that enable them to operate, communicate and collaborate more effectively. This technology enables the owner of a house to control household functions remotely. Conversely, this technology could give criminals access to household appliances. The day that someone from across the world can turn on a gas stove and spark a toaster to blow up another's house is near.

ENIAC	ARPANET	Intel 8080	Mac & IBM PCs	WWW	Internet2
1946	1969	1974	1980s	1991	1999

Figure 5.2

Time line of key events.

This history is necessarily brief and incomplete because it is still evolving and is not the focus of the text. For an excellent account of the history of networking see *A Short History of the Internet* by Bruce Sterling (1993).

NETWORK COMPONENTS AND OPERATIONS RELEVANT TO COLLECTION AND RECONSTRUCTION OF DIGITAL EVIDENCE

To begin with, there are some basic terms that investigators need to know to understand networks: host, network interface card, modem and router.

- Host – a computer connected to a network.
- Network Interface Card (NIC) – a piece of hardware used to connect a host to the network. Every host must have at least one network interface card. Every NIC is assigned a number called a Media Access Control (MAC) address[2].
- Modulator/demodulator (modem) – a piece of equipment used to connect computers together using a serial line (usually a telephone line). This piece of equipment converts digital data into an analog signal (modulation) and demodulates an analog signal into digits that a computer can process.
- Router – a host connected to two or more networks that can send network messages from one network to another.

Routers are a crucial component of computer networks, essentially directing data to the correct place. Though almost any host can be used as a router, most networks use custom-made routers like those produced by Cisco. Routers direct data from one network to another and many routers keep logs of noteworthy events and can be an excellent source of digital evidence. Many firewalls also keep detailed logs of successful and unsuccessful attempts to reach the computers that it protects and can be a good source of digital evidence (see Figure 5.3).

[2]*Individuals who are learning about networks for the first time will find that the convenience of using abbreviations and acronyms creates its own difficulties. For instance, the acronym for Media Access Control addresses (MACs) can easily be confused with the abbreviation for Macintosh computers (Macs). The Glossary organizes the terms, abbreviations and acronyms that are used in this text to assist the reader.*

Figure 5.3

Depiction of hosts with NICs connected to a router to form a network.

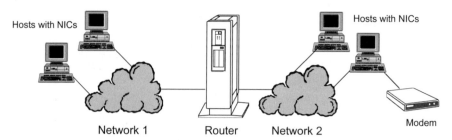

Hosts with NICs   Hosts with NICs

Network 1   Router   Network 2   Modem

NETWORK TECHNOLOGIES

Network technologies enable multiple hosts to share a single transmission medium. When hosts are sharing a transmission medium only one host can use the medium at any given time. This is analogous to a polite conversation between people in which one person talks and the others listen. If two computers were allowed to use the transmission medium at the same time, they would interfere with each other.

The easiest way to understand network basics is to imagine someone setting up a network. Suppose that Sarah has several computers and decides to set up a network to connect them to each other. The first thing Sarah must do is choose a network technology to connect the computers physically. Four network technologies: ARCNET, Ethernet, ATM and FDDI are briefly described here.

ATTACHED RESOURCE COMPUTER NETWORK (ARCNET)

ARCNET was one of the earliest network technologies and the latest version (ARCNET Plus) can transmit data at twenty megabytes per second (20 Mbps). ARCNET uses coaxial cables, similar to the ones used for cable television, to connect the Network Interface Card (NIC) in each computer to a central hub. If a single host is damaged or turned off, other computers on the network can still communicate with each other through the hub. However, if the hub is damaged or turned off, none of the hosts will be able to communicate with each other.

ARCNET uses a method called "token passing" to coordinate communication between each of the hosts connected to the central hub – i.e. the networked computers. Basically, a token is sent around on the network and when a host wants to send data it waits for the token, takes the token, and starts to transmit. When that host is finished transmitting, it relinquishes the token, passing it on to the other computers on the network thus allowing other hosts to communicate.

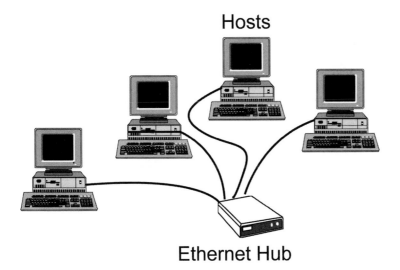

Hosts

Ethernet Hub

Figure 5.4

Hosts connected to a hub.

ETHERNET

Ethernet has gone through several stages of development and has become one of the most widely used network technologies because it is relatively fast and inexpensive. One of the most recent forms of Ethernet uses wires similar to regular telephone cords. These wires are used to connect the NIC in each computer to a central hub that essentially makes the hosts think that they are connected by a single wire (see Figure 5.4 on page 79).

Instead of token passing, Ethernet uses Carrier Sense Multiple Access with Collision Detection (CSMA/CD), to coordinate communication. Although CSMA/CD is a mouthful, the concept is straightforward. Computers using Ethernet are like people making polite conversation at a dinner party. At a polite dinner party, if two people start to speak at the same time, they both stop for a moment, one starts to talk again while the other waits. Similarly, when two computers using Ethernet start to transmit data at the same time, they both sense that the other host is transmitting and they both stop for a random period of time before transmitting again. Ethernet is described in more detail in Chapter 8.

FIBER DISTRIBUTED DATA INTERNETCONNECT (FDDI)

As the name suggests, FDDI uses fiber optic cables to transmit data by encoding it in pulses of light. This type of network is expensive but fast, transmitting data at 100 Mbps. Like ARCNET, FDDI uses the token passing technique but, instead of using a central hub, computers on an FDDI network are connected together to form a closed circuit. Data travels around this circuit through every host until it reaches its destination. Normally, data only travels in one direction around this circuit. However, if one of the computers on an FDDI network detects that it cannot communicate with its neighbor, it uses a second, emergency ring to send data around the ring in the opposite direction. In this way, a temporary ring of communication is established until the faulty host can communicate again.

Figure 5.5

Normal FDDI communication versus backup communication when a host is down.

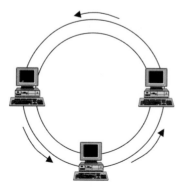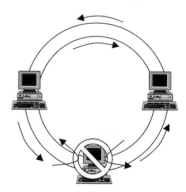

ASYNCHRONOUS TRANSFER MODE (ATM)

ATM uses fiber optic cables and specialized equipment (ATM switches) to enable computers to communicate at very high rates (gigabits per second). Telecommunications companies developed this technology to accommodate concurrent transmission of video, voice and data. Although it is very expensive, ATM is becoming more widely used. In Chapter 8, ATM is briefly compared with Ethernet to highlight their similarities and differences and describe how they both can be useful as a source of digital evidence.

ATM uses technology similar to telephone systems to establish a connection between two computers. Computers are connected to a central ATM switch and these switches can be connected to form a larger network. One host contacts the central switch when it wants to communicate with another host. The switch contacts the other host and then establishes a connection between them.

CONNECTING NETWORKS USING INTERNET PROTOCOLS

Like people who do not speak the same language, two computers using different network technologies cannot communicate directly. So, a computer using FDDI cannot communicate directly with a computer using Ethernet. There are two methods of enabling communication between computers using different network technologies: translators and common languages. As with the use of professional translators and common languages like

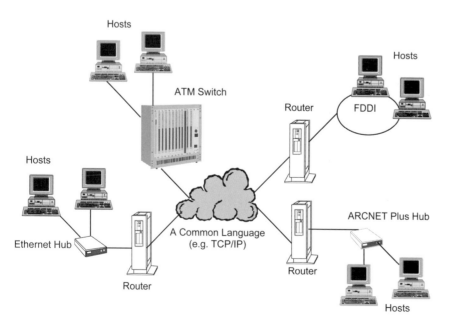

Figure 5.6

Dissimilar networks connected using a common language to form an internet[3].

[3]ARCNET Plus is an enhanced version of ARCNET that has the ability to use TCP/IP.

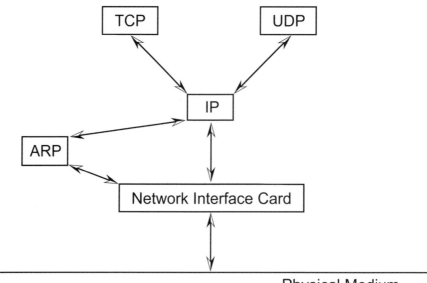

[4] *The word* internet *is used in lowercase when referring to any connection of dissimilar networks. The* Internet *(capitalized) refers specifically to the global network of interconnected networks.*

Esperanto, in the computer-networking world there are translators (e.g. gateways, translating bridges) and common languages – called internet protocols (e.g. TCP/IP, TP-4/CLNP)[4].

For instance, suppose that Sarah successfully networked her computers using Ethernet technology and now wants to connect with her friends' networks. Unfortunately, she discovers that they are using different network technologies. These networks are essentially speaking different languages. If Sarah just wanted to connect her network with one other network it might make sense to use a specialized translator. However, when connecting many dissimilar networks it is more efficient and effective to use internet protocols that every host can understand (see Figure 5.6 on page 81).

Currently, the most widely used internet protocols are the Transport Control Protocol (TCP), the User Datagram Protocol (UDP) and the Internet Protocol (IP). These protocols, along with a few supporting protocols, are collectively referred to as the TCP/IP internet protocol suite – TCP/IP for short. In some respects, TCP/IP is the Internet – every computer attached to the Internet uses TCP/IP to communicate (see Figure 5.7).

To deal with digital evidence on the Internet, investigators need a solid understanding of TCP/IP. To understand how TCP/IP works, it is useful to think of it in terms of layers as defined in the Open System Interconnection (OSI) reference model. The OSI reference model divides internets into seven layers: the application, presentation, session, transport, network, data-link, and physical layers. TCP and IP are transport and network layer protocols, respectively.

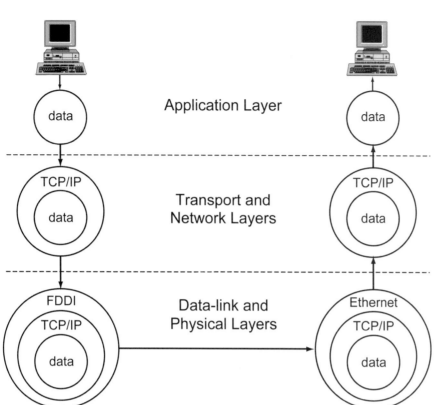

Figure 5.8

A simplified depiction of the Open System Interconnection layers.

Each layer of the OSI model performs specific functions and hides the complexity of lower layers. For example, Sarah's Ethernet network occupies the lowest layers of the Internet – the physical and data-link layers. A common language like TCP/IP at the network and transport layers enables computers on ARCNET Plus, Ethernet, FDDI and ATM networks to communicate with each other. The session, presentation and application layers make it easier for humans to use the network – hiding the inner workings of the lower layers. Provided all networks follow this model, they will be able to interconnect with relative ease.

The OSI reference model is described here briefly and is discussed in more detail in subsequent chapters. In a metaphorical sense, Chapters 6, 7 and 8 sequentially peel away the layers of the OSI model.

APPLICATION LAYER

The application layer provides the interface between people and networks, allowing us to exchange e-mail, view Web pages, and utilize many other network services. Some common Internet services are described later in this chapter. Without the application layer, we would not be able to access computer networks. This layer contains a large amount of digital evidence as demonstrated in Chapter 6.

PRESENTATION LAYER

When necessary, the presentation layer formats and converts data to meet the conventions of the specific computer being used. This reformatting is necessary because not all computers format and present data in the same way. Some computers have different data formats and use different conventions for representing characters (ASCII or EBCDIC). This is analogous to an exclusive restaurant or club that requires men to wear jackets and ties and will provide these items of clothing to those who do not have them to make them "presentable". Without the presentation layer, all computers would have to be designed in exactly the same way to communicate. Rather than design all computers to process data in exactly the same way, presentation layer protocols have been developed to facilitate communication (e.g. the OSI's ASN.1 and Sun's XDR). This layer does not have much evidentiary value and will not receive further attention in this text.

SESSION LAYER

The session layer coordinates dialog between computers, establishing, maintaining, managing and terminating communications. For example, the session layer verifies that the previous instruction sent by an individual has been completed successfully before sending the next instruction. Also, if the connection between two computers has been lost, the session layer can sometimes re-establish a connection and resume the dialog from the point where it was interrupted.

The clearest implementation of the session layer is Sun's Remote Procedure Call (RPC) system. RPC enables several hosts to operate like a single computer – sharing each other's disks, executing commands on each other's systems and sharing important system files (e.g. password files). On Unix, the Network File System (NFS) and Network Information System (NIS) protocols depend on RPC. Microsoft uses its own RPC system to enable computers to share resources.

The session layer is generally very interesting and useful, but it is not a rich source of digital evidence. Therefore, the session layer will not receive further attention in this text.

TRANSPORT LAYER

The transport layer is responsible for managing the delivery of data and has some features that are similar to the session layer. For example, the transport layer establishes, maintains, manages and terminates communications between computers. These functions exist in both the session and transport layers because they are so important.

The transport layer divides large messages into smaller, more manageable parts and keeps track of the parts to ensure that they can be reassembled or retransmitted when necessary. If desired, the transport layer will confirm receipt of data, like a registered mail service that gives the sender a confirmation when the letter reaches its destination. When data is lost in transit, the transport layer will resend it if desired. Without the transport layer, computers would only be able to engage in small talk, making it difficult to perform any complex task over a network. For instance, without the transport layer, it would not be possible to log into a remote computer and interact with it as if your keyboard was directly attached to it.

The transport layer is also responsible for keeping track of which application each piece of data is associated with (e.g. part of an e-mail message or Web page). Port numbers are used to help computers determine what application each piece of data is associated with. Port numbers will be described more fully in Chapter 7, as will the evidentiary aspects of the transport layer.

NETWORK LAYER

The network layer is responsible for routing information to its destination using addresses, much like a postal service that delivers letters based on the address on the envelope. If a message must pass through intermediate computers to get from one place to another, this layer will include appropriate instructions in the message to help the intermediate computers direct the message properly. The central switches in a telephone system are on the network layer of telephone systems (many people forget that telephone systems are computer networks). These switches direct calls based on telephone numbers. The Internet and other large networks also use switches (or slightly different machines called routers) to direct traffic based on unique network addresses.

DATA-LINK LAYER

While the upper layers enable communication between distant computers, the data-link layer enables basic connectivity between computers that are close to each other. For example, when two computers are connected by a single wire, the data-link layer puts data into a form that can be carried by the wire and processed by the receiving computer. Like the network layer, the data-link layer often uses addresses to direct data. However, addresses on the data-link layer are only used locally when data is being transmitted between computers that are not separated by routing equipment. In short, the data-link layer is responsible for local communications between computers and then, once routing, large distances and multiple networks

Figure 5.9

Graphical synopsis of the OSI reference model.

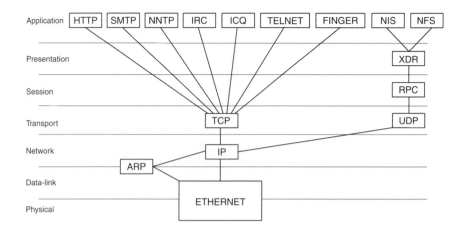

are involved, the network layer takes over. In addition to formatting and transmitting data according to the specifications of the network technology being used (e.g. Ethernet, FDDI, PPP), the data-link layer ensures that data has not been damaged during transmission. Without the data-link layer, data would be sent down from the upper layers and would reach a dead end. Computers would not be able to communicate at all.

PHYSICAL LAYER

The physical layers refers to the actual media that carries data (e.g. telephone wires; fiber optic cables; satellite transmissions). This layer is not concerned with what is being transported but without it, there would be no connection between computers.

SYNOPSIS OF THE OSI REFERENCE MODEL

Figure 5.9 shows how various things fit into the OSI reference model. We can see how the OSI model applies to the Internet by looking at how a Web browser accesses the Internet (see Figure 5.10).

INTERNET APPLICATIONS AND SERVICES

Applications and services are what most of us see and use on computer networks. A service is a program running on one host (called a server) and available to other hosts (called clients). An application is a piece of software that enables an individual to use a specific service (see Figure 5.11).

The Internet provides the infrastructure on which these services can run. Most people are familiar with the services available on the Internet – like e-mail and the World Wide Web. The Internet enables us to publish Web pages for the world to see and enables us to send messages to each other

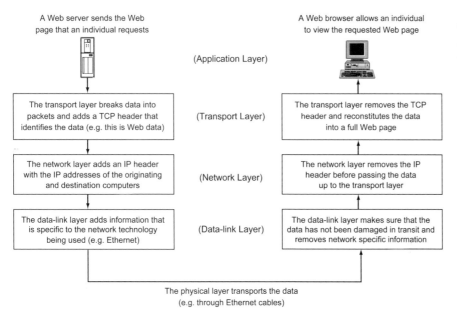

A Web server sends the Web page that an individual requests

(Application Layer)

A Web browser allows an individual to view the requested Web page

The transport layer breaks data into packets and adds a TCP header that identifies the data (e.g. this is Web data)

(Transport Layer)

The transport layer removes the TCP header and reconstitutes the data into a full Web page

The network layer adds an IP header with the IP addresses of the originating and destination computers

(Network Layer)

The network layer removes the IP header before passing the data up to the transport layer

The data-link layer adds information that is specific to the network technology being used (e.g. Ethernet)

(Data-link Layer)

The data-link layer makes sure that the data has not been damaged in transit and removes network specific information

The physical layer transports the data (e.g. through Ethernet cables)

Figure 5.10

How a Web browser accesses the Internet as seen through the OSI model.

using e-mail. Though many of us use these Internet services, we rarely access them directly. Instead we use applications (computer programs) that make it easier to use the services on a network. For example, many people use the Netscape Navigator application to access Web pages stored on distant Web servers. Similarly, Eudora is an application used to access e-mail on distant e-mail servers.

Although there are thousands of Internet services and applications, the process of understanding the Internet can be simplified by considering its four main services:

- World Wide Web (WWW or Web);
- e-mail;
- newsgroups (a.k.a. asynchronous discussion groups);
- synchronous chat networks.

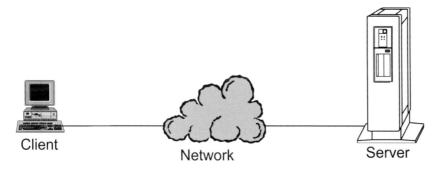

Client

Network

Server

Figure 5.11

A server provides services to clients over a network.

THE WORLD WIDE WEB

The Web first became publicly available in 1991 and has become so popular that it is often mistakenly referred to as the Internet. The Internet is the underlying infrastructure that enables the dissemination of information in the form of Web pages, e-mail messages, etc. Other Internet services including e-mail, Usenet, and synchronous chat networks are now accessible through Web pages. Web pages make it easier for individuals to interact with other Internet services – hiding the complexity with a user-friendly façade.

The popularity and rapid growth of the Web is mainly due to its commercial potential. Using the Web, organizations and individuals alike can make information and commodities available to anyone in the world. Browsers, like Netscape Navigator and Microsoft Internet Explorer, provide an easy to use graphical interface to the Web. Before 1990, some of this information was only available through less user-friendly programs like WAIS, FTP, Archie, Veronica and Gopher. The Web has incorporated these older services and continues to grow, producing the largest information repository in human history. By one count, there are more than sixteen million servers (computers from which information may be obtained) connected to the Internet.

As always, criminals go where the money is, and as the Web becomes more widely used to make monetary transactions, associated criminal activities grow. Some criminals use the Web to provide information to and communicate with fellow criminals. For example, there are an increasing number of recipes for illegal substances on the Web. Also, the Web contains a large amount of information about criminal activity including fraud, abuse and homicide (see Figure 5.12).

Because the Web contains so much loosely ordered information, searching for something in particular can be like looking for a needle in a haystack. This is why it is crucial to learn how to search the Web effectively. Search engines, like AltaVista and Hotbot, are the most useful tools for finding information on the Web. Although search engines are not particularly difficult to use, there is some skill involved. Each search engine has different contents, archiving methods, and search features. Getting to know which search engine is best for a particular type of search will greatly improve your ability to search the Web. This is covered in Chapter 6.

E-MAIL

E-mail, as the name suggests, is a service that enables people to send electronic messages to each other. Provided a message is correctly addressed, it will be delivered through cables and computers to the addressee's personal electronic mailbox. Every e-mail message has a header that contains

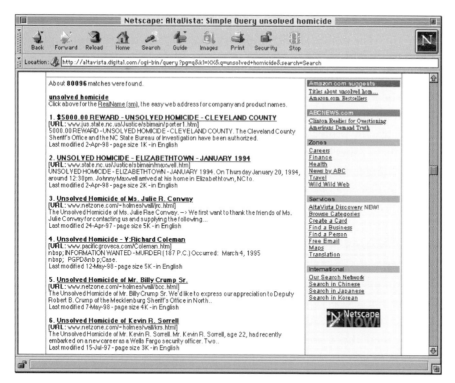

Figure 5.12

Searching the Web for unsolved homicides using Altavista.

information about its origin and destination. It is often possible to track e-mail back to its source and identify the sender using the information in e-mail headers. Even if a header is forged it can contain information that identifies the sender. For example, though the header in Figure 5.13 was forged to misdirect prying individuals, it still contains information about the sender, ec30@is4.nyu.edu.

It takes training and practice to learn how to identify the sender of an e-mail message and there is no single reliable method. However, learning how to read e-mail headers and becoming fluent with the tools used to track e-mail will enable you to adapt your approach to each message that you encounter.

Received: from NYU.EDU by is4.nyu.edu; (5.65v3.2/1.1.8.2/26Mar96-0600PM) id AA08502; Sun, 6 Jul 1997 21:22:35 -0400
Received: from comet.connix.com by cmcl2.NYU.EDU (5.61/1.34) id AA14047; Sun, 6 Jul 97 21:22:33 -0400
Received: from tara.eire.gov (ec30@IS4.NYU.EDU [128.122.253.137]) by comet.connix.com (8.8.5/8.8.5) with SMTP id VAA01050 for <eoghan.casey@nyu.edu; Sun, 6 Jul 1997 21:21:05 -0400 (EDT)
Date: Sun, 6 Jul 1997 21:21:05 -0400 (EDT)
Message-Id: <199707070121.VAA01050@comet.connix.com
From: fionn@eire.gov
To: achilles@thessaly.gov
Subject: Arrangements for Thursday's battle: spears or swords

Figure 5.13

A forged e-mail message.

Despite the identifying information that it contains, e-mail is one of the most important vehicles for criminal activity. It offers a high level of privacy, especially when encryption is used. It can be difficult to determine if e-mail is being used to commit or facilitate a crime because only the addressees receive the message. Although an e-mail message can be intercepted at many points along its journey or collected from an individual's computer, personal e-mail is usually protected by strict privacy laws, making it more difficult to obtain than other forms of evidence. Even if investigators can obtain incriminating e-mail, it can be difficult to prove that a specific individual sent a specific message. People can easily repudiate (reject the validity of) a message, claiming that they did not send the message.

NEWSGROUPS

Newsgroups are the Internet equivalent of public bulletin boards, enabling asynchronous communication that often resembles a discussion. Anyone with Internet access can post a message on these bulletin boards and come back later to see if anyone has replied. Most newsgroups are part of a global system called the User's Network (Usenet) that began in 1979. Because Usenet messages are broadcast to millions of people around the world, it is the perfect medium for individuals to communicate with a huge audience. Criminals use this global forum to exchange information and commit crimes, including defamation, copyright infringement, harassment, stalking, fraud, and solicitation of minors. Also, child pornography and pirated software is advertised and exchanged through Usenet.

There are archives that contain millions of messages from tens of thousands of newsgroups. These archives are invaluable tools for investigators because they contain a vast amount of detailed information about individuals and their interactions. However, these archives are not comprehensive and should not be depended on completely when dealing with Usenet. Few archives include message attachments and anyone can specify that they do not want their postings to be archived. Any newsgroup posting with "x-no-archive: yes" as its first line will be ignored by archiving software and there are some newsgroups that are not archived at all. Whenever possible, investigators should collect digital evidence from the actual newsgroups rather than the archives since the archives are incomplete.

Like e-mail, Usenet messages have headers containing information about the sender and the journey that the message took. However, the format of the headers in Usenet is slightly different from e-mail. For instance, instead of a Received header, Usenet messages have a Path: line that lists the primary computers that handled the message. As with e-mail, the header can be

Subject: Wanna Buy My Worn...Pantyhose...and Panties????
From: nancyc544@aol.com (NancyC544)
Date: 1996/05/15
Message-ID: <4nduca$2j4@newsbf02.news.aol.com
Newsgroups: alt.pantyhose
organization: America Online, Inc. (1-800-827-6364)
reply-to: nancyc544@aol.com (NancyC544)
sender: root@newsbf02.news.aol.com
            Hi! My name is Nancy. I am 25, have Blonde hair, green eyes am 5'6
            and weigh 121. Is anyone out there interested in buying my
            worn...pantyhose...or....panties? This is not a joke or a wacky internet
            scam. I am very serious about this. I live in the U.S. but I can ship them
            anywhere in the world. If you are serious you can e-mail me at:
            nancyc544@aol.com

Figure 5.14

A Usenet message.

modified to make it more difficult to identify the sender. With training and practice, investigators can learn to extract a great deal of information from Usenet (see Figure 5.14).

SYNCHRONOUS CHAT NETWORKS

Live conversations between users on the Internet exist in many formats (text, audio, video, and virtual reality), on a huge variety of topics, and take place 24 hours a day. IRC (Internet Relay Chat) is currently the largest chat network and can be used by anyone with Internet access. America Online has a substantial chat network but this is separate from the Internet and is only available to its subscribers. There are many smaller chat areas on the Internet, including text-based Multi User Domains (MUDs) that allow individuals to build virtual spaces and role play in them. There are even some chat networks that allow individuals to create three-dimensional representations of themselves and wander through a three-dimensional environment, meeting and chatting with others. Most synchronous chat networks allow individuals to create their own, self-titled rooms that often involve explicit, but not necessarily unlawful, sexual content.

The Internet Relay Chat (IRC) network, started in 1988, is accessible using free or low-cost, easy-to-use software. Two of the most popular IRC software programs are mIRC and PIRCH. There are thousands of chat rooms in operation worldwide on IRC at any given time. Many IRC chat rooms exist to facilitate the discussion of unlawful activities and the exchange of obscene photographs and videos. Computer crackers gather in IRC chat channels to collaborate and socialize. Child pornographers meet to exchange materials. IRC has even been used to broadcast live sessions of children being sexually abused.

Figure 5.15

A screen shot of IRC as seen through an IRC client.

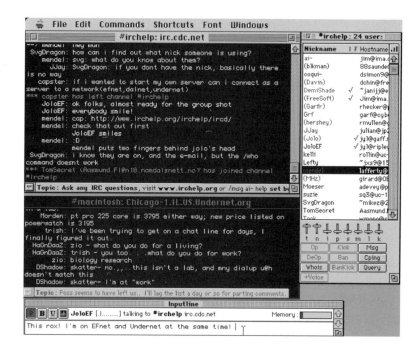

Using simple commands anyone can bypass the IRC servers, connect directly to another person's computer, and transfer pictures, video or data. This direct link between two computers leaves no digital evidence on the IRC servers. However, there will be other indications of this activity; it is just a matter of knowing where to look.

ICQ ("I seek you") is a relatively new live chat network with a difference. Instead of gathering in chat rooms, ICQ users must seek each other out and jointly agree to have a conversation. While this limits contact with others on the ICQ network, it enables more private conversations than on other chat networks. In this respect, misconduct facilitated by ICQ is more difficult to detect because a third party cannot participate in ICQ conversations unless invited. However, the same privacy makes ICQ a useful tool for business communication and collaboration, and it has many legitimate users and uses.

On IRC, ICQ and many other chat networks, you can find some basic information about an individual using tracking tools and techniques. However, since many chat networks enable people to create their own private areas and some chat programs allow users to initiate a direct connection with each other, bypassing the chat network altogether. Therefore, much of the information on chat networks is transient and sometimes difficult to find. To access this information, you must develop a solid understanding of the Internet, the chat network being used, and the search features built into the chat network.

The privacy, immediacy and impermanence of synchronous chat networks make them particularly conducive to criminal activity; predators can obtain victims immediately without leaving a trace of evidence. This, in turn, makes synchronous chat networks a valuable investigative tool. A surprising amount can be learned from the activities in the millions of online chat rooms.

CRIME AND EVIDENCE ON DIFFERENT NETWORK LAYERS

The criminal activity and digital evidence that can be found on the various layers is summarized here and presented in greater detail in subsequent chapters.

APPLICATION LAYER

Because the application layer is essentially the user interface to computer networks, it is the most widely used layer and so can be awash with evidence of criminal activity. On this layer, e-mail, the Web, Usenet, chat rooms and all of the other network services can facilitate a wide range of crimes. These crimes can include homicide, rape, torture, solicitation of minors, child pornography, stalking, harassment, fraud, espionage, sabotage, theft, privacy violations, and defamation.

CASE EXAMPLE
In one homicide case, involving arson, the application layer of the Internet played several roles in the investigation. On 22 March 1998, in his e-mail based support group, Larry Froistad made the following confession about killing his five-year-old daughter, Amanda, three years before:

My God, there's something I haven't mentioned, but it's a very important part of the equation. The people I'm mourning the loss of, I've ejected from my life. Kitty had to endure my going to jail twice and being embarrassed in front of her parents. Amanda I murdered because her mother stood between us. I let her watch the videos she loved all evening, and when she was asleep I got wickedly drunk, set our house on fire, went to bed, listened to her scream twice, climbed out the window and set about putting on a show of shock, surprise and grief to remove culpability from myself. Dammit, part of that show was climbing in her window and grabbing her pajamas, then hearing her breathe and dropping her where she was so she could die and rid me of her mother's interferences.

Froistad, a 29-year-old computer programmer, was arrested and extradited from California to North Dakota. He apparently confessed again while in police custody. However, upon mature reflection, Froistad pleaded innocent to the charge of murder, a charge that can lead to life imprisonment but not execution, since North Dakota does not have a death penalty. His lawyers argued that someone else could have sent the e-mail messages. However, while investigating Froistad's other Internet activities, the FBI found that he had traded child pornography and admitted to sexually abusing his daughter. This additional evidence could change the charge to sexual exploitation of a minor ending in the victim's death – and this could lead to a death sentence.

It is no secret that there are national and international pedophile rings, so it should be no surprise that these rings use the Internet. Nonetheless, the amount of evidence of child abuse on the Internet and the numbers of pedophile rings using the Internet has astonished the most veteran crime fighters.

CASE EXAMPLE
Richard Romero was charged with kidnapping a 13-year-old boy with the intent to engage in sexual activity. Romero befriended the boy on the Internet, initially posing as a young boy himself. Romero persuaded the boy to meet him at a Chicago hotel and travel with him to St Petersburg. After the boy's mother alerted police of her son's absence, a taxi driver reported driving Romero and the boy to a bus station and investigators were able to arrest Romero before he and the boy reached their destination. The FBI found child pornography on Romero's computer and evidence to suggest that Romero frequently befriended young boys on the Internet.

Most network applications create sources of digital evidence. For example, Web browsers often keep a record of all Web pages visited and temporary copies of materials that were viewed recently. There are many other Internet applications, each with their own investigative and evidentiary challenges. For example, Hotline Server is a very compact program that enables individuals to turn their personal computers into servers that provide a variety of services including file transfer and chat. Using a Hotline Client, anyone on the Internet can connect directly to a computer running the Hotline Server to upload or download files. Access to a Hotline Server can be password restricted. This is very similar to a Bulletin Board System (BBS) but is much easier to use. There is currently no reliable way to find Hotline Servers that people want to keep secret – and this makes it more difficult to detect illegal activity. Also, because no central servers are involved, the only evidence of a crime is on the individual computers involved. Fortunately, the Hotline Server can keep a record of every computer that connects to the server, and every file that is downloaded or uploaded will be noted. This can be a useful source of digital evidence. One should look carefully at every new computer application encountered to determine what kind of digital evidence it can provide.

TRANSPORT AND NETWORK LAYERS

The transport and networks layers are ripe with digital evidence. This is largely because these layers play such an important role in internetworking.

Addresses on the network layer (e.g. IP addresses) are used to identify computers and direct information. Technically proficient criminals can alter this addressing and routing information to intercept or misdirect information, break into computers, hide their identity (by using someone else's IP address) or just cause general mischief. Conversely, investigators can use this addressing information to determine the source of a crime.

For example, on Internet Relay Chat (IRC) networks, some criminals shield their IP address, a unique number that identifies the computer being used, to make it more difficult for an investigator to track them down. ICQ purposefully enables their users to hide their IP address to protect their privacy. However, an investigator who is familiar with the transport layer and network layers can uncover these hidden IP addresses quite easily (described in the TCP/IP section in Chapter 7).

Computer crackers often use programs that access and manipulate the transport and network layers to break into computers. The simple act of gaining unauthorized access to a computer is a crime in most places. However, the serious trouble usually begins after a computer cracker gains access to a host. A malicious intruder might destroy files or use the computer as a jump-off point to access other systems or commit other crimes. There is usually evidence on a computer that can show when an individual has gained unauthorized access. However, clever computer crackers will remove incriminating digital evidence.

It is important to note that many of the activities on the application layer generate log files that contain information associated with the transport and network layers. For example, when an e-mail message is sent or received, the time and the IP address that was used to send the message are often logged in a file on the e-mail server. Similarly, when a Web page is viewed, the time and the IP address of the viewer are usually logged on the Web server. There are many other potential sources of digital evidence relating to the transport and network layers. A clear understanding of these layers can help investigators locate these sources of digital evidence. Chapter 7 covers the basics of the transport and network layers and describes how investigators can use log files and state tables in an investigation.

DATA-LINK AND PHYSICAL LAYERS

The data-link and physical layers are a gold-mine from a digital evidence perspective. The Media Access Control (MAC) addresses described earlier in this chapter are part of the data-link layer and can be used to identify a specific computer on a network. These addresses are more identifying than network layer addresses (e.g. IP addresses) because they are associated with hardware inside the computer (IP addresses can be reassigned to different computers). Additionally, all information travelling over a network passes through the physical layer. Individuals who can access the physical layer have unlimited access to all of the data on the network (unless it is encrypted). Investigators can dip into the raw flow of bits traveling over a network and pull out valuable nuggets of digital evidence. Conversely, criminals can access the physical layer and gather any information that interests them.

It is not especially difficult to access the physical layer and eavesdrop on network traffic. One method of eavesdropping is to gain physical access to network cables and use specially designed eavesdropping equipment. However, it is much easier to gain access to a computer attached to a network and use that computer to eavesdrop. With the proper access privileges and software, a curious individual can listen into all traffic on a network. Computer crackers often break into computer systems and run programs called *sniffers* to gather information. Also, employees can run sniffers on their computers, allowing them to read their co-workers' or employer's e-mail messages, passwords, and anything else that travels over the network.

SUMMARY

Connecting computers together is inherently risky. An individual can gain unauthorized access to a distant network. Anyone can intercept transmissions between networks. Additionally, connecting networks enables individuals, including criminals, to communicate in ways that were not possible before, resulting in a new set of problems. However, for every disadvantage, there is an equal and opposite advantage. With the proper authority and precautions, investigators can gain access to and collect evidence from distant networks. Investigators can intercept digital evidence as it travels over a network, and computer networks enable investigators to communicate with each other and observe criminal activity and communication as never before.

The ultimate challenge for investigators is to follow cybertrails swiftly and thoroughly to find pockets of digital evidence before they are lost forever. This is challenging not only because evidence on a network is distributed and dynamic, but also because every network is different with unique combinations of hardware and software. Many networks have grown by a process of accretion, laying new technologies on top of old in a fairly haphazard manner. The result is almost organic: an entity that often seems to have a mind of its own. In some cases, even the people who are responsible for maintaining a network do not understand it completely. Therefore, it is unrealistic to expect an investigator to have full knowledge of a network before, or even after, an investigation. The most that can be expected of an investigator is to understand how computers and networks function in general and to have a familiarity with a variety of technologies and operating systems. Having a solid understanding of how networks function in general will enable an investigator to understand many different types of networks and will help determine when and what kind of expert is needed.

By learning how computer networks function and how forensic science can be applied to computer networks, investigators can take advantage of digital evidence and address the growing problem of cybercrime. The remainder of this text details how to recognize, collect, document, preserve, reconstruct, classify, compare, individualize and reconstruct various kinds of digital evidence found on computer networks, and how to use this evidence in an investigation. Specifically, Chapter 6 demonstrates how to scour the surface of a network for content and clues. Chapter 7 describes how to make use of the glue that holds large networks together (focusing on TCP/IP) and find evidence that is necessary for tracking down criminals. Chapter 8 goes to the core – the physical components and media that combine to make a network.

REFERENCES

Baran, P. (1964) *Introduction to Distributed Communications Networks*, RM-3420-PR. Santa Barbara, CA: The Rand Corporation [http://www.rand.org/publications/RM/RM3420/].

Comer, D. E. (1995) *Internetworking with TCP/IP. Vol. I: Principles, Protocols, and Architecture*, 3rd edn, Upper Saddle River, NJ: Prentice Hall.

Garfinkel, S. and Spafford, G. (1996) *Practical Unix and Internet Security*, 2nd edn, Cambridge, MA: O'Reilly & Associates, Inc.

Henry, P. H. and DeLibero, G. (1996) *Strategic Networking: From LAN and WAN to Information Superhighways*, Boston, MA: International Thomson Publishing Company.

National Computer Security Association (1997) *Internet Security: Professional Reference*, Indianapolis, IN: New Riders Publishing.

Sterling, B. (1993) *A Short History of the Internet*. Cornwall, CT: Magazine of Fantasy and Science Fiction [http://www.library.yale.edu/div/instruct/internet/history.htm].

## CHAPTER 6

DIGITAL EVIDENCE ON THE INTERNET

The application layer of any network contains a large amount of information. For example, many organizations use the application layer of their private networks to facilitate communication between employees and to make sales, payroll and other routine financial transactions more efficient. Also, Internet services like the Web, Usenet and IRC contain information about people, organizations and geographical areas. People use the Internet to communicate, explore new ideas and make purchases from the comfort of their homes.

This combination of social and financial activity makes the application layer an attractive place for criminals. Con artists find a large number of marks through e-mail, Usenet and the Web. Sexual predators have a wide selection of hunting grounds (e.g. chat networks) and victims to choose from. Stalkers use Internet services to obtain information about their victims and sometimes harass their victims using the Internet. Thieves break into private networks of organizations and steal credit card numbers and trade secrets.

This chapter focuses on investigating criminal activity on the application layer of the Internet (i.e. the Web, e-mail, Usenet, IRC). Scenarios are used to give a practical understanding of how the main services on the Internet can be involved in criminal activity and how they can be a source of digital evidence. The discussions of the Internet's application layer in this chapter can be generalized to any network. Collecting digital evidence at the application layer is like taking a surface scraping of a network. A lot of digital evidence can be obtained from the application layer, but there is a lot more below it that can be obtained with additional effort.

INVESTIGATING CRIME ON THE INTERNET

Only a limited amount of research has been performed to quantify and analyze criminal activity on the Internet. Most assertions about crime on the Internet are based on limited data and are often unverifiable.

CASE EXAMPLE

In 1995, the Georgetown University Law Review published a research paper by Martin Rimm, a student at Carnegie Mellon University (CMU). The paper described and classified the sexually oriented materials circulating on the Internet and quantified the relative amounts of obscene and illegal materials versus other kinds of materials.

Rimm's study generated a great deal of interest, reaffirming many people's view that the Internet was primarily used to exchange pornographic materials. Time magazine was so taken with the results that they published a special issue entitled Cyberporn featuring Rimm's study. The CMU administration was so concerned that their computer systems were being used to distribute illegal materials, they temporarily removed all sexually explicit images from the newsgroups on their servers.

Ultimately, the study did not stand under scrutiny – the research methodology and data analysis was flawed.

There are some general assertions that can be made about crime on the Internet. The Web does not contain much direct evidence of criminal activity because there is such a high risk of detection. Any illegal activity on the Web is carefully hidden (e.g. password protected), and only available to trusted individuals. Criminals utilize Usenet to collaborate (Mann and Sutton 1998) and to distribute pornography of all kinds including child pornography. Criminals feel relatively safe on Usenet because they can hide their identities and can prevent their messages from being archived, thereby reducing the risk of detection. Criminals that are determined to avoid detection while using the Internet use e-mail and synchronous chat networks.

In an effort to reduce the amount of criminal activity on synchronous chat networks, investigators often try to gain the trust of criminals by posing as children or fellow criminals. Although this approach has resulted in arrests, it is a time-consuming endeavor that is open to criticism. It is often argued that individuals on IRC tricked by investigators did not intend to commit a crime and were entrapped. Even when the individual travels to meet law enforcement officers expecting to find a potential victim, there is a question as to whether the individual had criminal intents[1].

[1] Any predisposition on the part of a defendant to commit a crime usually negates entrapment.

SEARCHING THE INTERNET

Given the magnitude of information on the Internet, it is crucial to learn how to search efficiently and effectively. There are many tools that make searching easier, including general search engines and topic-specific databases. Search engines are regularly updated catalogs of Web pages, recent Usenet messages, mailing lists, newspaper articles, and much more. Some excellent search engines are:

- Altavista: http://www.altavista.com
- Hotbot: http://www.hotbot.com
- Excite: http://www.excite.com
- Infoseek: http://www.infoseek.com

There are many other search engines – each with different contents, search features, and capabilities that change regularly. For instance, Excite uses a thesaurus-like feature called Intelligent Concept Extraction. As describe on the Excite Web page:

> ... when you enter a search query, Excite searches the entire Web for documents containing related concepts, not just keywords you entered. For instance, when you search for "dog care", Excite will bring you pages containing "pet grooming", even if the words "dog" and "care" are not actually on the page [http://www.excite.com/].

Excite also provides two other features to help individuals make searches more precise: Search Wizard, which suggests terms that can help narrow down a search, and Power Search, which helps perform advanced searches without learning any jargon. It is important for investigators to remain aware of such features so that they can use them or avoid them as necessary. Also, because no single search engine contains everything, it is important for investigators to become familiar with a number of search engines and learn which search engine is best for a particular type of search.

While search engines enable individuals to search through Web pages, newspaper articles, and a variety of other media for information on any topic, databases allow individuals to search within a specific subject area. For example, using Dejanews (http://www.dejanews.com) an investigator can search through Usenet messages that have been posted in the past few years. There are also databases on the Web that contain names, phone numbers, e-mail addresses, and street addresses. Additionally, using the Internet, investigators can access databases containing information about sexual predators, missing children, individuals' assets and credit history, medical information, and more (Lane 1997).

There are several approaches to searching the Internet.

1   Geographical: useful when investigators are interested in a specific geographical region. There are many resources on the Internet that organize information by geographical region.

2   Organizational: useful when investigators want to know more about a specific organization. The Internet can contain quite a bit of information about an organization and many organizations have searchable Web sites.

3   Individuals: a search for an individual can require a combination of geographical and organizational searching in addition to some broader search criteria like the name, e-mail address, and other identifying information of individuals.

4 Subject: a search for information on a particular subject is the most general search of all.

Regardless of the type of search, it is generally necessary to narrow the search. An initial search will usually result in hundreds or thousands of resources that are of no interest to the investigator. To eliminate large amounts of extraneous information, investigators can use the language of the database or search engine to refine a search. For example, some databases and search engines understand words like AND, OR, NOT and NEAR. Some search engines also allow symbols such as '–' to exclude terms for the search and '+' to include terms.

For instance, in Altavista, the following commands can be used to find documents containing the words "unsolved" and "homicide" but not the words "mystery" or "mysteries":

```
+homicide +unsolved –mystery –mysteries

homicide AND unsolved NOT myster*

homicide & unsolved !myster*
```

Keep in mind that searching for obviously illegal terms will rarely turn up anything illegal. Many Web sites use illegal terms to attract interest, but actual criminals make some effort to hide their activities using euphemisms. For instance, the term *warez* refers to software that is distributed in violation of copyright. Sometimes these euphemisms will turn up during the initial searches, in which case it will be necessary to expand the search using this new knowledge and gradually narrow the search again.

E-MAIL FORGERY AND TRACKING

Suppose you receive the following e-mail from Bill Gates containing a copy of the commercial software, Microsoft Office:

```
Date: Sun, 6 Jul 1997 21:21:05 -0400 (EDT)

From: Bill.Gates@microsoft.com

To: you@emailaddress.com

Subject: Microsoft Office
As the richest man in the world, I think that it is safe to say that I have taken
enough money from you. It is time to give something back. Please accept this
complimentary copy of Microsoft Office. If you are feeling similarly generous,
please send what you can to:

Charity Donations
P.O. Box 5356
New York, NY 10003
```

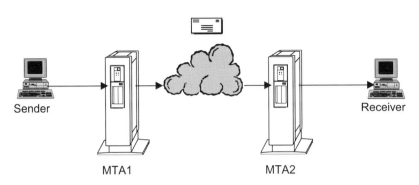

Figure 6.1

Message Transfer Agent.

You suspect that Bill Gates did not send this e-mail message but how can you be sure? Also, you might be wondering who sent this e-mail and the method they used. Did some prankster break into Microsoft and use Mr Gates' personal computer to send the message? To answer these questions it is necessary to understand how e-mail is created and transmitted.

Electronic mail is similar to regular mail in many ways. There are computers on the Internet, called Message Transfer Agents (MTA), which are the equivalent of post offices for electronic mail. When you send an e-mail message, it first goes to your local MTA. Just as a post office stamps letters with a postmark, your local MTA puts the current time and the name of the MTA along with some technical information, at the top of your e-mail message. This e-mail equivalent of a postmark is called a *Received header*. Your message is then passed from one MTA to another until it reaches the destination MTA (see Figure 6.1).

Every MTA that receives the message puts a Received header at the top of the message. A simple analogy to this is a stack of pancakes; newer ones are on top. This means that the last computer to handle the message is listed at the top of the header, and the first computer is listed near the bottom. Therefore, to track an e-mail message back to the sender you simply retrace the route that the e-mail traveled by reading through the e-mail's Received headers[2].

Here is the entire e-mail message from Bill Gates along with Received headers:

Received: from atrustingmta.com by yourmailserver.emailaddress.com (5.61/1.34) id AA14047; Sun, 6 Jul 97 21:22:33 -0400

Received: from fake.message.com (corpus-delicti.com [207.244.93.93]) by atrustingmta.com (8.8.5/8.8.5) with SMTP id VAA01050 for <you@emailaddress.com; Sun, 6 Jul 1997 21:21:05 -0400 (EDT)

Date: Sun, 6 Jul 1997 21:21:05 -0400 (EDT)

Message-Id: <199707070121.VAA01050@atrustingmta.com

From: Bill.Gates@microsoft.com

To: you@emailaddress.com

Subject: Microsoft Office

[2]Most e-mail applications will display e-mail headers. For example, while viewing an e-mail message in Netscape Mail select the Options - Show Headers menu, in Eudora click on the "Blah, Blah, Blah" button at the top of the message, and in Pine type H.

> As the richest man in the world, I think that it is safe to say that I have taken enough money from you. It is time to give something back. Please accept this complimentary copy of Microsoft Office. If you are feeling similarly generous, please send what you can to:
>
> Charity Donations
>
> P.O. Box 5356
>
> New York, NY 10003

According to the earliest Received header, this message was sent from *corpus-delicti.com* via *atrustingmta.com*. Now that you are certain that this message was not sent from *microsoft.com*, you are probably curious about the actual sender. In addition to searching the Web, Usenet and ICQ, there are several services on the Internet that can help you learn more about the sender of an e-mail message (e.g. finger, ph, Telnet). The most direct method of finding contact information for a given host is to search the Whois databases (http://whois.arin.net/whois/arinwhois.html).

The Whois databases contains the names and contact information of people who are responsible for the many computer systems that make up the Internet. You can contact these people for assistance if your query involves their computer system. For example, searching the Whois database for *corpus-delicti.com* returns the following information:

> Registrant: Brent Turvey (CORPUS-DELICTI-DOM)
>
> Knowledge Solutions LLC; 1271 Washington Ave #274
>
> San Leandro, CA 94577 US
>
> Domain Name: CORPUS-DELICTI.COM
>
>
> Administrative Contact:
>
> Troyer-Turvey, Barbara (BT4009) troyturv@CORPUS-DELICTI.COM
>
> 510-483-6739
>
> Technical Contact, Zone Contact:
>
> John Miker, Debi (JM2073) John@INFOBOARD.COM
>
> 781-592-6675 (FAX) (781)592-3042
>
> Billing Contact:
>
> Troyer-Turvey, Barbara (BT4009) troyturv@CORPUS-DELICTI.COM
>
> 510-483-6739

A court order could be used to compel the responsible individuals to check the e-mail logs on their computers to determine which individual used their system to send the forged Bill Gates message.

The final open question is, "How was this e-mail created?" The first thing to realize is that when you send e-mail, the Message Transfer Agents that handle the message do not always verify that you are who you say you are. Therefore, if you can find a trusting MTA that will relay your e-mail, you can pretend to be Bill Gates when sending e-mail[3].

There are many trusting computers on the Internet that will allow anyone to connect to them and create forged e-mail. Many entrepreneurs have discovered this fact and abuse the trusting computers by relaying unsolicited junk e-mail through them. This junk e-mail is called SPAM (in honor of a Monty Python skit) and is excellent food for practice if you would like to develop your e-mail tracking skills.

To understand how this e-mail forging is done, it is helpful to know how to use Telnet and to understand how MTAs exchange messages. Telnet is a simple but powerful protocol that enables individuals to log onto a remote host and type commands as if their keyboard were directly connected to the remote machine[4]. Using Telnet, individuals can connect directly to an MTA and defraud it provided they know the protocol (language) to use[5] (see Figure 6.2).

MTAs exchange e-mail using a protocol called Simple Mail Transfer Protocol (SMTP). Remember, a protocol is nothing fancy, it is just an agreed-upon way of "speaking." As the name suggests, Simple Mail Transfer Protocol is quite simple. In four broken English sentences (helo, mail from, rcpt to, data) one MTA (mta.sending.com) can say "helo" and ask another MTA (mta.receiving.edu) to pass an e-mail message on to its destination. This process is shown below with SMTP commands in upper case and acknowledgements in bold[6].

[3]When people first learn about e-mail forgery they make the mistake of thinking that they have to use their ISP to relay the e-mail. This is not the case — an individual can use any one of the thousands of trusting MTAs out there to relay forged e-mail.

[4]Telnet comes with Windows and Unix operating systems. To run Telnet on a Windows machine, click on the Start button, select Run, type telnet and click OK.

[5]To access an MTA directly using Telnet use the command telnet hostname 25. For example, on a Windows machine, click on the Start button, select Run, type telnet mail.berkeley.com 25 and click OK. The number 25 specifies the port number that you want to Telnet to access. Ports are discussed in Chapter 7.

[6]The numbers "250" and "349" in this example are not relevant and can be ignored.

```
% telnet mail.berkeley.edu 25
Trying 128.32.136.21...
Connected to nak.Berkeley.EDU.
Escape character is '^]'.
220 nak.berkeley.edu ESMTP Sendmail 8.8.5/8.8.5; Mon, 26 Apr 1999 17:57:31 -0700
 (PDT)
HELO fake.message.com
250 nak.berkeley.edu Hello infobsun11.infoboard.net [206.243.183.148], pleased t
o meet you
MAIL FROM: Bill.Gates@microsoft.com
250 Bill.Gates@microsoft.com... Sender ok
RCPT TO: you@emailaddress.com
571 you@emailaddress.com... We do not relay for infobsun11.infoboard.net
QUIT
221 nak.berkeley.edu closing connection
Connection closed by foreign host.
%
```

Figure 6.2

Telnet being used to connect to a MTA and issue commands. Note that this MTA will not be fooled into sending a forged e-mail message.

```
> HELO Fake.message.com

250 mta.receiving.edu welcomes mta.sending.com

> MAIL FROM: Bill.Gates@microsoft.com

250 Bill.Gates@microsoft.com... Sender ok

> RCPT TO: you@ emailaddress.com

250 you@emailaddress.com... Recipient ok

> DATA

354 Enter mail, end with "." on a line by itself

Subject: Sending an e-mail message

This is the contents of the e-mail message. To end a

message you must type a period on a line by itself.

.

250 MAA06130 Message accepted for delivery

> QUIT
```

If you use Eudora, Netscape Mail, or another e-mail client program that uses SMTP, you might notice these SMTP commands flash by when you send a message. These e-mail clients can be configured with false information to make e-mail appear to come from somebody else. For an example of how to reconfigure Netscape to send forged e-mail see *Net Crime, Don't be a Victim* (Ferrell 1997) (this article does not mention that you will have to find a trusting MTA to relay your forged message).

Some people mistakenly think that using a free e-mail service like Hotmail (www.hotmail.com) or Netaddress (www.netaddress.com) will protect their identity. However, e-mail sent from these free services contain information about the originating computer that can be used to track down the sender.

```
Received: from NYU.EDU by is4.nyu.edu; (5.65v3.2/1.1.8.2/26Mar96-0600PM) id
AA29416; Wed, 5 Nov 1997 23:19:10-0500

Received: from hotmail.com ("port 4044"@F59.hotmail.com) by cmcl2.nyu.edu
(PMDF V5.1-10 #24942) with SMTP id

<0EJ700A13INX7S@cmcl2.nyu.edu> for ec30@is4.nyu.edu; Wed, 5 Nov 1997
23:19:09 -0500 (EST)

Received: (qmail 3403 invoked by uid 0); Thu, 06 Nov 1997 04:17:52 +0000
Received: from 128.122.253.141 by www.hotmail.com with HTTP; Wed, 05 Nov
1997 20:17:52 -0800 (PST)

Date: Wed, 05 Nov 1997 20:17:52 -0800 (PST)

From: Casey O'Connor
```

Subject: Test

To: eoghan.casey@nyu.edu

Message-Id: <19971106041752.3401.qmail@hotmail.com>

Content-Type: text/plain

X-Originating-Ip: [128.122.253.141]

Contents Removed

Get Your Private, Free Email at http://www.hotmail.com

For example, this message was sent through Hotmail. Reading the header from bottom to top, you will notice that it contains the IP address of the computer that was used to send the message (128.122.253.141). IP addresses can be very useful for tracking down criminals as described in Chapter 7 and in the following case example:

CASE EXAMPLE
Police in California were seeking Troy A. Mayo for several months in connection with the death of a pregnant 17-year-old named Serina Adele Ely. The girl's body had been found in Mayo's apartment. Several weeks after his disappearance, Mayo e-mailed a relative using Hotmail. Police used the IP address of the originating machine to determine that Mayo was using a computer at the University of California library in Berkeley. They waited near the computer that Mayo commonly used until he appeared.

USENET FORGERY AND TRACKING

Usenet is made up of news servers (computers running special software) all over the world that communicate using the very simple Network News Transport Protocol (NNTP). To view a newsgroup on Usenet you need a newsreader such as the Messenger in Netscape Communicator. In the newsreader you must choose a server and view the newsgroups stored on that server (see Figure 6.3 on page 108). Each server subscribes to a selection of newsgroups and stores a copy of each Usenet newsgroup it subscribes to. There is no centralized server that coordinates Usenet – it is a cooperative network.

More specifically, when you first post a message to a newsgroup, your message is only stored on the news server you are connected to. At a prearranged time, this news server automatically sends your message – along with all of the other new messages that it has – to a prearranged set of neighboring servers. These servers add their names to the message header and pass the messages on to other servers, and so on. In this way, your message eventually is passed along to all of the other people who participate,

Figure 6.3

The alt.2600.warez Usenet newsgroup viewed on the news.yale.edu server as seen through Netscape Communicator's Messenger.

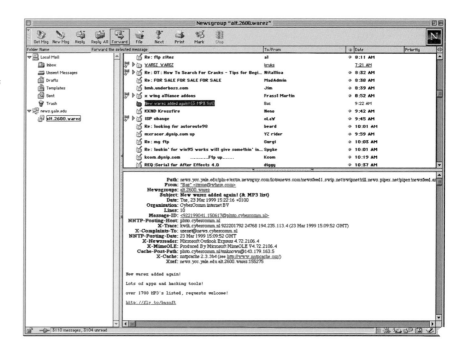

to create the global Usenet network. Like e-mail, the path a Usenet message takes can often be traced back to the computer used to send it. The following message is not trying to hide anything and is therefore easy to track:

```
Path: news.corpus-delicti.com!pln-e!extra.newsguy.com!lotsanews.com!
newsfeed.gamma.ru!Gamma.RU!demos!newshub.northeast.verio.net!
howland.erols.net!EU.net!EUnet.yu!not-for-mail


From: "kruks" <arcus@eunet.yu>
Newsgroups: alt.2600.warez
Subject: WAREZ WAREZ
Date: Tue, 23 Mar 1999 13:21:47 +0100
Organization: Public news server of EUnet Yugoslavia
Lines: 5
Message-ID: <7d8108$obu$1@SOLAIR2.EUnet.yu>
NNTP-Posting-Host: p-199.166.eunet.yu
X-Trace: SOLAIR2.EUnet.yu 922191688 24958 194.247.199.166 (23 Mar 1999
12:21:28 GMT)
X-Complaints-To: abuse@EUnet.yu
NNTP-Posting-Date: 23 Mar 1999 12:21:28 GMT


OVER 5000 PROGRAMS
FULL CD  80$
PRICE INCLUDE SHIPPING
```

The *NNTP-Posting-Host* line indicates that the individual who created this message was connected to a Yugoslavia ISP, called *Eunet.yu,* through a dialup connection (p-199.166.eunet.yu). The Path header (reading from right to left and ignoring the "not-for-mail") shows that this message was first posted on a news server run by *Eunet.yu.* The *message ID* and *X-trace* headers near the bottom of the message confirm that the new server's full name is *SOLAIR2.Eunet.yu.* This news server transferred the message to another news server named *howland.erols.net,* which then passed the message on to a server called *newshub.northeast.verio.net.* This continued until the message reached all of the cooperating servers. Unlike e-mail, which is transferred the moment it is received by a Message Transfer Agent, Usenet can take several hours to distribute a message to all of the news servers around the world.

In some cases Usenet messages are not so easy to track. For instance, the NNTP-Posting-Host and Path headers in the following message are contradictory. The NNTP-Posting-Host line indicates that the message was created on a computer called *cheat.usenet.com,* but the first news server in the Path header is a seemingly unrelated computer named *masters0.news.internet.net:*

```
Path: news.corpus-delicti.com!pln-e!extra.newsguy.com!lotsanews.com!
news.maxwell.syr.edu!newsfeed.wli.net!su-news-hub1.bbnplanet.com!
news.bbnplanet.com!newsfeed.concentric.net! masters0.news.internet.net!usenet

From: nobody (nobody@hotmail.com)

Newsgroups: alt.abuse.recovery

Subject: Something pithy

Date: Fri, 25 Sep 1998 10:51:29 -0700

Organization: Nobody's Home

Message-ID: <8pF762$Flg@masters0.Internet.net>

Reply-To: nobody@hotmail.com

NNTP-Posting-Host: cheat.usenet.com
```

What is going on here? This message was forged. The best way to learn more about a piece of digital evidence is to reconstruct it by either recreating the sequence of events or the environment that created the evidence. In this instance, the commands that resulted in this Usenet message can be recreated by connecting to the news server and constructing a forged message[7] (see Figure 6.4 on page 110).

This process is shown below with Network News Transport Protocol (NNTP) commands are in upper case, and acknowledgements are in bold.

[7]To access an news server directly using Telnet use the command telnet hostname 119. For example, on a Windows machine, click on the Start button, select Run, type telnet news.berkeley.com 119 and click OK. The number 119 specifies the port number that you want to Telnet to access. Ports are discussed in Chapter 7.

Figure 6.4

Telnet being used to connect to a news server and issue commands. Note that this news server will not be fooled into sending a forged e-mail message.

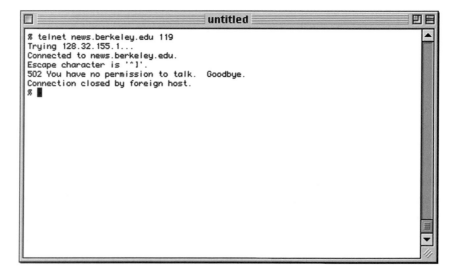

```
% telnet news.berkeley.edu 119
Trying 128.32.155.1...
Connected to news.berkeley.edu.
Escape character is '^]'.
502 You have no permission to talk.   Goodbye.
Connection closed by foreign host.
%
```

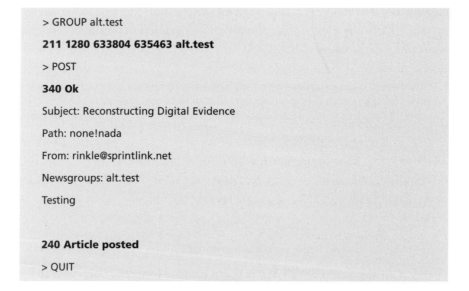

```
> GROUP alt.test

211 1280 633804 635463 alt.test

> POST

340 Ok

Subject: Reconstructing Digital Evidence

Path: none!nada

From: rinkle@sprintlink.net

Newsgroups: alt.test

Testing


240 Article posted

> QUIT
```

This sequence of commands would cause the following forged message to be posted to the Usenet group alt.test, complete with the fake e-mail address (rinkle@sprintlink.net) and fake news servers (none!nada) inserted during the forging process:

```
Path: news.nyu.edu!pln-e!extra.newsguy.com!lotsanews.com!
Howland.erols.net!newsfeed.concentric.net!
Masters0.news.internet.net!none!nada

From: rinkle@sprintlink.net
```

Newsgroups: alt.test

Subject: Reconstructing Digital Evidence

Date: 27 Sep 1998 17:37:13 GMT

Message-ID: <6ult49$fha@masters0.Internet.net>

NNTP-Posting-Host: possibly.Forged.com

Testing

In this instance, the header does not contain information about the original sender so it would be necessary to contact the system administrators of *masters0.news.internet.net* and ask them to check their log files for an entry corresponding to the forged message. If a log entry exists, it would only contain the name of the computer that the sender used but sometimes a little lead can make a big difference.

IRC TRACKING

IRC is made up of subnets such as Undernet, DALnet, Efnet, and IRCnet. Each subnet is simply a server, or combination of servers, run by a different group of people. Though they are all part of IRC, the subnets are physically separate. So, if you are on Undernet, you will not be able to access the chat rooms (a.k.a. channels) on DALnet. To connect to IRC you need to download an IRC client from the Internet. Two popular IRC clients are mIRC (http://www.irchelp.org) for IBM compatibles and IRCle for Macs (http://www.ircle.com). Anyone can create a channel on IRC and only allow certain people to participate. Some people make their channels publicly accessible while others set up private channels and only notify people that they trust.

IRC is different from the Web or Usenet in two fundamental ways. Firstly, activities on IRC are not archived so there is no reason to expect any record of a specific event. Secondly, IRC enables people to communicate with each other directly, bypassing the IRC network entirely. This concept can be difficult to grasp and requires some clarification. Suppose that two people are connected to the Internet through their ISPs. They open their IRC client (e.g. mIRC or Ircle) and connect to an IRC subnet (e.g. DALnet or Undernet). They meet each other in a channel and decide to set up a direct line of communication. Using either IRCs direct chat mode(DCC) or file server (fserve), they bypass the IRC network's computers and send directly to each other[8]. In more technical terms, the IRC client program sends information directly to the IP address of the other computer instead of

[8]Actually, the data passes through both of their ISPs before reaching them, but the point is that they bypass the IRC network.

sending it through the IRC network. Therefore, the IRC network has no opportunity to make a record of the transaction.

This direct communication is very much like making a telephone call. Fortunately, many people keep personal logs (knowingly and unknowingly) of the direct, private communications that they have on IRC. Therefore, there is a chance that you will find logs of private communications on a person's computer. This is not as likely as finding old e-mail messages but it is still a possibility, so always look for IRC logs.

There are two general reasons for wanting to track a person on IRC. Either you become aware of the person through IRC and you want to learn more about him/her, or you learn about the person somewhere other than IRC and you suspect that he/she uses IRC. Though few people use the latter approach because they are not very familiar with IRC and it is time consuming, in either situation you can find some information about an individual using tracking tools and techniques described here. However, keep in mind that the individual you want to track has to be using IRC at the time (and has to be on the same IRC subnet) for these tracking tools to work. All of the IRC commands mentioned here can be accessed by typing them in your IRC window (some commands are also accessible through menus in your IRC client program). When you type a command in any IRC window you must precede it with a "/" to indicate that you are typing a command as opposed to a communication. Also, the results of many commands only appear in your main (Console) IRC window. If this window is not visible you will not see the results of your commands.

One of the most useful commands for tracking on IRC is the *whois* command. The whois command on IRC is not the same as the Whois database mentioned earlier. The whois command uses a person's IRC nickname to get the person's e-mail address, the chat channels the person is in, and the IP address (explained in Chapter 7). An IP address can be used to determine where a person is located and is therefore very important from an investigative viewpoint. Figure 6.5 shows information obtained about a user with the nickname "eco" using whois (note that eco is "Not Telling" his real name).

As you can see from Figure 6.5, the whois command tells you which channels eco is in (#my_cats and #cp580) and which IRC server he is on (webbernet.mi.us.dal.net). More importantly, it shows the IP address that he is using to connect to the Internet (130.132.187.144). If people leave IRC or change their nicknames while you are tracking them you might still find information using the *whowas* command and their old nickname. This is because IRC servers keep a temporary cache of nicknames.

Another powerful IRC command called *who* enables you to search in a

Figure 6.5

Output from the whois command.

particular subnet (e.g. DALnet or Undernet). Though you have to know which subnet the person is on, this command can be useful if you do not know the nickname an individual is using but you know his/her ISP or some other identifying information that you can search for. For example, if you give the who command a domain name preceded by an asterisk (*netcom.com) it will tell you all of the people on IRC who are coming from that domain[9]. Also, the who command can search for any word that might occur in a person's hostname or personal information. So, in the above example, the who command would have found eco using "/who *eoghan*" or "/who *telling*" as Figure 6.6 on page 114 demonstrates.

Sometimes it is not necessary to use any of these IRC search commands. For instance, when you use DCC or fserve to connect directly to another person's computer, that person's IP address is immediately visible. The following log shows "snoop" (an investigator) connecting directly to "DeGeNeRaTiOn-KiD_'s" computer (fserve turns a personal computer into a file server on IRC).

[9]*The asterisk is known as a wildcard because it can represent anything.*

Session Start: Mon Jan 19 17:23:50 1998

DCC Chat session

Client: DeGeNeRaTiOn-KiD_ (207.67.107.76)

Acknowledging chat request...

DCC Chat connection established

<DeGeNeRaTiOn-KiD_> mIRC32 v5.02 File Server K.Mardam-Bey

<DeGeNeRaTiOn-KiD_> Use: cd dir ls get read help quit

<DeGeNeRaTiOn-KiD_> [\]

<snoop> Rules

<DeGeNeRaTiOn-KiD_>

<DeGeNeRaTiOn-KiD_> Welcome to my FSERVE!!

<DeGeNeRaTiOn-KiD_> 1. ONLY upload jpg's gif's and mpg, or avi movies.

<DeGeNeRaTiOn-KiD_> 2. ONLY upload preteen & teen pics, and movies ages 2-19.

<DeGeNeRaTiOn-KiD_> 3. I will also except preteen stories or xxx passwords.

Session Start: Mon Jan 19 17:24:39 1998

<DeGeNeRaTiOn-KiD_> UPLOAD of file 12,0 SUCK16.JPG completed. New Credit: 4,0 76939

<snoop> ls

<DeGeNeRaTiOn-KiD_> [*.*]

<DeGeNeRaTiOn-KiD_> 10yr3way.jpg   11-12&13.jpg   11bath.avi 11blonde.jpg

<DeGeNeRaTiOn-KiD_> 11fk10.jpg   11fk11.jpg   11hghscl.jpg   11oooh.jpg

<DeGeNeRaTiOn-KiD_> 11sister.jpg   11suck.jpg   124aastr.htm   12anal.jpg

<DeGeNeRaTiOn-KiD_> 12asia3.jpg   12bj.avi   12jenny.txt   12sprea5.jpg

<DeGeNeRaTiOn-KiD_> 12suckdick.jpg 12toilet.jpg   13cortn.jpg   13yosex!.mpg

<DeGeNeRaTiOn-KiD_> 14&17_yr.jpg   14&uncle.jpg   14.jpg   14cute2.jpg

<DeGeNeRaTiOn-KiD_> 14sue8.jpg   14yroldgoddess.jpg 15&15fck.jpg

<DeGeNeRaTiOn-KiD_> 9thgrad.jpg   PRETEEN   TEEN-A   TEEN-B

<DeGeNeRaTiOn-KiD_> End of list.

Session Close: Mon Jan 19 17:48:30 1998

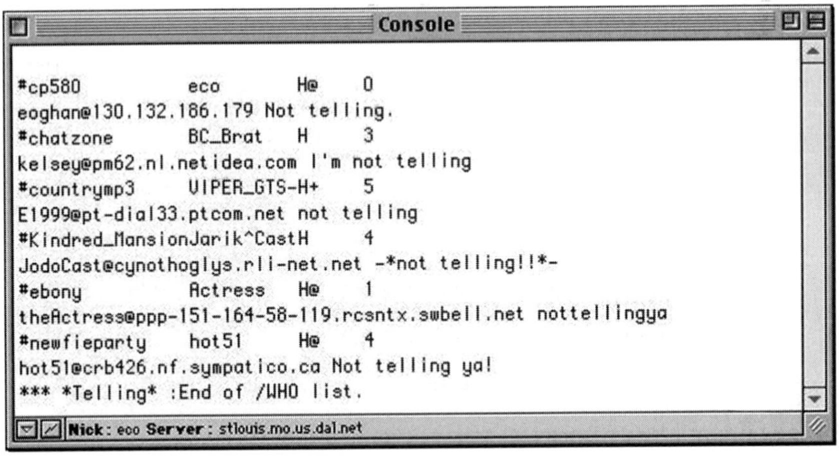

Figure 6.6

The results from typing /who
telling in IRC.

```
┌─────────────────────────────── Console ───────────────────────────────┐
│                                                                        │
│ #cp580            eco        H@     0                                   │
│ eoghan@130.132.186.179 Not telling.                                    │
│ #chatzone         BC_Brat    H      3                                   │
│ kelsey@pm62.nl.netidea.com I'm not telling                             │
│ #countrymp3       VIPER_GTS-H+     5                                    │
│ E1999@pt-dial33.ptcom.net not telling                                  │
│ #Kindred_MansionJarik^CastH     4                                      │
│ JodoCast@cynothoglys.rli-net.net -*not telling!!*-                     │
│ #ebony            Actress    H@     1                                   │
│ theActress@ppp-151-164-58-119.rcsntx.swbell.net nottellingya           │
│ #newfieparty      hot51      H@     4                                   │
│ hot51@crb426.nf.sympatico.ca Not telling ya!                           │
│ *** *Telling* :End of /WHO list.                                       │
│                                                                        │
│ Nick: eco Server: stlouis.mo.us.dal.net                                │
└────────────────────────────────────────────────────────────────────────┘
```

The beginning of this session is an automated introduction, telling you what fileserver is being used, what commands to use, and most importantly, the IP address (207.67.107.76) of the computer you are connecting to. Different fileservers work slightly differently but you can usually figure out what you need to know from the introductory messages. Using mIRC's "DDC Send" (not shown), specifying DeGeNeRaTiOn-KiD_ as the receiver, the investigator ("snoop") send an image called SUCK16.JPG to the file server. After sending this image, "snoop" gets a list of available files using the "ls" command, and can get any file from DeGeNeRaTiOn-KiD_ using the self-explanatory "get" command.

In some cases, the operators on IRC (IRCops) can be of assistance in learning more about an individual on IRC. Also, searching the Web and Usenet for the nickname and other individualizing information can lead to more information. The most direct way to uncover the identity of an individual on IRC is using the IP address that the individual is using to connect to the Internet. IP addressed are discussed in Chapter 7.

DIGITAL EVIDENCE GUIDELINES FOR THE APPLICATION LAYER

With some adaptation, the forensic science methods described in Chapter 4 can be applied to digital evidence on the Internet. Digital evidence on the Internet is slightly different from digital evidence stored on a single computer. Digital evidence on the Internet is often stored on remote computers (e.g. Web pages, Usenet messages) or is not stored anywhere unless an effort is made to capture it (e.g. live chat sessions). Therefore, investigators should make extra efforts to demonstrate that digital evidence on the Internet is authentic and has not been modified while it was being transmitted or collected. This section describes some approaches to collecting digital evidence on the Internet[10].

[10]These guidelines are not intended to be comprehensive procedures and cannot substitute for thorough training.

When a remote computer contains a large amount of important digital evidence, try to obtain direct access to the computer instead of collecting all of the evidence over the Internet. For instance, when a Web server has hundreds of files that are important to an investigation, do not risk collecting the digital evidence remotely – gain access to the computer and apply the methods described in Chapter 4.

RECOGNIZING DIGITAL EVIDENCE ON THE INTERNET

Recognition of digital evidence at the application layer usually involves active searching. Searching can be a time-consuming process when a network is involved because evidence can be stored in so many places. Become familiar with common search tools and be aware of their limitations. For example, each Web search engine contains different information and has slightly different search methods.

Keep in mind that computers that are used to access the Internet have quite a bit of digital evidence on them. Web browsers keep records of the pages that were viewed, e-mail clients contain copies of messages that have been sent and received, newsgroup activity leaves a variety of traces on a computer and live chats are sometimes logged to files on an individual's computer. Therefore, in some cases examining a personal computer can give investigators a clear picture of how a suspect or victim used the Internet.

- Use search engines, directories, utilities, and other methods for finding information on the Web. Use geographical and organizational searches when appropriate. When interested in an individual, search for real names, nicknames, e-mail addresses, and segments of e-mail addresses. Some people protect themselves by using computer-smart nicknames such as En0ch|an instead of Enochian. The zero instead of an "o" and the pipe (|) instead of an "i" confound search algorithms. In such cases, clever use of search engine syntax (e.g. AND, OR, NEAR) is required.

- Look in Usenet archives (http://www.dejanews.com) for messages about or from the subject by searching real names, nicknames, e-mail addresses, and segments of e-mail addresses. Search for computer-smart nicknames and simple variations of e-mail addresses and nicknames.

- Monitor areas that would attract the individual. For example, if the subject has a torture fantasy, look in newsgroups that play into torture fantasies. As another example, if the offender targets young victims, look in newsgroups that attract youth. While monitoring these areas, look for possible acquaintances of the individual, performing a search of the Internet using their name, e-mail address, etc.

- Larger synchronous chat networks have limited search utilities. Search for real names, nicknames, full e-mail addresses, and segments of e-mail addresses. Whenever possible search for unusual interests. Participate in discussions when necessary to gather information and learn more about possible suspects.

- Use what is known about MO (described in Chapter 3), victimology, etc. (described in Chapter 9) to focus searches of the application layer.

PRESERVATION, COLLECTION AND DOCUMENTATION

When information is stored on remote computers, it might not be possible to get the original files from the disk that they are stored on. Therefore, it is imperative to make every possible effort to document the fact that evidence was stored on a remote computer, detailing where the original evidence was, when, and how it was collected. It is also important not to modify evidence while collecting it. For instance, do not change files names and do not edit the contents of files to make them more readable unless you are working with a copy of a previously collected piece of evidence.

- Consider photographing, videotaping and capturing the evidence using screen captures or automatic logging utilities. Also consider printing evidence. Collecting and documenting the same evidence in multiple ways will enable cross comparison. To verify that one form of evidence has not been altered (a log file, for example) one can look at the other forms (like a video).

- Maintain a chronological list of dates, times, programs used, and actions taken during a search. Make a note of important information and possible leads. With large amounts of information it is sometimes difficult to remember when and where you noticed a lead.

- Calculate the message digests of files as soon as feasible for the purpose of demonstrating integrity. This can only be used to demonstrate that the file was not changed after it was collected and documented. What happened to the evidence as it was transferred over the Internet is open to question – photographs or screen captures can be used to show the state of the evidence before it was collected. Additionally, sign the evidence to indicate that it is authentic.

- Keep a list of possible aliases. Many people have (or have had) multiple Internet accounts and Internet aliases, especially individuals who want to protect their true identity.

- Keep a list of possible Internet acquaintances. If a search fails to turn up anything on one individual, following the activities of acquaintances can lead to relevant information.

CLASSIFICATION, COMPARISON AND INDIVIDUALIZATION

- Carefully examine digital evidence for characteristics that can be used to classify it – traits that differentiate it from other digital objects. Ask questions like: is it a Web page or and e-mail message? what program was used to create it? was it created on a machine running Windows, Mac OS, Unix?

- Look for individualizing characteristics. For example, attempt to identify the source of the e-mail message using the information in the header. If the header was modified, try to determine if the modification was just necessary to hide the sender's identity or was also satisfying a psychological need (e.g. a threatening nickname).

- When searching for information about an offender, note any indications of employment, skill level, education, hobbies, personal interests, relationship status, unusual or repeated verbal behaviors, level of planning and forethought, precautionary acts and any other potentially individuating information. Also, note potential MO behaviors (Chapter 3).

RECONSTRUCTION

A criminal can be several places on a network at any given time using several windows or application on computer or using several computers. This makes the reconstruction process more complicated and arduous but does not change the basic approach. As mentioned earlier, it is often easiest to reconstruct certain aspects of the crime separately before trying to combine them into complete reconstruction.

- Recover deleted or damaged digital evidence. For instance, Web pages might require reconstruction before images appear and interactive aspects of the page will work. Reconstructing Web pages requires knowledge of how they are constructed (HTML, Javascript, etc.). Consult an expert to assist in the reconstruction process when necessary.
- If possible, replicate the process that created the digital evidence. Trying to replicate the process can improve investigators' understanding of the evidence and the criminal.
- Reconstruct relational aspects of the crime. Determine where digital evidence was in relation to the other evidence or to the crime.
- Reconstruct functional aspects of the crime. Determine the purpose of each piece of digital evidence, how it works or how it was used.
- Reconstruct temporal aspects of the crime – when events occurred.

REFERENCES

Ferrell, K. (1997) "Net Crime, Don't be a Victim," CNET, 2 June [http://www.cnet.com/Content/Features/Dlife/Crime/index.html].

Lane, C. (1997) *Naked in Cyberspace: How to Find Personal Information Online*, Wilton, CT: Pemberton Press.

Mann, D.and Sutton, M. (1998) "Netcrime: More Change in the Organization of Thieving," *British Journal of Criminology*, 38 (2).

RESOURCES

WEB
Altavista: [http://www.altavista.com]
Hotbot: [http://www.hotbot.com]
Excite: [http://www.excite.com]
Infoseek: [http://www.infoseek.com]
Whowhere: [http://www.whowhere.com]
Whitepages: [http://www.whitepages.com]

E-MAIL TRACKING
Sam Spade, Spam Hunter [http://www.blighty.com/spam/spade.html]

Get that Spammer: [http://kryten.eng.monash.edu.au/gspamt.html]
Arin – [http://whois.arin.net/whois/arinwhois.html]

USENET

Dejanews [http://www.dejanews.com]

SYNCHRONOUS CHAT NETWORKS

ICQ [http://www.icq.com]
IRC [http://www.mirc.co.uk/], [http://www.irchelp.org/index.html],

- Efnet [http://www.efnet.net/]
- IRCnet [http://www.ircnet.org/]
- Dalnet [http://www.dalnet.com/]
- Undernet [http://www.undernet.org/]

## CHAPTER 7

DIGITAL EVIDENCE AT THE TRANSPORT AND NETWORK LAYERS

For a communication system to work it must have an addressing mechanism. Often, there is also a need for some form of verification that a message reached its destination. Take a postal service as an example. Addresses are used to direct letters and, when necessary, the postal service will inform the sender when a letter has been delivered. Similarly, computer networks require an addressing scheme and sometimes a method for confirming that information has been delivered. The transport and network layers are responsible for these important aspects of computer networks.

Activities on the transport and network layers generate information that can be very useful in an investigation. Log files contain information about activities on the network, when they occurred, and the addresses of the machines involved. These addresses can be used to determine the point of origin of a crime, thus leading investigators to likely suspects. Collecting and analyzing evidence on the transport and network layers is like digging into the glue that holds a network together. This digging can turn up a lot of information but you have to be willing to roll up your sleeves and get your hands dirty. In other words, you have to become familiar with the technical details of these layers to take advantage of them as a source of digital evidence.

To understand how the transport and networks layers work it is helpful to examine a specific example. TCP/IP is a good example because it is the most commonly used implementation of the transport and network layers – it is a fundamental part of the Internet. This chapter describes some of the ways that TCP/IP can be involved in crimes and explains the evidentiary value of information on the transport and network layers. Analogies are used to clarify technical concepts and many minute details are omitted for the sake of simplicity. References are provided at the end of the chapter for investigators wishing to learn more about TCP/IP.

In addition to describing TCP/IP in detail, this chapter provides a brief overview of wireless networks. Cellular phones and other hand-held devices depend on computer networks that are similar to the Internet in many respects. These similarities are emphasized to enable investigators to generalize their knowledge of the transport and network layers and use that knowledge to understand other internetworks. This chapter closes with detailed examples of log files and state tables that contain digital evidence on the transport and network layers.

TRANSPORT CONTROL PROTOCOL (TCP) AND USER DATAGRAM PROTOCOL (UDP)

Remember from Chapter 5 that TCP/IP is a combination of protocols that includes the User Datagram Protocol (UDP), Transport Control Protocol (TCP) and Internet Protocol (IP).

TCP operates on the transport layer – acknowledging receipt of information and resending information when necessary. UDP is a very simple protocol that some applications use instead of TCP when an acknowledgement of receipt is not desired. These transport layer protocols are designed to ameliorate the common problems that arise on a network, including hardware failure, network congestion and data delay, loss, corruption and sequencing errors (see Figure 7.1).

Figure 7.1

TCP/IP diagram with OSI layers superimposed.

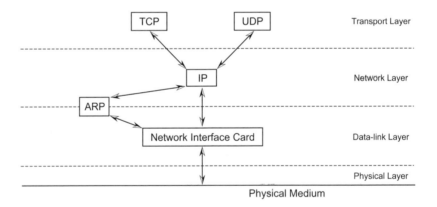

PACKETS

When a large number of computers are competing to use the same wires and hardware on a network, some fair method of sharing these resources is necessary. To enable equal sharing of the network, TCP and UDP break data into small packets before transmitting it.

Breaking data into packets prevents large messages from monopolizing the network and enables two computers to open multiple lines of communication on a single physical wire. For example, two computers can exchange e-mail, Web pages, and Usenet messages simultaneously by breaking the information into packets and putting the packets on the network, leaving it up to the other computers on the network to direct packets to their destination and reconstitute the information at the receiving end. This type of network is called a packet-switched network to differentiate it from the more expensive and reliable circuit-switched networks.

> Circuit-switched networks operate by forming a dedicated connection (circuit) between two points. The US telephone system uses circuit switching technology – a telephone call establishes a circuit from the originating phone through the local switching office, across trunk lines, to a remote switching office, and finally to the destination telephone … The advantage of circuit switching lies in its guaranteed capacity: once a circuit is established, no other network activity will decrease the capacity of the circuit. One disadvantage of circuit switching is cost: circuit costs are fixed, independent of traffic. For example, one pays a fixed rate for a phone call, even when the two parties do not talk.

> Packet-switched networks, the type used to connect computers, take an entirely different approach … The network hardware delivers the packets to the specified destination, where software reassembles them into a single file again. The chief advantage of packet-switching is that multiple communications among computers can proceed concurrently, with intermachine connections shared by all pairs of machines that are communicating. The disadvantage, of course, is that as activity increases, a given pair of communicating computers receives less of the network capacity. That is, whenever a packet-switched network becomes overloaded, computers using the network must wait before they can send additional packets. (Comer 1995)

PORTS

When a computer receives packets of an e-mail message, a Web page and a Usenet message at the same time, how does it distinguish between the different types of data? How does the computer know which packets contain pieces of the e-mail and which packets contain pieces of the Web page? Computers use numbers, called *ports*, to identify different types of data (see Figure 7.2).

The standard port numbers for Web pages, e-mail and newsgroups are 80, 25 and 119 respectively. Therefore, when a server receives a packet with the number 25 in the port field, the server assumes that the packet is e-mail

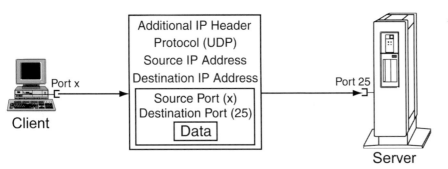

Figure 7.2

UDP packet with port number in the heading being transmitted to a server.

related. If the packet is not e-mail related, the e-mail server will not know what to do with the data and will return an error, crash, or do nothing at all. Similarly, when a server receives a packet with the number 119 in the port field, the server assumes that the packet is newsgroup (Usenet) related. This fact was alluded to in Chapter 6 when discussing e-mail and Usenet forgery, using Telnet to send packets directly to specific ports on a server.

SESSION MANAGEMENT

Remember that on a packet-switched network, computers are not connected using dedicated circuits. Instead, to make large-scale internetworking more reliable, TCP creates what are called *virtual circuit*s, establishing, maintaining and terminating connections between computers.

To establish a connection, TCP performs a three-way handshake. First, host A asks host B for a connection by sending what is commonly known as a SYN packet[1]. Second, host B acknowledges host A's request by returning a packet containing the special acknowledgement (ACK) bit (this acknowledgement packet also contains a SYN bit to enable the host to synchronize). Third, host A sends a packet containing data (with the ACK bit) to host B thus establishing a connection (see Figure 7.3).

A SYN packet contains the special SYN bit that indicates that host A wants to synchronize sequence numbers with host B. TCP uses sequence numbers to keep packets in order.

Once a connection is established, TCP has the very important responsibilities of verifying that a packet reaches its destination, reassembling packets into their original form, and controlling the rate at which data is transmitted – making sure that data is not sent faster than the receiver can process it.

The concept behind TCP's session management is simple – it keeps a record of everything that it sends until it receives an acknowledgement that the information reached its destination. If TCP does not receive an acknowledgement after a set amount of time, it assumes that the information was lost and resends it. So, if one packet is lost or damaged in transit, TCP will resend just that packet, not the entire message.

As simple as this may seem, it is actually quite ingenious. If a major portion of a network is destroyed, TCP assumes that the network will be repaired quickly and continues to retransmit data – patiently waiting for an

Figure 7.3

TCP establishing a connection using a three-way handshake.

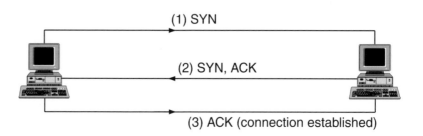

(1) SYN

(2) SYN, ACK

(3) ACK (connection established)

acknowledgement. If the network is not repaired quickly, TCP will eventually stop trying to resend information. However, if the network is repaired quickly, TCP will resume communication between two computers despite the interruption. This differs from a telephone call, which is terminated when the connection is broken.

When two hosts have finished communicating, TCP terminates the session by sending a packet containing the FIN bit. There are some nuances to the way that TCP uses sequence numbers and controls the rate that data is sent that are beyond the scope of this text. Additional information about TCP can be found in Comer's *Internetworking with TCP/IP Vol I* (Comer 1995) and Hunt's *TCP/IP Network Administration* (Hunt 1998).

Watching information move around the Internet is like watching ants work. Tiny entities move around quickly, bumping into each other and occasionally getting lost or damaged, but an overall order is maintained by TCP.

INTERNET PROTOCOL (IP)

On the network layer, the Internet Protocol (IP) is primarily responsible for addressing and routing information. After TCP breaks data into packets, IP addresses each packet and adds some other information.

| Additional IP Information |
| Source IP address | IP Header |
| Destination IP address |
| TCP Header |
| Data |

Table 7.1

TCP/IP packet.

IP ADDRESSES

Each computer attached to the Internet has a unique address, called an IP address. Each IP address comprises two parts, the network number and the host number. To accommodate networks of different sizes, three classes of addresses were agreed upon (Table 7.2).

Table 7.2

IP address classes. There are some special network numbers like 127.0.0.0 and 10.0.0.0 that have specific purposes and are not used in the same way as other IP addresses.

[2]Massachusetts Institute of Technology (MIT) has a Class A network. Such large networks are usually divided into subnets to make them more manageable.

	IP ADDRESS RANGE	EXAMPLE NETWORK # (n) AND HOST # (h)
Class A	1.0.0.0 – 126.0.0.0	124.11.12.13 is network 124, host 11.12.13
Class B	128.0.0.0 – 191.0.0.0	156.134.15.16 is network 156.134, host 15.16
Class C	192.0.0.0 – 223.0.0.0	192.132.12.13 is network 192.132.12, host 13

These classes of IP addresses are like real estate on the Internet. Class A is prime real estate because you can fit hundreds of thousands of computers on it, whereas if you have a Class C network you can only fit a couple of hundred computers on it[2].

Figure 7.4

IP addresses are conceptually the same as phone numbers.

UC Berkeley
area code = 510
network# = 128.32.0.0

Yale University
area code = 203
network# = 130.132.0.0

New York University
area code = 212
network# = 128.122.0.0

As you might expect from the terminology, the network number is a unique number that identifies a computer network attached to the Internet and the host number is a unique number that identifies a computer on that network. This is conceptually the same as a telephone number that has an area code and a local number[3] (see Figure 7.4).

[3]Extending this analogy, port numbers are like telephone extension numbers that large organizations assign to individuals or departments.

Although computers work well with numbers, people are more comfortable with names. For convenience, the Domain Name System (DNS) was created to assign names to IP addresses. For example, the canonical name for 128.122.253.152 is *acf2.nyu.edu* and the name for 130.132.143.37 is *mars.its.yale.edu*. Whenever you use a name to refer to a computer (e.g. when you type the name of a Web site into your browser), the Domain Name System works behind the scenes to determine the associated numerical IP address.

IP ROUTING

Once addressed, a packet is ready to venture out onto the Internet where it will be directed to the destination specified in the IP header. For example, when *acf2.nyu.edu* sends information to *mars.yale.edu,* the information must pass through several intermediate routers. The IP software on each router contains a routing table that it uses to determine where to send information.

An analogy might clarify how routing tables works. Imagine you are driving from New York City to New Haven and you reach a junction. You do not have a map and you are not familiar with the route so you depend on the signs to guide you. One sign indicates that Brooklyn is straight ahead, another sign indicates that Queens is to the left and a third sign indicates that all other locations are to the right. Therefore, you go right and drive until you reach another junction. You repeatedly follow the signs until you find one that says "New Haven" and you know you have reached your destination. All that you have to do then is find the specific building that you are looking for. Routing tables are the road signs on the information superhighway. When a packet is travelling from New York to New Haven, the routers that it passes through are like junctions and the routing tables are used to determine where the packet should go next to reach its destination.

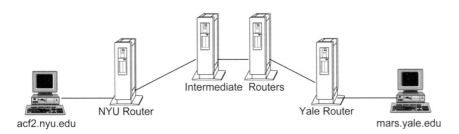

Figure 7.5
IP routing.

Intermediate Routers

NYU Router

Yale Router

acf2.nyu.edu

mars.yale.edu

When the packet finally reaches the network that it is destined for, all that remains is for a router to direct the packet to the correct host.

You might have expected routers to be a bit more intelligent, finding the "best" route between computers. However, this is not the case. Information traveling between any two computers will follow the same route unless a person physically changes a routing table (effectively creating a detour) for some reason.

A program called *traceroute* provides a list of routers that information passes through to reach a specific host. Many operating systems come with the traceroute program (in Microsoft Windows the program is called *tracert*). The route between *mars.its.yale.edu* and *acf2.nyu.edu* is shown in Figure 7.5 as an example. You will notice that routes between computers remain the same even though the Internet was designed to be flexible. Many people make the mistake of thinking that packets traveling between two specific computers on the Internet will take different routes. Although this it is technically possible it is rarely practiced at present. Therefore, it is safe to assume that all packets traveling between New York University and Yale University take the same route[4].

[4]*The route that a packet takes between two points will only change if a router is reconfigured to direct packets differently.*

```
acf2> traceroute mars.its.yale.edu

   route started from acf2.nyu.edu (128.122.253.152)
1 WWHGWA-FDDI-10-0.NYU.NET (128.122.253.129) 1 ms 0 ms 1 ms
2 NYUGWA-FDDI-2-0.NYU.NET (128.122.253.65) 1 ms 1 ms 1 ms
3 EXTGWA-FA1-0-0.NYU.NET (192.76.177.66) 1 ms 1 ms 1 ms
4 at-gw2-nyc-4-0-T3.appliedtheory.net (169.130.13.17) 3 ms 2 ms 3 ms
5 at-bb2-nyc-1-0.appliedtheory.net (169.130.10.8) 4 ms 4 ms 3 ms
6 sl-gw6-nyc-1-1-0-T3.appliedtheory.net (169.130.2.66) 9 ms 4 ms 3 ms
7 sl-bb10-nyc-3-2.sprintlink.net (144.232.7.69) 3 ms 4 ms 3 ms
8 sl-bb10-chi-3-0.sprintlink.net (144.232.8.202) 23 ms 23 ms 24 ms
9 sl-bb4-chi-4-0-0.sprintlink.net (144.232.0.166) 23 ms 27 ms 22 ms
10 h1-1-0.chi-bb1.cerf.net (134.24.32.37) 26 ms 25 ms 25 ms
11 atm9-0.phl-bb1.cerf.net (134.24.46.165) 40 ms 41 ms 42 ms
12 pos6-1-155M.phl-bb2.cerf.net (134.24.29.174) 25 ms 24 ms 24 ms
13 atm5-0-2.bdl-bb1.cerf.net (134.24.46.226) 38 ms 31 ms 34 ms
14 yale-gw.bdl-bb1.cerf.net (134.24.49.2) 33 ms 34 ms 34 ms
15 cerf-yale-dmz.bdl-bb1.cerf.net (134.24.49.6) 36 ms 36 ms 34 ms
```

16 sloth.net.yale.edu (130.132.1.17) 35 ms 44 ms 35 ms
17 mars.its.yale.edu (130.132.143.37) 37 ms * 34 ms

It can be seen from these traceroute results that NYU connects to the Internet through a company named Applied Theory[5], Yale connects through an organization called CERF, and Sprint owns the network in-between.

The traceroute program is very useful for determining which computers were involved in the transport of information on the Internet – and intermediate routers sometimes have relevant digital evidence in log files. All of the computers that the data passed through are potential sources of digital evidence. Also, the path that the data took can clarify which borders and boundaries were crossed during the perpetration of a crime. Recall that whois databases contain contact information for the people who are responsible for each router. For example, searching the US Whois database for *nyu.edu, appliedtheory.net, sprintlink.net, cerf.net,* and *yale.edu* will return the contact information for all of the routers involved in the above example.

SETTING UP A SMALL ISP

A scenario might help you tie all of this together. Imagine that you want to set up a small, "Mom and Pop" ISP to give your friends and neighbors access to the Internet. You purchase several computers and connect them together using some networking technology (e.g. Ethernet). You also buy some modems to enable your friends and neighbors to dial into your little network. However, you still have to connect the little network to the global Internet. The first step to getting on the map, as it were, is to get a network address on the Internet. So, you contact one of the organizations that assigns IP addresses (www.arin.net for U.S.; www.ripe.net for Europe; www.apnic.net for Asia). For a fee, the organizations will assign you a set of sequential IP addresses and will name your block of addresses "momandpop.com" so that everyone else on the Internet will know that they belong to you.

Once you have a block of IP addresses, you can keep a few for your own computers (let's call them moms.momandpop.com; pops.momandpop.com) and you start assigning the rest to family and friends. Since you are only providing for a small number of people you may decide to give them their own IP address – a static IP address (another option is considered later). Now, suppose that your neighbor John Doe dials into one of your modems and connects to the Internet through your little network. When John requests any information from the Internet (e.g. a Web page) this information will first pass through a router on your little momandpop.com network before going to John's computer (e.g. johndoe.momandpop.com).

[5]Traceroute only shows one IP address for each router but keep in mind that a router has an IP address for every network that it is connected to. For example, NYU's "external gateway" to the Internet (EXTGWA-FA1-0-0.NYU.NET) is connected to both NYU's network and Applied Theory's network so it has two IP addresses – one beginning with 192 and another beginning with 128.

Similarly, any information that John sends out (e.g. e-mail) will come from John's computer, pass through your router, and go out into the Internet. There are two obvious implications of this arrangement. Firstly, you could keep a log of all of John's activities. Secondly, most things that John sends through the Internet will indicate that they originated from *johndoe.momandpop.com* so someone could contact you, the owner of *momandpop.com,* in relation to John's activities on the Internet and, if you have kept logs, you could check them for "johndoe.momandpop.com."

STATIC VERSUS DYNAMIC IP ADDRESS ASSIGNMENT

Now suppose that this Mom and Pop operation becomes very popular and there are not enough IP addresses for every customer. Now, rather than giving each person a unique IP address, you decide to assign IP addresses temporarily when individuals need them to connect to the Internet. This type of dynamic IP assignment has become the norm for many ISPs that provide Internet dial-up access to a large number of people. This dynamic assignment can make it more difficult to determine who was using an IP address at a given time. Fortunately, a log is usually kept for a short time (a few days), listing who was assigned a particular IP address during a specific period.

- Static IP address: a unique IP address assigned to a specific computer for as long as the computer exists. Whenever that computer is connected to the Internet it has the same IP address. The IP address for *is4.nyu.edu* is static.

- Dynamic IP address: each time the computer is connected to the Internet it is assigned a new IP address. This is primarily used by larger service providers who do not want to dedicate an IP address to each of their customers. The names associated with the dynamic IP addresses often contain the words "dial," or "ppp," or have numbers in them (e.g. cz052.cyberia.com). These numbers are usually part of a sequence of dynamic IP addresses (e.g. cz051.cyberia.com, cz052.cyberia.com, cz053.cyberia.com). Some dynamic IP addresses have the abbreviations of cities and/or geographic regions that can be helpful in determining a rough location for an IP address.

PROTOCOLS FOR ASSIGNING IP ADDRESSES

Some networks use the Bootstrap Protocol (BOOTP) and others use Dynamic Host Configuration Protocol (DHCP) for assigning IP addresses to all hosts, even ones with static IP addresses. These protocols are used to prevent computers from being configured with incorrect IP addresses. Sometimes computers are misconfigured accidentally, causing two computers to interfere with each other. Also, sometimes individuals purposefully assign their computers with someone else's IP address to hide their identity. Using BOOTP or DHCP prevents these situations from occurring by centrally administering IP addresses.

BOOTP and DHCP are quite similar – both require hosts to identify themselves (using a MAC address) before obtaining IP addresses. When a computer is booting up, it sends its MAC address to the BOOTP or DHCP server. If the server recognizes the MAC address it sends back an IP address and makes a note of the transaction in its log file. The server can be configured to assign a specific IP address to a specific MAC address thus giving the effect of static IP addresses.

All of these acronyms can be confusing but the idea is simple. A central computer keeps track of which hosts are using which IP addresses. Under certain circumstances, the log files on these central BOOTP and DHCP servers will show the times a specific computer connected to and disconnected from the network. This could be used to determine when a computer dialed into a network or when a host that is usually part of the network was turned on and turned off.

ADDRESSING AND ROUTING ON WIRELESS NETWORKS

Wireless communication has existed for quite a while but has only recently become reliable and inexpensive enough to be useful on a large scale. Wireless networks can use radio frequency, infrared, lasers and microwaves to carry data. A powerful example of wireless networking involves cellular voice telephone systems that use radio frequencies to transmit information.

Cellular networks are made up of cell sites that enable individuals within a certain geographical area to place and receive calls. Cell sites are connected to central computers (switches) that process and route calls and keep logs that can be used for billing, maintenance, and investigations. Although cellular networks are primarily used as circuit-switched networks (making direct connections between telephones) they can also function as packet-switched networks (making virtual circuits between computers). To function as a packet-switched network, additional equipment is required that extracts packets of data from the wireless network and routes them to their destination.

It is with wireless packet-switched networks that the power of the OSI reference model becomes vividly apparent. Using a network technology called Cellular Digital Packet Data (CDPD) at the data-link layer and Connectionless Network Protocol (CLNP) at the network layer, a cellular network can quickly route data to a mobile individual who is using a wireless connection[6].

[6]The Connectionless Network Protocol (CLNP) was developed along with the OSI reference model as a standard for network layer protocols.

The following scenario describes the potential of wireless packet-switched networking if you were traveling between Los Angeles and Las Vegas:

> You boot up your notebook computer with its CDPD wireless modem enroute to your office in Los Angeles. The ride from Las Vegas to Los Angeles will take several hours, but you can't wait. You've got to check your e-mail for an important message regarding your biggest client. Let's look at the concepts that allow you to do this.
>
> When your wireless modem initiates a connection, a registration process is started that provides your remote device with access to your home carrier's wireless network. Your wireless modem is homed to a specific router that will keep track of your location and all messages intended for you will be forwarded to that router.
>
> When you move out of your home [region], this home router will forward your packets to another router, which in turn directs traffic within the group of [neighboring regions] you are in at that particular time. This method keeps routing updates to a minimum and allows you to roam freely, from [region] to [region] or city to city. (Henry and DeLibero 1996)

This technology is becoming widely available and increasingly popular. Organizations that depend on mobility (e.g. airlines, package delivery companies) have equipped their employees with hand-held devices that communicate over CDPD wireless networks. Also, organizations that want to avoid the expense of installing cables in their offices are adopting wireless networks. It is generally agreed that wireless networking will be much more popular and will develop far more rapidly than the Internet as we know it.

TCP/IP AS EVIDENCE

There are several challenges that investigators will encounter when dealing with TCP/IP as evidence. For instance, IP headers only contain information about computers, not people, so it is difficult to prove that a specific individual created a given packet. However, an investigator can use the source IP address to get closer to the point of origin of the crime. Knowing the point of origin of TCP/IP traffic can also help identify suspects. For example, only a small group of individuals might have access to a given computer or the ability to use a specific IP address.

Another challenge arises when criminals change their IP address frequently (using dynamic IP addresses). Individuals who exchange illegal information and materials by turning their personal computers into file servers (as described in Chapter 6) can avoid detection by regularly changing the IP address of the server. For instance, by dialing into a large ISP, such a criminal will be assigned an IP address that others then use to connect to the computer being used as a file server. After a few hours, the criminal might decide that it is time to move. Disconnecting and redialing will often result in the criminal being assigned a different IP address. The only difficulty on the criminal's end is notifying a select group of people using the criminal's computer as a file server about the new IP address. Investigators find it difficult to find and monitor these roaming servers. However, once found, the IP address of a server can lead investigators to the culprit.

Another significant challenge arises when information in the IP header is falsified. It is possible to create a packet with a false source IP address making it appear that data is coming from one computer when it is actually coming from another. For example, a malicious program will purposefully insert a false source IP address into packets, before interrupting service on a network (e.g. by flooding a network with data or crashing a central machine on the network). When the administrators of the flooded network try to track down the culprit, they find that the information in the packets is false – making it difficult to trace information back to the sender. When a source IP address has been falsified, tracking becomes a lengthy and tedious process of examining log files on all of the routers that the information passed through. When multiple ISPs are involved, the time and effort that it takes to get everyone's cooperation is rarely justified and there is a high probability that the trail will be too cold to follow.

Being able to falsify the source IP address is a well-known vulnerability that has led to many security problems.

> In 1985, R. T. Morris described a vulnerability in the TCP/IP protocol that would let a hostile system appear to have another host's address (Morris 1985). If the targeted system is using a protocol that relies on address-based authentication, a hostile host has the ability to subvert that authentication and access the target system as a trusted host. In 1989, Steve Bellovin published a paper that generalized this type of attack and reported other new security-related problems with TCP/IP protocol (Bellovin 1989). These vulnerabilities include session hijacking and IP spoofing … (Boulanger 1998)

IP spoofing is a technically complicated process of gaining access to a computer system by pretending to be a computer that the target system trusts. One of the most highly publicized IP spoofing attacks occurred in December 1994 when someone broke into a well-known security expert's computers. This attack and the subsequent investigation is well described in Tsutomu Shimomura's book, *Shakedown*, and his description of the digital evidence he found hints at how challenging such investigations can be[7]:

> One of [the pieces of evidence] was a mysterious program, Tap, that I had seen when I peered into Osiris's memory the day before. It was a transient program that someone had created and placed in my computer's memory for a specific task. When the computer was turned off or rebooted it would vanish forever. And what about the ghost of the file oki.tar.Z, whose creation suggested that someone was after cellular telephone

[7] Shimomura's computers were named Osiris and Ariel. After gaining access to the computers, the intruder bundled the cellular telephone software that he wanted a compressed file called oki.tar.Z. The intruder deleted the compressed file after transferring a copy to another machine that he had broken into.

software ... There was another crucial discovery from looking at Ariel's data; the intruder had tried to overwrite our packet logs, the detailed records we keep of various packets of data that had been sent to or from our machines over the Internet. The erased log files revealed that in trying to overwrite them the intruder hadn't completely covered over the original file. It was as if he had tried to hide his footprints in the sand by throwing buckets of more sand on top of them. But here and there, heels and toes and even a whole foot were still visible. (Shimomura 1996)

Fortunately, most criminals do not know how to fake IP addresses and so an IP address can usually be used to determine which computer was used to commit a crime.

RECOGNITION

Digital evidence on the transport and network layers can be found in log files that show past connections and in state tables that show recent and current connections between computers (see Figure 7.6).

LOG FILES

Log files can contain a large amount of information about an individual's use of a computer and can be an excellent source of digital evidence. Log files contain IP addresses – enabling investigators to determine which computer was used to perform a specific action at a given time. For example, a log file can be used to determine what time someone logged into a computer and from where.

Server logs often record which IP addresses used a specific service at a specific time. For instance, when an individual sends an e-mail message, this action is recorded in the e-mail server log file. Also, when individuals view Web pages, the IP addresses of their computer are noted in the Web server access log. Dial-up modem banks and BOOTP/DHCP servers create log files of IP address assignments. Additionally, firewalls and routers are sometimes configured to keep a log of the TCP/IP traffic that passes through them.

It is worth noting that most log files contain information about incoming traffic, but not outgoing traffic. This makes it relatively easy to determine what an individual was doing to a computer but makes it difficult to determine what an individual was doing from a specific computer. However, there are a few exceptions to this and some system administrators install IP

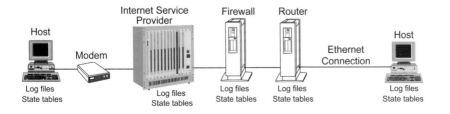

Figure 7.6

A single line of communication can contain many sources of digital evidence.

auditing software on their computers that creates detailed logs of all TCP/IP traffic incoming and outgoing.

LOG FILES ON UNIX

Most computers only log a selection of events so some of these log files might not be present on certain machines.

FILE	DESCRIPTION
acct or pacct	These accounting logs contain every command typed by every user on the computer. This can be very useful for determining what a specific user was doing at any given time.
Aculog	If modems are attached to the computer, this log contains a record of when the modems were used to dial out.
lastlog	This log file contains a record of each user's most recent login (or failed login).
loginlog	Records failed logins.
messages or syslog	The messages or syslog file (depending on the type of Unix) is the main system log file that contains a wide range of messages from many applications. These main log files often contain information that is also found in other log files, e.g. failed logins. Additionally, routers and firewalls can be configured to add their messages to a computer's message or syslog file.
sulog	This file records every attempt to log in as the administrator of the computer (root). This is a very important log because only a few authorized individuals should be able to become administrator of any system because this account gives a person full access to the computer.
utmp and utmpx	These files contain a record of all users currently logged into a computer. The "who" command accesses this file.
wtmp and wtmpx	These files contain a record of all of the past and current logins and records system startups and shutdowns. The "last" command accesses this file.
vold.log	This file contains a record of errors that are encountered when accessing external media (e.g. CD-ROMs and floppy disks).
xferlog	This file contains a record of all files that were transferred from a computer using the file transfer protocol (FTP).

Newer versions of Unix store their log files in /var/adm or /var/log whereas older versions store them in /usr/adm. The only exception are the two log files *utmp* and *wtmp*, which are sometimes stored in /etc. Two commands make it easier to view the *wtmp* and *utmp* files. The "who" command displays the contents of the *utmp* log and the "last" command displays the contents of the *wtmp* log. Other log files must be viewed directly using a text viewer (e.g. more) or editor (e.g. vi). For instance, to view the *syslog* file an investigator might type "more /var/log/syslog."

In the following segment taken from the Unix *syslog* file, someone tried to break into "mycomputer" through the e-mail server (called Sendmail) using vulnerabilities that are/have been fixed in newer versions of Sendmail. Then another individual tried to send two pieces of junk mail through "mycomputer" but was denied.

```
Oct 5 17:14:24 mycomputer sendmail[11668]: "debug" command from
hacker.dhp.com (199.245.105.25)
Oct 5 17:14:24 mycomputer sendmail[11668]: "wiz" command from
hacker.dhp.com (199.245.105.25)
Oct 5 22:42:25 mycomputer sendmail[17936]: TAA17936: ruleset=check_rcpt,
arg1=<someone@hotmail.com>, relay=08-162.015.popsite.net [207.240.169.162],
reject=550
<21freeto@flashmail.com>... Relaying denied
Oct 5 22:44:26 mycomputer sendmail[17936]: TAA17936:
from=<smoke@www.lg.co.kr>,
size=0, class=0, pri=0, nrcpts=0, proto=SMTP, relay=08-162.015.popsite.net
[207.240.169.162] , reject=550 < someone@hotmail.com >... Relaying denied
```

The IP addresses and names of the hosts that were used to attack
"mycomputer" can be seen in this log segment. The individual trying to
break into "mycomputer" was using 199.245.105.25 (hacker.dhp.com) and
the individual trying to relay junk mail was using 207.240.169.162 (the
numbers in the host name 08-162.015.popsite.com suggest a dial-up
connection). Without these IP addresses, it would not be possible to
determine who attacked "mycomputer."

Similarly, IP addresses are logged in the *syslog* file when a computer tries
to log in remotely. For example, in the following log excerpt, a cracker tried
to gain unauthorized access to "mycomputer" using several methods
including some account names that come with certain operating systems
(e.g. bin, lp, root, uucp).

```
May 11 15:12:14 mycomputer rshd[7373]: Connection from 199.245.105.25 on
illegal port 2066
May 11 15:12:15 mycomputer ftpd[7375]: connection from hacker.dhp.com
May 11 17:11:27 mycomputer login[7593]: failed: ?@ hacker.dhp.com as +
May 11 17:11:29 mycomputer login[7595]: failed: ?@ hacker.dhp.com as bin
May 11 17:11:30 mycomputer login[7596]: failed: ?@ hacker.dhp.com as daemon
May 11 17:11:31 mycomputer login[7597]: failed: ?@ hacker.dhp.com as lp
May 11 17:11:33 mycomputer login[7599]: failed: ?@ hacker.dhp.com as nuucp
May 11 17:11:34 mycomputer login[7600]: failed: ?@ hacker.dhp.com as root
May 11 17:11:42 mycomputer login[7604]: failed: ?@ hacker.dhp.com as user
May 11 17:11:43 mycomputer login[7605]: failed: ?@ hacker.dhp.com as uucp
May 11 17:14:02 mycomputer ftpd[7654]: connection from hacker.dhp.com
May 11 17:14:02 mycomputer telnetd[7653]: ttloop: peer died
May 11 17:14:02 mycomputer rshd[7652]: Connection from 199.245.105.25 on
illegal port 4128
```

The log file shows that the cracker was using the IP address
199.245.105.25, which refers to hacker.dhp.com. Because the IP address is
the same in both attacks, there is a distinct possibility that the same
individual is responsible for both.

LOG FILES ON WINDOWS NT

Windows NT stores its log files in the %systemroot%\system32\config\ directory (most commonly c:\winnt\system32\config\). The easiest way to access these log files is using the Event Viewer (see Figure 7.7).

Also, by default, Microsoft's Web and FTP servers keep logs in C:\WINNT\SYSTEM32\Log Files in the W3SVC and MSFTPSVC directories, respectively.

Table 7.4

Log files on Windows NT.

FILE	DESCRIPTION
appevent.evt	Contains a log of application usage
secevent.evt	Records activities that have security implications such as logins
sysevent.evt	Notes system events such as shutdowns

STATE TABLES

State tables are like log files except that they are transient. State tables contain information about current or very recent connections between computers – and entries in these tables are usually cleared in less than an

Figure 7.7

Windows NT Event Log.

Event Viewer - Security Log on \\ORGO

Log View Options Help

Date	Time	Source	Category	Event	User	Computer
4/20/99	10:50:03 AM	Security	System Event	515	SYSTEM	ORGO
4/20/99	10:50:03 AM	Security	Privilege Use	577	SYSTEM	ORGO
4/20/99	10:49:58 AM	Security	Privilege Use	576	ANONYMOUS	ORGO
4/20/99	10:49:58 AM	Security	Logon/Logoff	528	ANONYMOUS	ORGO
4/20/99	10:49:55 AM	Security	Privilege Use	576	Eoghan	ORGO
4/20/99	10:49:55 AM	Security	Logon/Logoff	528	Eoghan	ORGO
4/20/99	10:49:43 AM	Security	Logon/Logoff	529	SYSTEM	ORGO
4/20/99	10:49:39 AM	Security	Privilege Use	577	SYSTEM	ORGO
4/20/99	10:49:39 AM	Security	System Event	515	SYSTEM	ORGO
4/20/99	10:49:38 AM	Security	Privilege Use	577	SYSTEM	ORGO
4/20/99	10:49:38 AM	Security	System Event	515	SYSTEM	ORGO
4/20/99	10:49:38 AM	Security	Privilege Use	577	SYSTEM	ORGO
4/20/99	10:49:38 AM	Security	System Event	515	SYSTEM	ORGO
4/20/99	10:49:38 AM	Security	System Event	515	SYSTEM	ORGO
4/20/99	10:49:38 AM	Security	Privilege Use	577	SYSTEM	ORGO
4/20/99	10:49:37 AM	Security	System Event	514	SYSTEM	ORGO
4/20/99	10:49:37 AM	Security	System Event	512	SYSTEM	ORGO
4/20/99	10:27:23 AM	Security	Privilege Use	578	eoc3	ORGO
4/20/99	10:26:46 AM	Security	Logon/Logoff	538	eoc3	ORGO
4/20/99	10:26:46 AM	Security	Privilege Use	576	eoc3	ORGO
4/20/99	10:26:46 AM	Security	Logon/Logoff	528	eoc3	ORGO
4/20/99	10:26:37 AM	Security	Logon/Logoff	529	SYSTEM	ORGO

Event Viewer - System Log on \\ORGO

Log View Options Help

Date	Time	Source	Category	Event	User	Computer
4/20/99	10:50:09 AM	NETLOGON	None	5719	N/A	ORGO
4/20/99	10:50:06 AM	Service Control Mar	None	7026	N/A	ORGO
4/20/99	10:49:37 AM	Serial	None	8	N/A	ORGO
4/20/99	10:49:37 AM	Serial	None	3	N/A	ORGO
4/20/99	10:49:37 AM	Serial	None	29	N/A	ORGO
4/20/99	10:49:15 AM	EventLog	None	6005	N/A	ORGO
4/20/99	10:49:15 AM	EventLog	None	6009	N/A	ORGO
4/20/99	10:49:33 AM	Dhcp	None	1005	N/A	ORGO
4/20/99	10:27:52 AM	EventLog	None	6006	N/A	ORGO

hour. For instance, typing "netstat" on a computer running Unix or Windows will list the current and recently terminated TCP/IP connections. Table 7.5 shows open and recently closed connections to www.forensic-science.com.

% netstat -f inet		
TCP		
Local Address	**Remote Address**	**State**
www.forensic-science.com.telnet	23.oakland-01.ca.world.net.2048	ESTABLISHED
www.forensic-science.com.telnet	sdn-ar-004njnbruP047.dial.net.1754	ESTABLISHED
www.forensic-science.com.80	dial55175.mru.ru.1084	ESTABLISHED
www.forensic-science.com.80	proxy-354.public.net.43883	TIME_WAIT
www.forensic-science.com.80	line1.old.net.4667	FIN_WAIT_2

Table 7.5

State table for www.forensic-science.com using netstat. The netstat command has many options to control the information that it displays. On some types of Unix, the -f inet option restricts the output to IP connections.

The first two lines show telnet sessions initiated from dial-up accounts on world.net and dial.net. The last three lines show Web connections; the first is fully established and the last two are in different stages of terminating. Firewalls, routers and many other pieces of network equipment also maintain state tables (e.g. FastPath, Gatorbox).

CASE EXAMPLE
A man who was using ICQ to harass a woman believed that he could not be caught because he had configured his ICQ client to hide his IP address. However, the woman consulted with a computer expert and learned that if she could initiate a TCP/IP connection with the man's computer, she could view his IP address using the "netstat" command. So, the next time the woman was harassed by this man, she sent an ICQ instant message to him, and used netstat to obtain his IP address. The woman contacted his Internet Service Provider and the harassment stopped. This method of finding an individual's IP address is not limited to ICQ. If the harasser had used IRC, AOL Instant Messenger or any other application that uses TCP/IP to transfer data the same method could have been used to track him down.

COLLECTION, DOCUMENTATION AND PRESERVATION

Collecting digital evidence at the transport and network layers can be quite challenging from a forensic science standpoint. Although log files are similar to regular files and can be collected like any other digital file, they contain a large amount of information, some of which investigators might not be authorized to seize. For example, one log file can contain information about the activities of many people who use the computer. To protect the privacy of their users, many organizations only divulge the portions of a log file that relates specifically to an investigation. Also, state tables are not neatly prepackaged in files and are only available for a short time. In addition, collecting the hardware for future examination is not an option because a state table will be lost when the hardware is turned off. Therefore, it is often necessary to cut and paste information from a state table into a file.

Cutting and pasting and collecting segments of log files is not entirely satisfactory from an evidentiary standpoint because it makes it more difficult to prove authenticity and integrity of the digital evidence. Therefore, it is advisable to take extra precautions to document digital evidence at the transport and network layers. For example, investigators should consider taking print screens and/or photographs of a state table *in situ* before collecting it. When investigators are only permitted to collect a portion of a log file, they should obtain the message digest of the log file and arrange for a copy to be preserved by a trusted party in the event that it is required later in court. Once the file is properly documented and preserved, investigators can collect the portion that relates to their investigation.

Although it takes time and experience to become familiar with the log files, programs and techniques related to the network and transport layers, it is not as difficult as it first seems. The main challenge is to obtain access to a computer on which you can try out the tools and techniques at your leisure. However, even expensive simulations cannot cover all possible scenarios since every network is different and there are new ways to commit cybercrimes and to hide/destroy digital evidence are constantly emerging. The bottom line is that if you want to become adept at collecting digital evidence related to the transport and network layers, you have to seek out opportunities to investigate cybercrimes.

CLASSIFICATION, COMPARISON AND INDIVIDUALIZATION

Log files and state tables can contain information about the source and nature of the crime being investigated. Log files on a computer contain the IP addresses of hosts that connect to it and information about what the remote host was doing or trying to do. State tables – for a short time – contain IP addresses of remote hosts that connected to the local computer recently and some information about what type of connection was established. All of this information can be used to classify and individualize digital evidence.

Remember that classifying evidence involves finding common characteristics. A log file or state table can be classified as a whole (e.g. a Linux 5.2 *wtmp log*, a Solaris *syslog*, a state table from a Windows NT Primary Domain Controller) and can then be compared with similar samples to determine what makes a specific piece of evidence unique. For instance, the time a log file was created or last modified is an individualizing characteristic that can be very telling. Many criminals purposefully change the times of files to hide their activities.

In addition to classification and comparison of logs as a whole, the contents of log files and state tables are a rich source of evidence that can be identified, compared and individualized. There are many types of TCP connections (e.g. telnet, e-mail, Web) that can be classified. After classifying the type of connection or transmission, investigators can compare it with similar samples of the same class to find individualizing characteristics. Alternately, if a particular log entry or IP packet does not fit into a familiar class, investigators can compare it with known types of log entries or packets to pinpoint the differences. The individualizing characteristics of digital evidence at the transport and network layers can be very useful when reconstructing the crime, linking it with other crimes and determining the criminal's motivations.

For example, investigators can determine quite a bit by examining a single packet of data. Unusual packets are sometimes created to cause computers to crash. Determining how these packets differ from regular ones can help investigators to understand what is happening, and can be used to link similar occurrences. Once it is known that the packets are devised solely to crash a specific type of Web server, the motivation of the offender may become clearer. It may be that the offender is targeting the particular Web server in retaliation for some perceived wrong, or developing confidence and experience with this type of activity. More commonly, individualizing characteristics can be used to determine if the same computer cracker is responsible for multiple intrusions. If the same uniquely fabricated packet is used to crash several Web servers in an organization, the likelihood is that the same individual is responsible for all of the incidents.

RECONSTRUCTION

Recall from Chapter 4 that there are two sorts of reconstruction: (a) digital evidence that has been damaged can be reconstructed through various processes and (b) digital evidence can also be used to help reconstruct events surrounding a crime.

(a) As with any form of digital evidence, it might be necessary to reconstruct messages and packets that have been damaged or partially deleted. The process of recovering deleted evidence was described in Chapter 4 and can be applied to the transport and network layers. In his book *Takedown*, Shimomura describes how he and his assistant retrieved a partially deleted log file:

> We agreed that Andrew would write his conventional program for retrieving the packet information, while I would write one to look for patterns on the disk and then attempt to reassemble them into something that resembled the original file ... I wrote a program called Hunt to search the disk that I ran for the first time at about 2:45 in the morning, and a second program called Catch, which was designed to organize what Hunt found ... In the end, we both succeeded in retrieving the data. (Shimomura 1996)

(b) When dealing with digital evidence, especially large amounts that have been collected from the transport and network layers, it is often necessary to reconstruct small portions separately and then attempt to string them all together. When a criminal is doing several things simultaneously, either on a single computer or on different computers, it is easiest to process each thread of events individually and tie them together rather than try to reconstruct them all at the same time.

CASE EXAMPLE

Individuals break into Web sites and vandalize the pages to make, in retaliation for a perceived wrong and/or to assert their power over the owner(s) of the site. An obvious part of investigating this type of occurrence is to examine the log files of the Web server that was broken into for information about the intruders. Of course, this is obvious to intruders as well, so if they cannot delete the log files on the Web server they often break in from another computer that they have compromised. Typically, intruders will delete all of the digital evidence on the host that they use to break into the Web server, making it difficult for an investigator to track them down.

Fortunately, investigators can take advantage of a vandal's behavior and the Web server access log to narrow the pool of suspects. A vandal usually looks at the page after (and sometimes before) modifying it. The Web server access log contains IP addresses of computers that accessed the Web page. Therefore, by looking at entries in the log file around the time of the vandalism, investigators often find the IP address of the vandal. In many cases vandals use the browser on their personal computer to view the Web page so the IP address in the Web server access log is a direct link, bypassing any intermediate hosts that the vandal used to break into the Web server. Although it is not conclusive this IP address can help investigators reconstruct the crime and find suspects.

DIGITAL EVIDENCE GUIDELINES FOR THE TRANSPORT AND NETWORK LAYERS

The following guidelines provide suggestions for dealing with digital evidence at the transport and network layers. When collecting digital evidence on the transport and network layers, it is usually necessary to have direct access to the computer that contains the evidence. When accessing a computer directly, remember to consult the guidelines provided in Chapter 4. For the sake of brevity, the guidelines in Chapter 4 are not reproduced here. The following guidelines summarize the key points in this chapter, focusing primarily on TCP/IP log files and state tables.

RECOGNITION

- Search for log files on all hosts, including Web servers, file servers, routers, firewalls and DHCP servers. Consider the possibility that there are logs that are unique to the network (e.g. logs of who dialed into a system). Interview several individuals to determine what log files are kept (different people know about different logs).

■ Look for state tables on hosts, especially servers, routers and firewalls. Again, interview several individuals to determine which equipment keeps state tables.

COLLECTION, DOCUMENTATION AND PRESERVATION

■ Keep notes to help remember details and reconstruct events. Seemingly insignificant details can prove to be significant later.

■ Note the current date/time and the date/time on the computer (note any discrepancy).

■ Print out as much as possible, signing and dating each page immediately to preserve the chain of evidence.

■ Make two copies of all evidence to your own disks. Whenever possible, check each copy on another computer to ensure that the copy was successful.

■ Inventory contents of all disks, including file creation and modification dates. Calculate the message digest of all files and disks using message digest programs.

■ If investigators are not authorized to collect entire log files, calculate the message digest of the files, arrange for a copy of the files to be held by a trusted party in case they are needed later, and then collect the portion that is relevant to your investigation.

■ Take print screens and/or photographs of all state tables before saving them to a file. Once saved, process the file like any other – calculate the message digest, make two copies, print and sign.

■ Collect programs that might have been used to commit the crime, processing them like any other file that contains digital evidence.

IDENTIFICATION, COMPARISON AND INDIVIDUALIZATION

■ Find individualizing aspects of log files, state tables, log files and patterns. For example, note the timestamps and message digest of files.

■ Carefully examine all log files and state tables to determine what they contain. Identify important or unusual portions.

■ Compare the information in log files and state tables with other similar samples to find distinguishing characteristics.

■ Compare system programs and commands with originals. For example, compare the timestamps, message digests, and contents for discrepancies.

■ Classify any other programs that are related to the crime and find their individualizing characteristics by comparing them with other, similar programs. For example, if a file containing financial information is found during an investigation, compare it to similar financial files to determine if anything has been changed, added or removed.

RECONSTRUCTION

- Reconstruct packets to form entire messages.

- Recover deleted or damaged digital evidence. If log files are damaged or partially deleted, attempt to recover and reconstruct what remains using system utilities of data recovery programs that are specially designed for the task.

- Reconstruct relational aspects of the crime. Determine where digital evidence was in relation to the other evidence or to the crime.

- Reconstruct functional aspects of the crime. Determine the purpose of each piece of digital evidence, how it works, or how it was used.

- Reconstruct temporal aspects of the crime – when events occurred. For example, reconstruct events from log files.

- In cases where an IP address is being used to identify the point of origin of a crime, an effort should be made to verify that the computer was actually using the IP address. This step in the reconstruction process requires knowledge of the Physical Layer as described in the next chapter.

SUMMARY

Few networks are designed to make evidence collection simple. Evidence is scattered and there is rarely one person in an organization who has access to, or even knows about, all of the possible sources of digital evidence on their network. Also, every network is unique, comprising many different components that are sometimes held together by little more than the digital equivalent of duct tape. Therefore, it is impractical to create a general checklist of all potential sources of evidence with an associated method of collection. A set of rough guidelines is provided here but keep in mind that each network will require a unique approach. As was mentioned before, as digital evidence becomes utilized more, some organizations will develop digital evidence maps of their networks to save time and protect themselves against liability. However, without a map, looking for digital evidence on a network is a matter of exploration and interviewing knowledgeable people.

REFERENCES

Bellovin, S. (1989) "Security Problems in the TCP/IP Protocol Suite," *Computer Communications Review* 19 (2), April: 32–48.

Boulanger, A. (1998) "Catapults and Grappling Hooks: The Tools and Techniques of Information Warfare," *IBM Systems Journal*, 37 (1) [http://www.research.ibm.com/journals/sj/371/boulanger.html].

Comer, D. E. (1995) *Internetworking with TCP/IP. Volume I: Principles, Protocols, and Architecture*, 3rd edn, Upper Saddle River, NJ: Prentice Hall.

Henry, P. and De Libero, G. (1996) *Strategic Networking: From LAN and WAN to Information Superhighways*, Boston, MA: International Thomson Computer Press.

Hunt, C. (1998) *TCP/IP Network Administration*, 2nd edn, Sebastepol, CA: O'Reilly.

Morris, R. T. (1985) "A Weakness in the 4.2BSD UNIX TCP/IP Software," *Bell Labs Computer Science Technical Report 117*, 25 February [available at http://www.eecs.harvard.edu/~rtm/papers.html].

Sheldon, T. (1997) *Windows NT Security Handbook*, Berkeley, CA: Osborne McGraw Hill.

Shimomura, T. and Markoff, J. (1996) *Takedown: The Pursuit of Kevin Mitnick, America's Most Wanted Computer Outlaw – By the Man Who Did It*, New York, NY: Hyperion.

## CHAPTER 8

DIGITAL EVIDENCE ON THE DATA-LINK AND PHYSICAL LAYERS

The data-link and physical layers provide the foundation for everything else on a network. The physical layer is the medium that carries data – such as the cables, radio waves, microwaves, and lasers. The data-link layer joins a computer with the physical layer. For example, Network Interface Cards (NICs) are part of the data-link layer – connecting computers to the network cables. The data-link layer also includes the transmission method (e.g. CSMA/CD) as mentioned in Chapter 5.

To understand the data-link and physical layers as a source of digital evidence, it is necessary to understand how the data-link layer works. The most effective way to learn about the data-link layer is to examine a specific example in detail. This chapter describes Ethernet in detail to provide a sense of how a network technology functions. Ethernet is a good example because it is one of the most widely used network technologies. Also, a familiarity with Ethernet makes it easier to understand how other network technologies operate.

To highlight the similarities and differences between Ethernet and other network technologies, Ethernet is briefly compared to Asynchronous Transfer Mode (ATM). ATM is quickly becoming the standard for high-speed networking.

Once you are equipped with a general understanding of these technical details of network technologies, it will be easier to deal with evidence at the data-link and physical layers. Like IP addresses on the network layer, addresses at the data-link layer (MAC addresses) can be used to determine which computer was used to commit a crime. In fact, MAC addresses are more identifying than IP addresses because an IP address can be easily reassigned to different computers whereas a MAC address is usually directly associated with the NIC in a computer.

Eavesdropping on a network is another approach to gathering digital evidence on the data-link and physical layers. With the help of a network monitoring tool (a sniffer), investigators and criminals can capture large amounts of information as it travels through a network.

ETHERNET

As described in Chapter 5, specific combinations of NIC, cable, and transmission method are called *network technologies*. For instance, Ethernet cables, Ethernet cards, and the method that Ethernet cards use to transmit data (CSMA/CD) are jointly referred to as *Ethernet*. Ethernet is one of the most widely used network technologies and it has gone through several revisions. Some networks still use the original Ethernet technology that was created at Xerox PARC in the 1970s. However, most networks now use one of the newer versions of Ethernet (i.e. 10Base5, 10Base2, 10BaseT, 100BaseT, 1Base5 and 10Broad36)[1].

[1]*1Base5 and 10Broad36 are not widely used and will not be described here. For more information, see* Ethernet Networks *(Held 1994).*

10BASE5

The 10Base5 standard closely resembles original Ethernet, relying on a continuous piece of thick (½ inch) yellow coaxial cable – the ether. The technology is called 10Base5 because:

1 it can transmit data at 10 megabits per second;
2 only one computer can transmit while the other listens (this is known as baseband);
3 the maximum recommended cable length is 500 meters (thus the 5 in 10Base5).

To connect a computer to a 10Base5 cable, you look for a black mark on its yellow plastic sheath, stab a transceiver through the yellow sheath to "tap into the ether" and then connect the transceiver to the NIC inside the computer using a drop cable. The technical name for this drop cable is Attachment Unit Interface (AUI) (see Figure 8.1).

10BASE2

The 10Base2 standard (called thin Ethernet) is a cheaper, less cumbersome form of Ethernet. Thin Ethernet does not require a separate tap, transceiver

Figure 8.1

Old Ethernet configuration (modern configurations are conceptually the same).

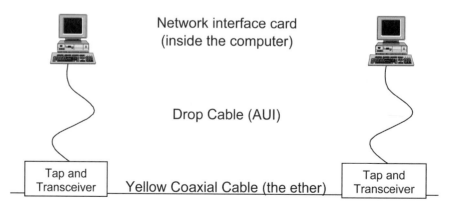

and drop cable, only a NIC and a thin, flexible coaxial cable joining adjacent computers. Although 10Base2 cable is cheaper and easier to bend around corners, it can only carry data about 200 meters whereas 10Base5 cable can carry data for up to 500 meters. Another disadvantage of thin Ethernet is that each host is an active part of the network and if one host breaks, the entire network is disabled.

10/100BASET

The most popular form of Ethernet, 10BaseT, uses unshielded twisted-pair (UTP) cables similar to regular telephone cords (two pairs of copper wires twisted together to reduce electrical interference). These cables are used to connect hosts to a central hub. A hub (also called a concentrator) is simply a box that tricks the computers into thinking that they are all attached to a single Ethernet cable (Figure 8.2).

The latest version of Ethernet is 100BaseT, basically the same as 10BaseT except faster. It is important to be able to recognize the different technologies. Table 8.1 summarizes the main distinguishing features of these standards. If possible, visit a local business, ISP or university that uses Ethernet and ask them to show you their network wiring and equipment.

IEEE 802.3 STANDARD	CABLE	MAX CABLE LENGTH	SPEED
10Base5 (thick Ethernet)	1/2" yellow coaxial	500 meters	10Mbps
10Base2 (thin Ethernet)	1/4" coaxial	185 meters	10Mbps
10BaseT (twisted-pair Ethernet)	Twisted pair	100 meters	10Mbps
100BaseT	Twisted pair	100 meters	100Mbps

Table 8.1

Different types of Ethernet.

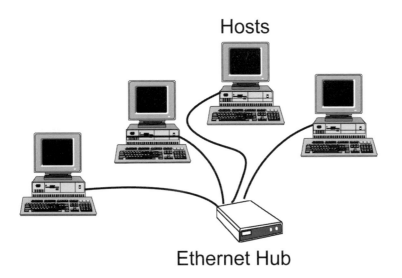

Hosts

Ethernet Hub

Figure 8.2

Computers on a 10BaseT network plugged into a hub.

CSMA/CD

Although Carrier Sense Multiple Access with Collision Detection (CSMA/CD) is a mouthful, the concept is straightforward: it is a "listen before acting" access method. Recall the analogy of polite dinner conversation described in Chapter 5. At a polite dinner party, an individual who has something to say waits for a break in the conversation before speaking. If two people start to speak at the same time, they both stop for a moment before starting to speak again. Similarly, when two computers using Ethernet start to transmit data at the same time, they both sense that the other computer is transmitting and they both stop for a random period of time before transmitting again. This method of communication works well as long as there are not too many computers connected to the same wire. Having too many computers on the network will result in many collisions and not enough successful communication.

LINKING THE DATA-LINK AND NETWORK LAYERS – ENCAPSULATION

In addition to connecting computers to the network, the data-link layer prepares data for its journey through the physical layer. For example, before sending an IP packet, Ethernet adds a header and checksum (a number used to verify the integrity of the data), encapsulating the packet in an *Ethernet frame*. Table 8.2 shows the segments of an IP packet encapsulated in an Ethernet frame.

Table 8.2

An Ethernet frame (IEEE 802.3 Standard) encapsulating an IP packet. Ethernet frames are actually composed of binary digits but are often examined in hexadecimal form as described later in this chapter.

Why are two types of addresses required – an IP address and a MAC address? Each address serves a different purpose. Put simply, Ethernet enables communication between computers on the same network using MAC addresses while TCP/IP enables communication between computers on different networks using IP addresses. Ethernet computer applications use TCP/IP to communicate, regardless of the network technology involved and computers themselves use the local network technology to exchange data. So, before an IP packet can be transmitted through the data-link and physical layers, it must be encapsulated in the local language (e.g. Ethernet, ATM, FDDI). For instance, at the data-link layer, Ethernet uses a particular

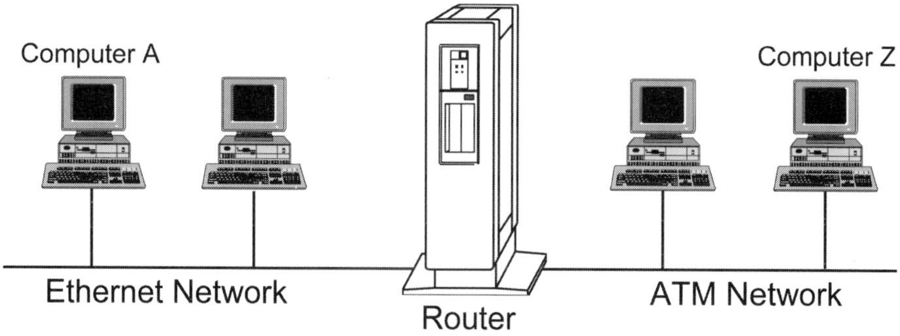

Figure 8.3

A router joining an Ethernet network and an ATM network.

kind of MAC addresses (e.g. 08-00-56-12-97-A8) to direct data, encapsulating IP packets into Ethernet frames as shown in Table 8.2.

Recall from Chapter 7, when a computer on one Ethernet network needs to send information to a computer on another network, it must send the information through a router (see Figure 8.3).

To deliver data to computer Z, computer A must first deliver it to the router. So, computer A puts the data in an IP packet addressed to computer Z and then encapsulates the IP packet in an Ethernet frame addressed to the router. When it receives the frame, the router peels off the Ethernet header and sees computer Z's IP address. Once it sees that the IP packet is addressed to computer Z on an ATM network, the router re-encapsulates the packet in an ATM cell (the ATM equivalent of an Ethernet frame) and sends it directly to computer Z.

When computer Z receives the ATM cell, it does the opposite of what computer A did to send the data. The data-link layer on computer Z peels off the ATM header and passes the IP packet to the TCP/IP software. Then, the TCP/IP software peels off the TCP and IP headers and passes the data to the appropriate application (e-mail, Web, Usenet, IRC, etc.) (see Figure 8.4 on page 150).

One key point about MAC addresses is that they do not go beyond the router. Unlike IP addresses, MAC addresses are only used for communication between computers on the same network. Therefore, when a packet is sent through the Internet, it does not contain the MAC address of the computer that created it, only the local router that delivered it. If the router keeps logs of the data that it received, investigators can track data back to its source using MAC addresses. This is only practical if a few routers are involved.

ADDRESS RESOLUTION PROTOCOL (ARP)

Computers on a network do not necessarily know each other's MAC addresses. For example, when a computer wants to send an IP packet, it only

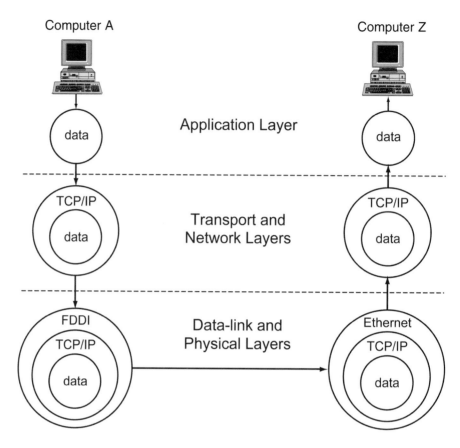

Figure 8.4

Computer A sending data to computer Z.

knows the IP address of the destination computer. To discover the MAC address of the destination computer, a host simply asks every other host on the network: is this your IP address? The host with that IP address responds with its MAC address. This simple exchange is called the Address Resolution Protocol (ARP).

ARP is part of TCP/IP but is usually considered a part of the data-link layer (see Figure 8.5). The easiest way to think about ARP is to imagine it straddling the network and data-link layers. This address discovery process might seem like a lot of effort that could be replaced by a list of IP → MAC address associations. However, every computer would have to have such a list and whenever a computer was added to the network, the list on each computer would have to be updated. As a compromise, computers keep a temporary list of IP → MAC address associations. So, two computers that communicate frequently will not have to constantly remind each other of their respective IP addresses. This temporary list is called an ARP cache and can be viewed on Unix and Windows NT machines using the "arp -a" command. If the record in the ARP cache is not used for a while (usually between 20 minutes and 2 hours), it is deleted.

```
        TCP              UDP            Transport Layer
---------------------------------------------------------
                    IP                  Network Layer
      ARP  ---------------------------------------------
          Network Interface Card       Data-link Layer
---------------------------------------------------------
                                        Physical Layer
            Physical Medium
```

Figure 8.5

Summary diagram of TCP/IP separated by OSI layer.

POINT TO POINT PROTOCOL (PPP) AND SERIAL LINE INTERNET PROTOCOL (SLIP)

The use of modems to connect computers to the Internet deserves a quick mention here. Many people dial into an ISP to connect to the Internet – transmitting data over a copper phone line instead of an Ethernet or fiber optic cable. This type of connection is much less sophisticated than network technologies like Ethernet, FDDI and ATM. An addressing scheme is not required since the modem in a person's home is connected directly to one of their ISP's modems through telephone wires. All that is required is a simple method of encapsulating IP packets and sending them over the telephone wires. Several protocols do just this, including Point to Point Protocol (PPP) and Serial Line Internet Protocol (SLIP). Although this is open to debate, think of PPP and SLIP as being on the data-link layer and the serial line that they use as being on the physical layer in a dial-up connection.

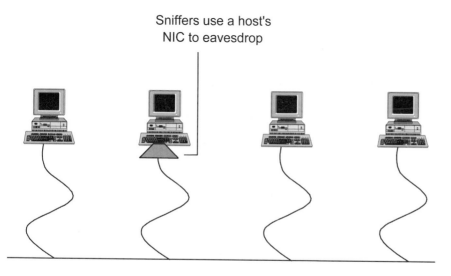

Sniffers use a host's
NIC to eavesdrop

Figure 8.6

Computers connected at the physical level are vulnerable to eavesdropping.

EAVESDROPPING

Any computer on the network can be configured to listen in on communications between other computers on the same network. Sniffers put Network Interface Cards (NIC) into "promiscuous mode," forcing them to listen in on all of the communications that are occurring on the network (see Figure 8.6 on page 151).

Many sniffers can be configured to collect only certain information, making it easier to filter out the vast amounts of irrelevant information on the network. Sniffers capture entire frames, so this form of eavesdropping also collects evidence from the transport and network layers. An actual Ethernet frame (encapsulating an IP packet) looks like this in hexadecimal[2]:

[2]Hexadecimal uses base 16 as opposed to base 10 used in decimal. Letters are used in hexadecimal – the decimal sequence 1, 2, 3, 4, 5, 6, 7, 8, 9, 10, 11, 12, 13, 14, 15, 16, 17, 18 is equivalent to the hexadecimal sequence 1, 2, 3, 4, 5, 6, 7, 8, 9, a, b, c, d, e, f, 10, 0b, 0c.

```
08 00 5a 47 43 58 08 00 20 21 fb 7d 08 00 45 00 00 1d c0 fa 00 00 3c 11 00 a2 0a
17 2d 43 0a 17 2d 4414 0e 0f d4 00 0d 3c bc 72 6f 6f 74 00 00 00 00 00 00 00 00
00 00 00 00 00 00
```

which breaks down as shown in Table 8.3.

Table 8.3

Breakdown of an Ethernet frame in hexadecimal.

08 00 5a 47 43 58	Source Ethernet address
08 00 20 21 fb 7d	Destination Ethernet address
08 00	denotes the fact that this frame contains an IP packet
45 00 00 1d c0 fa 00 00 3c	part of the IP header
11	indicates that the packet contains UDP data (11) as opposed to TCP data (06)
00 a2	checksum used to verify that the packet was not damaged in transit
0a 17 2d 43	source IP address (10.23.45.67)
0a 17 2d 44	destination IP address (10.23.45.68)
14 0e 0f d4 00 0d 3c bc	UDP source port, destination port , header length and checksum
72 6f 6f 74	The word "root" in hexadecimal
00 00 00 00 00 00 00 ...	The rest is padding

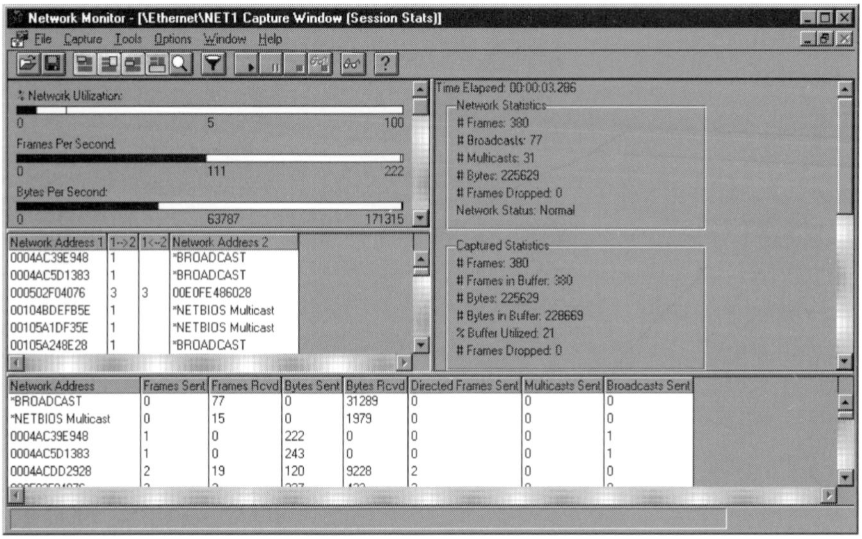

Figure 8.7

Network Monitor, a sniffer that comes with Microsoft Back Office, makes it easier to collect and examine a large number of captured Ethernet frames.

Investigators can use network-monitoring tools (sniffers) to collect data as it travels through the physical layer of a network, eavesdropping on communications between computers. A sniffer makes it much easier to collect and sort through thousands of such frames (see Figure 8.7).

Be aware that it is not possible to use a sniffer when connected via modem. For a sniffer to work, the computer must be on the same network as the computers being sniffed. Since there are only two modems connected to a dial-up connection (one at each end) there are no other computers to sniff.

In addition to sniffing, cables can be tapped physically, and wireless communication is particularly easy to listen in on. Although it is very difficult to tap a fiber optic cable, it can be done. Also, there are many sophisticated eavesdropping techniques that do not require direct access to the physical layer – emissions from the cables and other physical components of the network can be picked up using specialized equipment. However, in an investigation, eavesdropping should be used as a last resort because the process is time-consuming and invasive, very much like wire-tapping.

Clever criminals take steps to protect themselves against eavesdropping. There are many ways to prevent physical eavesdropping, like encasing cable in thick metal tubes or using triple layered coaxial cable (to prevent radiation) with pressured gas inside so that any tampering will result in a discernable drop in pressure. However, the best way to protect data against eavesdropping is by using encryption. It is virtually impossible to break strong encryption. Computer crackers who are aware that investigators might try to monitor sessions will encrypt them using software like Secure Shell (SSH).

Even if data is encrypted, sniffing a network and analyzing traffic can be informative. For instance, if hundreds of packets containing encrypted data were traveling between two individuals while one of them committed a crime, the second person may well be an accomplice and there may be probable cause to search the second person's computer or property.

Not so clever criminals have been known to record themselves unwittingly with their own sniffers when they return to examine the sniffers' log files. This is analogous to someone setting up a video camera to tape an area, returning to check that the camera is working (recording themselves in the process) and leaving the camera to tape more activities. Obtaining such a recording makes it easier to track a criminal. Therefore, when investigating a cybercrime, look for sniffers.

ETHERNET VERSUS ATM NETWORKS

As mentioned in Chapter 5, ATM uses fiber optic cables and specialized equipment (ATM switches) to enable computers to communicate at very high rates (gigabits per second). ATM networks were originally developed by the telecommunications industry to handle multimedia communications (combined video, voice and data). Therefore, it is no coincidence that ATM works like voice telephone systems. Switches establish circuits between computers on a network (like a telephone call) and ATM network addresses use the same standard as telephone numbers – they have a local network number and then a prefix (like an area or country code) for communication between distant networks[3].

Notice that this circuit establishment is different from Ethernet. Like Ethernet, ATM encapsulates data into what are called *ATM cells*. However, ATM cells are not addressed in the same way as Ethernet frames. Instead of addressing a cell using the MAC address of the destination computer, ATM uses a number which identifies the circuit that the ATM network has established between two computers. Two computers will use the same circuit for the duration of their communication.

Although ATM uses a form of ARP (called ATMARP) to discover Machine Access Control (MAC) addresses, the approach that ATM takes is slightly different. Instead of allowing individual computers to respond to ARP requests, ATMARP uses a central server to keep track of IP → MAC address associations. This central server responds to all ARP requests on a given ATM network.

Although there are some differences between Ethernet and ATM, the digital evidence on each is similar. There are log files, MAC addresses, ARP caches, and encapsulated data traveling through the network cables – all of which can be a source of digital evidence.

WIRELESS COMMUNICATION

CELLULAR NETWORKS (PACKET-SWITCHED)

Cellular networks use a network technology called Cellular Digital Packet Data (CDPD) at the data-link layer that is very similar to Ethernet. Wireless devices use a protocol called Digital Sense Multiple Access with Collision Detection (DSMA/CD) that works just like CSMA/CD described earlier in this chapter. Before transmitting data, a device listens to make sure that the transmission medium is not in use. If the medium is clear, the device sends data, otherwise it waits. Just as a computer on a network can be configured to eavesdrop, a wireless device can be configured to eavesdrop on a cellular network.

[3] ATM addresses contain information that is used for routing so there is some network layer functionality in ATM. However, for the purposes of this text it is sufficient to think of ATM as the data-link and physical layers.

CELLULAR NETWORKS (CIRCUIT-SWITCHED)

Cellular telephones have two numbers that uniquely identify them – an Electronic Serial Number (ESN), and a telephone number or Mobile Identification Number (MIN). When a cellular phone is manufactured, its microchip is programmed with a unique ESN and when the telephone is given to a subscriber it is assigned a telephone number that people used to call the subscriber. These numbers are used by telephone companies to direct calls to the correct mobile phone and are used by investigators to locate the phone. Special electronic tracking equipment enables investigators to lock onto an ESN/MIN pair and track it to a general geographical area. Within a given geographical area, triangulation can be used to pinpoint the cellular phone. Investigators require the assistance of cellular telephone companies to perform this type of tracking[4].

Most cellular telephone companies maintain communication with all of their cellular phones at all times even when the telephone is not in use (the phone must be turned on). This constant communication is used to notify subscribers of voice mail and can be used to track a cellular phone even when it is not being used to make calls.

In addition to tracking, cellular telephone companies can provide investigators with call details, toll records and wiretaps. This information can be used to determine the geographical location, calling patterns and even the specific activities of a criminal.

SATELLITE NETWORKS

Satellite networks have been growing over the past few years, ever since the Federal Communications Commission (FCC) allowed private companies (e.g. Hughes, Lockheed, Martin, Loral, Motorola) to develop and operate their own satellite networks. Satellites are becoming more widely used to convey Internet traffic around the globe. Some satellite networks use a variety of networking technologies including ATM and Very Small Aperture Terminal (VSAT).

WIRELESS COMPUTER NETWORKS

In addition to large-scale cellular and satellite communication, smaller wireless networks are on the rise. For instance, wireless Ethernet is becoming popular because it reduces the need for cables that must be replaced when better network technologies emerge. Using small antennae to transmit and receive high frequency radio waves, an Ethernet link can be established between two locations that are relatively close. For instance, wireless networks are often set up to connect two buildings on either side of a busy street. Putting a transceiver on the roof is cheaper and more convenient than putting cables underground.

[4]*If criminals can obtain an ESN and MIN, they can reprogram a cellular telephone to mimic someone else's telephone. Any calls made from the criminal's phone will be billed to the valid subscriber. Additionally, it becomes harder to capture criminals when they change the ESN/MIN in their phones. This has become such a problem in the late 1990s that most cellular telephone companies use encryption to protect the ESN and MIN of their telephones.*

DIGITAL EVIDENCE ON THE DATA-LINK AND PHYSICAL LAYERS

The data-link and physical layers are among the richest sources of digital evidence on a network. Data-link layer addresses (MAC addresses) are more identifying than network layer addresses (e.g. IP addresses) because a MAC address is usually directly associated with the Network Interface Card in a computer whereas an IP address can be easily reassigned to different computers. Eavesdropping can provide a large amount of evidence that can give investigators a detailed view of what a criminal is doing. Also, data captured using a sniffer can be very useful for reconstructing a crime or verifying that other sources of digital evidence contain accurate information. For example, the accuracy of log files that summarize events can be called into question, and data captured using a sniffer can be used to confirm entries in the logs.

Unlike previous chapters, guidelines for dealing with digital evidence on the data-link and physical layers are not provided here. The general approach to processing and analyzing digital evidence described in Chapter 4 and applied to the other layers of computer networks can also be useful for dealing with digital evidence on the data-link and physical layers of a network. However, digital evidence on the data-link and physical layers is very dynamic and can only be collected and examined using special tools and techniques, some of which are presented in the following sections.

ARP CACHE AND LOG FILES

If a criminal reconfigures his computer with someone else's IP address to hide his identity, investigators can still identify the computer by its MAC address. How? The criminal's computer must use the Address Resolution Protocol (ARP) to receive data from a router and ARP requires the actual MAC address of the computer. Therefore, the router would have an entry in its ARP cache showing a particular computer (identified by its MAC address) using someone else's IP address.

Some routers keep a log of hosts that use the incorrect IP address. Network administrators use these logs to detect misconfigured computers and investigators use these logs to identify computers that have been purposefully reconfigured to hide a criminal's identity. If there are no logs, investigators might be able to obtain relevant IP → MAC address associations from the ARP cache on a computer. Although every host on a network has an ARP cache, the ARP cache on a router is the most useful because it contains the IP→MAC address associations for all of the hosts it communicated with recently (Table 8.4).

% arp -a NET TO MEDIA TABLE DEVICE IP ADDRESS	MAC ADDR
e0 serv3.forensic-science.com	08:00:20:75:d3:fb
e0 serv7.forensic-science.com	08:00:20:1c:1f:67
e0 serv4.forensic-science.com	08:00:20:1c:6a:ff
e0 serv9.forensic-science.com	00:60:83:24:1f:4d
e0 serv2.forensic-science.com	08:00:20:7d:40:9c
e0 sim.forensic-science.com	08:00:20:80:fe:34
e0 serv5.forensic-science.com	08:00:20:7f:17:3c
e0 serv6.forensic-science.com	08:00:20:7d:e3:94
e0 serv8.forensic-science.com	00:04:ac:44:3f:4e
e0 wise.forensic-science.com	08:00:20:1c:5b:df
e0 db.forensic-science.com	08:00:20:87:2c:73
e0 serv1.forensic-science.com	08:00:20:86:4a:cf
e0 pobox.forensic-science.com	08:00:20:87:a5:bb
e0 mail.forensic-science.com	08:00:20:86:e2:5c
e0 news.forensic-science.com	08:00:20:7e:2d:ef

Table 8.4

"arp -a" shows the MAC addresses of hosts on a network. In general, use the Domain Name System (DNS) to convert names to IP addresses – the command "nslookup hostname." The hostnames in this table are not in the Domain Name System and, therefore, cannot be resolved to an IP address.

Investigators can document and collect the ARP cache by taking photographs or print screens and then cutting and pasting the contents into a file.

SNIFFING

Sniffing should only be used as a last resort because it is expensive and invasive. After capturing data with a sniffer, save it to a file and process the file like any other. Investigators should become familiar with sniffers. There are sniffers for MSDOS and Windows NT but the less expensive ones have limited functionality (e.g. *Gobbler*) and the more helpful ones are quite expensive (e.g. *Network Monitor* in Microsoft's Systems Management Server). There are also sniffers available for Unix (e.g. *TCPdump, snoop, linsniff*) but you must have administrator access on a Unix machine. The safest and most honest way to gain administrator access on a Unix machine is a complicated process. First, obtain Linux (a free version of Unix) and install it on a computer, then get a sniffer, compile it on your system and run it. Remember that you have to be connected to a network through a network interface card for this to work. Sniffers do not work with modems.

MAC ADDRESSES

MAC addresses can be used to identify individual machines and can sometimes be used to classify the type of machine. For example, Ethernet MAC addresses comprise 12 hexadecimal digits (e.g. 00-10-4B-DE-FC-E9). The first six hexadecimal digits refer to the vendor of the Network Interface Card (NIC) and the last six digits are the serial number for the particular

NIC. Table 8.5 lists a small selection of vendors and their associated Ethernet MAC address prefix. A more complete list can be found at http://www.cavebear.com/CaveBear/Ethernet/vendor.html. Note that large companies use different blocks of addresses (e.g. Cisco, 3Com) for different product lines and sometimes

Table 8.5

MAC addresses of different manufacturers.

PREFIX	MANUFACTURER	PRODUCT (WHEN APPLICABLE)
001007	Cisco Systems	Catalyst 1900
00100B	Cisco Systems	
00100D	Cisco Systems	Catalyst 2924-XL
001011	Cisco Systems	Cisco 75xx
00101F	Cisco Systems	Catalyst 2901
001029	Cisco Systems	Catalyst 5000
00102F	Cisco Systems	Cisco 5000
00104B	3Com	3C905-TX PCI
00105A	3Com	Fast Etherlink XL in a Gateway 2000
080020	Sun	
08003E	Motorola	
080056	Stanford University	
08005A	IBM	
09006A	AT&T	
10005A	IBM	
100090	Hewlett-Packard	
3C0000	3Com	dual function (V.34 modem + Ethernet) card
444553	Microsoft	Windows95 internal "adapters"

RECONSTRUCTION

It is often necessary to reconstruct related packets into complete messages or sessions. For example, data contained in captured frames might be reassembled to form an e-mail message or Web page. Also, by reconstructing a sequence of packets and comparing the sequence with other activities, individualizing differences can emerge. Some computer security tools have been developed that can recognize specific types of malicious behavior by monitoring packet sequences. These security tools use attack signatures to detect and thwart intrusion attempts. Also, captured packets can be played back to recreate the actions of the intruder. Some excellent examples of replaying an intruder's activities can be viewed at http://www.takedown.com/evidence/anklebiters/mlf/.

SUMMARY

Although it might be tempting to gloss over the technical details in this chapter, it is important to have a solid conceptual understanding of how data travels between computers. Data-link addresses (e.g. Ethernet addresses) enable data to travel between two computers on the same physical network while network layer addresses (e.g. IP addresses) enable the same data to travel across multiple physical networks. If all computer networks used the same network technology, two addressing schemes would not be necessary – all computers would already be speaking the same language. However, since there are many different network technologies, computer applications require a common language to communicate over dissimilar networks – TCP/IP.

Networked computers use the Address Resolution Protocol (ARP) to determine which MAC address is associated with (bound to) which network layer address. Every computer has an ARP cache that can be used to determine which computers were communicating and what their MAC and IP addresses were at the time of the communication. ARP tables do not keep permanent records and must be examined shortly after a communication occurred or the evidence will be lost. Fortunately, some systems keep limited logs of unusual ARP activity such as computers using incorrect IP addresses.

Complete logs are rarely kept of activities at the data-link and physical layers, simply because there is so much going on. Logging every piece of information that passes through a network, including all of the ARP requests and replies, would result in huge log files that would fill up a computer. There are limited logs but the majority of evidence is transient. The ARP cache on most computers only keeps entries for twenty minutes and data traveling through the network is only available for capture for a fraction of a second. Therefore, unlike the transport and network layers, to obtain evidence from the data-link and physical layers investigators must be quick and/or persistent. Investigators must be quick to obtain evidence of past activities and must be patient and persistent to obtain evidence of ongoing activities.

Eavesdropping is one of the primary means of collecting evidence from the physical layer. Sniffers can be connected to a network to capture any information traveling on it and more sophisticated techniques enable investigators to eavesdrop without being physically connected to the network. These advanced eavesdropping techniques depend on emissions from the physical layer. Eavesdropping should only be used as a last resort because the process is time consuming and invasive, very much like wiretapping. There are strict laws that must be adhered to when intercepting communications as described in Chapter 13.

At this point, the reader should now have a strong understanding of computer networks, from the application·layer that most people use, to the physical layer that carries data. It should be clear that digital evidence is everywhere in the air and cables around us. With an understanding of technology and how to deal with the associated digital evidence, you are ready to bring it all together in an investigation. The following chapters describe some general investigative methods and some specific types of situations that investigators commonly encounter.

REFERENCES

Comer, D.E. (1995) *Internetworking with TCP/IP Vol. 1: Principles, Protocols, and Architecture*, 3rd edn, Upper Saddle River, NJ: Prentice Hall.

Held, G. (1994) *Ethernet Networks*, New York, NY: John Wiley & Sons, Inc.

## CHAPTER 9

USING DIGITAL EVIDENCE AND BEHAVIORAL EVIDENCE ANALYSIS IN AN INVESTIGATION

Computers and networks contain vast amounts of information and allow various levels of anonymity, making it difficult to find the perpetrator(s) of, and digital evidence relating to, a specific crime. Therefore, there is a need for a methodical approach to help investigators manage and make use of digital evidence in an investigation. Behavioral evidence analysis (Turvey 1999) is an ideal tool in this situation, since its primary purpose is to condense evidence into a form that helps focus an investigation, narrow the suspect pool, understand offender choices, and interview suspects. Behavioral evidence analysis can also help investigators understand an offender's behavior, giving them a better sense of where the offender might go and what he might do to fulfill his individual needs (motives and fantasies).

The process of behavioral evidence analysis does not involve psychic abilities and it does not endeavor to implicate a specific individual. The foundation of this process is evidence and involves carefully and objectively examining that evidence to gain a more complete understanding of the crime, the people involved, their motives and their relationship with each other.

When people first encounter behavioral evidence analysis, they often think that it is either just good investigative work or merely common sense. While this may or may not be true, studies have shown that few people investigators have the patience or training to actually get involved with, understand and exploit evidence on the level that the deductive criminal profiling process requires.

> ... the use of physical evidence and application of the forensic sciences, in spite of the popular perception to the contrary, are not prominent in reality; systematic sleuthing and scientific successes do not characterize the criminal investigative process or what might be called, in other words, detective work. (Horvath and Meesig 1996)

This chapter presents the basic elements of behavioral evidence analysis (equivocal forensic analysis, victimology, risk assessment, and crime scene characteristics) to help investigators improve their investigative practices and take full advantage of digital evidence. This chapter is not intended to help investigators determine offender characteristics such as age, sex, race and marital status. The aim of this chapter is to raise investigators' appreciation for a methodical and thorough approach to investigating crime.

EQUIVOCAL FORENSIC ANALYSIS

In any investigation it is important to examine incoming evidence as objectively as possible, questioning everything and assuming nothing. In many situations, evidence will be presented to an investigator along with an interpretation (e.g. this is evidence of a computer intrusion or death threat). Investigators should not accept another person's interpretation without question but should instead verify the origins and meanings of the available evidence themselves to develop their own hypotheses and opinions. This is the basic concept behind equivocal forensic analysis[1].

In essence, an equivocal forensic analysis is the process of familiarizing oneself with the evidence without leaping to conclusions. This is the point in an investigation where investigators should closely follow the stages of digital evidence examination repeated throughout this text: recognition, collection, preservation, documentation, classification, comparison, individualization and reconstruction. In addition to physical and digital evidence, an equivocal forensic analysis should include interviews with victims and witnesses whenever possible. Simply because computers are involved does not mean that people should not be questioned about the situation.

During an equivocal forensic analysis, potential patterns of behavior may begin to emerge and gaps in the evidence may appear. The hope is that evidence will begin to fit together into a coherent whole, like pieces of a jigsaw puzzle, and will combine to form a more complete picture in which any holes will become more evident[2]. Additional evidence will be required to develop these patterns and fill in gaps – but some basic things may become clear quite early on in the analysis.

First, it needs to be clearly established that a crime has been committed. The *corpus delicti*, or body of the crime, refers to those essential facts that show that a crime has taken place. If these basic facts do not exist, it cannot be reliably established that there was indeed a crime. For example, to establish that a computer intrusion has taken place, investigators should look for evidence such as a point of entry, programs left behind by the criminal, destroyed or altered files and any other indication of unauthorized access to a computer. In some cases, investigators mistakenly think that an intrusion has occurred. In other cases, clever intruders cover their tracks, even going

[1] *'Equivocal' refers to anything that can be interpreted in more than one way or where the interpretation is open to question. An equivocal forensic analysis is one in which the conclusions regarding the physical and digital evidence are still open to interpretation.*

[2] *Investigators can never get the entire picture of what occurred at a crime. Forensic analysis and reconstruction only includes evidence that was left at a crime scene and is intrinsically limited.*

so far as to fix the vulnerability that they used to gain entry. During an equivocal forensic analysis, all possibilities must be entertained and the evidence must be the guide.

Secondly, it may become evident early on that there is enough evidence to generate investigative leads, identify suspects, link suspects to the victim, link suspects to the crime scene, link similar cases to the same perpetrator, and disprove or support witness testimony. In some situations, there simply is not enough evidence to generate any leads and it is necessary either to look for more evidence or halt the investigation until further leads develop.

If there is a risk of additional crimes or if it becomes clear that a large amount of evidence is missing, it is worth documenting the scope of the problem in what Turvey (1999) describes as a *threshold assessment*. A threshold assessment summarizes the existing evidence, indicates potential risks and suggests additional evidence that should be sought.

VICTIMOLOGY

One aspect of a crime that is often overlooked is the victim. Because the aim of an investigation is to find the offender, investigators concentrate on evidence relating to the offender. However, a victim is at the center of every crime.

> The victim is the last person to witness the crime. If alive, the victim can tell a great deal about the crime. If the victim is deceased, however, the crime scene must tell the story. In either instance, the profiler should be as interested in the activities of the victim as in any element of the submitted packet of information accompanying the request for a profile. (Holmes 1996)

Furthermore, offenders usually pick victims after some deliberation, even if the deliberation is only momentary. Understanding an offender's choice of victim can tell a lot about the offender and can help investigators warn and protect other potential victims.

Victimology is the process of learning about the victim(s) of a crime. Victimology involves understanding why an offender has chosen a specific victim and what risks the offender has been willing to take to acquire that victim. If investigators can understand how and why an offender has selected a particular victim, they may also be able to establish a link of some kind between the victim and that offender. These links may be geographical, work-related, schedule-oriented, school-related, hobby-related, or the link can be more substantial – the offender might be related to or intimate with the victim.

In addition to considering the circumstances surrounding the crime and victims' medical and social histories, it is important to get to know victims as people. Examine victims' personal effects and visit their personal environments (hangouts, work, school, home/bedroom) to get a better sense of how they perceived themselves, wanted to be perceived and how they felt about their lives in general (Turvey 1999).

CYBERTRAIL AND VICTIMOLOGY

As a rule, victimology should include a thorough search for cybertrails. It might not be obvious that a victim used the Internet but if a thorough Internet search is not performed, information that could drastically change victimology might be missed. Consider Sharon Lopatka, the woman who traveled from Maryland to North Carolina to meet her killer (case described at the beginning of Chapter 1). Friends described Lopatka as a normal woman who loved children and animals. However, Lopatka's activities on the Internet give a very different impression. Lopatka was evidently interested in sex involving pain and torture. Victimology that did not include her Internet activities would have been incomplete, lacking the aspects of her character most relevant to the crime being investigated and would probably describe her as a low-risk victim when in fact she was quite a high-risk victim.

Investigators should try to determine the what, why, where, how and when of the victim's Internet activities by asking questions like:

- What did the victim do on the Internet?
- What did the victim get from the Internet that was not accessible otherwise?
- How did the victim access the Internet, e.g. their own account, a parent's account, friend's account or stolen account?
- From where did the victim access the Internet, e.g. at home, work, a café or bar?
- Why did the victim pick that location to access the Internet, e.g. privacy, business, or to meet people face to face?
- What Internet services did the victim use and why?
- Did the victim try to make money on the Internet?
- Did the victim exhibit any behavior that might shed light on the victim's mental state, sexuality, lifestyle, intelligence, or self-image? For example, was the victim involved in abuse recovery newsgroups or mailing lists? If so, why?
- Are there discernable patterns in the victim's Internet activities that suggest habits or schedules?

VICTIM–OFFENDER RELATIONSHIPS

A major part of victimology is identifying possible links between the victim and offender. Any event or activity that could have brought the victim and offender into contact is worth investigating. Consider the possibility that the offender knew the victim in some capacity. For example, the offender could work with the victim or could have befriended the victim in their local bar/pub. Investigators should ask themselves whether or not the acquisition of a victim was dependent on some sort of routing or schedule, and who could be aware of that schedule. Investigators should also ask themselves whether or not some surveillance was required to acquire the victim.

When looking for offender–victim relationships, it is helpful to create a very detailed timeline of the 24 hours leading up to the crime. The 24 hours leading up to the crime often contains the most important clues regarding the relationship between the offender and the victim[3]. Such a timeline can organize the many details of a day and thus clarify how a victim came into contact with an offender. When reconstructing the period before the crime, include any Internet activity. If the victim did not use the Internet during that time, determine if that is unusual or significant. Whenever possible, individuals with whom the victim interacted on the Internet should be interviewed.

[3]*Cyberstalking and computer cracking can extend over several weeks or months, in which case investigators can look for pivotal moments and focus on those during the reconstruction process.*

RISK ASSESSMENT

One of the most informative aspects of offender–victim relationships is the risk that an offender was willing to take to obtain a victim and/or target. An offender who goes to great lengths to target a specific victim/target while hiding his identity has a specific reason for doing so – and these reasons are key to understanding the offender's intent, motives and even his identity. For example, the offender might know the victim well and would be understandably concerned that the victim might recognize him. If the risks present during the crime are not understood the relationship between the offender and victim cannot be well understood.

In any investigation involving computers, there is victim risk, target risk and offender risk.

- Victim risk: Low-risk victims are individuals whose personal, professional and social lives do not normally expose them to a possibility of suffering the type of harm or loss under investigation (e.g. children who are constantly supervised while using the Internet). High-risk victims are individuals whose personal, professional and social lives continuously expose them to the danger of suffering harm or loss (e.g. children who are not supervised while using the Internet). Victim risk on the Internet is not separate from victim risk in the physical world. If an individual's Internet activities attract the attention of a criminal, the criminal might try to gain physical access to the potential victim.

- Target risk: Target risk follows the same guidelines as victim risk. In most situations, a computer that is connected directly to the Internet is a high-risk target whereas a computer behind a firewall is a low-risk target. Ironically, when computers are behind a very restrictive firewall, some individuals connect modems to their computers so that they can access them from home. Thus, a seemingly low-risk target can actually be high risk upon close examination. Crackers often use automatic dialing programs (known war dialers) to look for modems behind a firewall. Because of this, some security-conscious organizations fire employees who connect modems to their computers. Target risk is discussed further in Chapter 10.

- Offender risk: Offender risk is the amount of exposure to harm, loss or identification and capture that an offender perceives when attempting to acquire a victim. An offender who takes precautions not to be caught and only targets high-risk victims is considered a low-risk offender. For example, by robbing a high-risk victim in a dark alley and wearing a mask during the attack an offender risks less than robbing a low-risk victim in a park at lunchtime without wearing a mask. The risks and precautions that an offender takes to obtain a specific victim can tell you what the offender desires and is willing to do to achieve that desire. The first robber in the example was primarily concerned with not being caught whereas the second robber's compelling need to satisfy his desires overrode his fear of being caught (or he has some reason for believing that he would not be caught).

Risk assessment on the computer network works in the same way as in the physical world, as the comparisons in Table 9.1 demonstrate.

Table 9.1

Risk assessment, Internet v. physical world.

RISK	PHYSICAL WORLD	INTERNET
High victim risk	Unattended child who talks with strangers walking home from school.	Unattended child in an Internet chat room who talks with strangers.
High offender risk	Offender who acquires victims in an area that is surveyed using security cameras.	Offender who acquires victims in an area of the Internet that is monitored or recorded.
Low victim risk	Individual who avoids going into certain areas unaccompanied and does not give personal information to strangers.	Individual who avoids using areas of the Internet unaccompanied and does not give personal information to strangers.
Low offender risk	Offender who wears a mask and performs covering behavior to avoid detection.	Offender who uses anonymity provided by the Internet and performs covering behavior to avoid detection.

CRIME SCENE CHARACTERISTICS

The primary assumption in behavioral evidence analysis is that everything an offender does while committing a crime reveals aspects of his behavior. In addition to choosing a specific victim and/or target, an offender chooses (consciously or unconsciously) a location and time to commit the crime and a method of approaching the victim/target. Additionally, while committing a crime, an offender does and says things for a specific reason (e.g. to control victims, to avoid capture, to satisfy a psychological need). Therefore, even the most barren crime scene is deeply imprinted with the offender's behaviors. Closely examining crime scenes and determining the significance of crime scene characteristics is a key to developing a complete behavioral evidence analysis.

Crime scene characteristics are the distinguishing features of a crime scene as evidenced by an offender's behavioral decisions regarding the victim and the offense location, and their subsequent meaning to the offender. (Turvey 1999)

As investigators analyze crime scenes, certain aspects of the criminal's behavior may begin to emerge. Specifically, the behaviors that were necessary to commit the crime (*Modus Operandi* oriented behavior) and behaviors that were not necessary to commit the crime (signature oriented behavior) may be become evident if enough evidence is available.

CRIME SCENE LOCATION AND TYPE

The location of a crime scene and ways a criminal used it are two fundamental characteristics of a crime scene that can flood an investigator's mind with questions. Why did the offender choose this location? Was the choice intentional, accidental, or simply a convenience? Who frequents this location? How did the victim and offender get to this location? Is this where the offender initially encountered the victim? Is this where the crime occurred or where evidence was dumped? Are there other crime scenes and if so, how does this location relate to the location of others?

Investigators should attempt to answer these questions and any others that will help determine the significance of the crime scene from the offender's perspective. Analyzing a crime scene in this way can help investigators understand the offender more fully and can influence their search strategy. For example, if an offender met the victim in one place and went to another location to commit the crime, investigators can expect to find more physical evidence at the primary crime scene than at the point of contact and should search accordingly.

Networks add complexity to crime scene analysis by allowing offenders to be in a different physical location than their victims or targets and furthermore allowing them to be in multiple places in cyberspace. In essence, criminals use computer networks as virtual locations, thus adding new characteristics and dimensions to the crime scene. For example, chat rooms and newsgroups are the equivalent of town squares on the Internet providing a venue for meetings, discussions and exchanges of materials in digital form. Criminals use these areas to acquire victims, convene with other criminals, and coordinate with accomplices while committing a crime.

CASE EXAMPLE
Some groups of computer crackers meet on IRC to help each other gain unauthorized access to hosts on the Internet. If the owner of a system that has been broken into does not notice the intrusion, word gets around and other computer crackers take advantage of the compromised system. Thus, a group of computer crackers become squatters, using the host as a base of operations to

experiment and launch attacks against other hosts. IRC functions as a staging area for this type of criminal activity and investigators can sometimes find relevant information by searching IRC using individualizing characteristics of the digital evidence that the crackers left at the primary crime scene: the compromised host.

Criminals choose specific virtual spaces that suit their needs and these choices and needs provide investigators with information about the offender's behavior. An offender might prefer a particular area of the Internet because it attracts potential victims or because it does not generate much digital evidence. Another offender might choose a virtual space that is associated with their local area to make it easier to meet victims in person. Conversely, an offender might select a virtual space that is far from their local area to make it more difficult to find and prosecute them (see Figure 9.1).

Analyzing a crime scene for clues about the offender's needs and behavior requires time, patience and a great deal of concentration. Just remember that every aspect of the crime scene reveals something about the offender. Some crime scene characteristics might only expose a little about the offender but together, these small details can disclose a lot. As investigators learn to hold the details of a crime in their mind and mentally review these details from multiple perspectives (i.e. as seen by the offender, victim, or an objective observer) they will find it easier to piece the details together and understand their significance.

METHOD OF APPROACH AND CONTROL

How the offender approaches and obtains control of a victim or target is significant, exposing the offender's confidences, concerns, intents, motives, etc. For example, an offender might use deception rather than threats to approach and obtain control over a victim or target because he does not want to cause alarm. Another offender might be less delicate and simply use threats to gain complete control over a victim quickly.

Figure 9.1

Offender in Europe, victim in US, crime scenes spread around the world on personal computers and servers (AOL in Virginia).

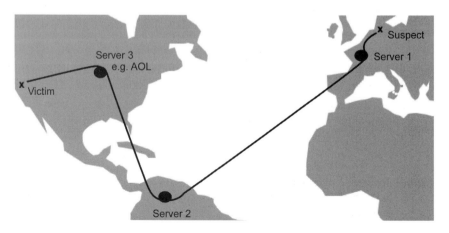

An offender's choice of weapon is also significant. For practical or personal reasons an offender might choose a lead pipe, a gun, or a computer connected to a network to get close to and gain control over a victim or target. Criminals use computer networks like a weapon to terrorize victims and break into target hosts. Although a criminal could visit the physical location of their victims or targets, using a network is easier and safer, allowing a criminal to commit a crime from home (for comfort) or from an innocuous cybercafe (for anonymity).

When an offender uses a network to approach and control a victim, the methods of approach and control are predominantly verbal since networks do not afford physical access/threats. These statements can be very revealing about the offender so investigators should make an effort to ascertain exactly what the offender said or typed. The way a computer cracker approaches, attacks and controls a target can give investigators a clear sense of the offender's skill level, knowledge of the computer, intents and motives. Crime scene characteristics of computer intrusions are described more fully in Chapter 10.

Different offenders can use the same method of approach or control for very different reasons so it is not possible to make broad generalizations based on these crime scene characteristics. For example, one offender might use threats to discourage a victim from reporting the crime whereas another offender might simply want control over the victim regardless of the surrounding circumstances. Therefore, it is necessary to examine crime scene characteristics in unison, determining how they influence and relate to each other.

OFFENDER ACTION, INACTION AND REACTION

Seemingly minor details regarding the offender can be important. Therefore, investigators should get in the habit of contemplating what the offender brought to, took from, changed or left at the crime scene. For instance, investigators might determine that an offender took valuables from a crime scene, indicating a profit motive. Alternately, investigators might determine that an offender took a trophy or souvenir to satisfy a psychological need. In both cases, investigators would have to be perceptive enough to recognize that something was taken from the crime scene.

Although it can be difficult to determine if someone took a copy of a digital file (e.g. a picture of a victim or valuable data from a computer), it is possible. Investigators can use log files to glean that the offender took something from a computer and might even be able to ascertain what was taken. Of course, if the offender did not delete the log files investigators should attempt to determine why the offender left such a valuable source of digital evidence. Was the offender unaware of the logs? Was the offender unable to delete the logs? Did the offender believe that there was nothing of concern in the logs? Small questions like these are key to analyzing an offender's behavior.

It is also important to remember that an offender is rarely in complete control – there can be unexpected occurrences or victims can react unpredictably. The pressures of unforeseen circumstances can cause an offender to reveal aspects of his personality, desires or identity that he would otherwise conceal. One extreme example is an offender calling the victim by name while appealing for cooperation, indicating that the offender knows the victim. Therefore, investigators should examine the victim–offender interactions and the events surrounding the crime to determine how an offender reacted to events that he could not have anticipated.

SUMMARY

Behavioral evidence analysis can lead to a very useful understanding of the choices made by an offender. It is difficult to imagine a case that would not benefit from a clear-headed review of existing evidence, a search for additional sources of evidence to fill in any gaps, and a summary of what is known about the offender, including MO, and signature behaviors. The level of detail that can be achieved by performing an equivocal forensic analysis, developing victimology and analyzing crime scenes can be surprising, leading many people to believe that some extraordinary mental ability is required. Admittedly, there is a lot of work involved but the process is methodical and repeatable and the reward of identifying and understanding a culprit makes up for the lost sleep.

REFERENCES

Geberth, V. (1996) *Practical Homicide Investigation*, 3rd edn, New York, NY: CRC Press.

Holmes, R. (1996) *Profiling Violent Crimes: An Investigative Tool*, 2nd edn, Sage Publications.

Horvath F. and Meesig, R. (1996) "The Criminal Investigation Process and the Role of Forensic Evidence: A Review of Empirical Findings," *Journal of Forensic Sciences*, 41 (6) (1996): 963–969.

Turvey, B. (1999) *Criminal Profiling: An Introduction to Behavioral Evidence Analysis*, London: Academic Press.

## CHAPTER 10

COMPUTER CRACKERS

New ways of breaking into and interfering with computers seem to be developed every day. Programs that automatically scan a target computer for common vulnerabilities are widely available at no cost on the Internet. With a little knowledge of computer networks, almost anyone can obtain and use the necessary tools to be a nuisance – or even dangerous (e.g. breaking into a computer and erasing its contents). It takes skill and experience, however, to break into a computer system, commit a crime, and cover your tracks.

In many cases, only people who are intimately familiar with a specific computer system possess the skills required to break into or tamper with it. As a result, a significant percentage of computer crimes are committed by individuals inside an organization (Carter and Katz 1996). However, the number of external attacks has grown, becoming as numerous as internal attacks. Specifically, organizations are finding that the attacks on their system are perpetuated through their connections to the Internet. Also, there has been a dramatic increase in the number of computer security breaches overall and a corresponding increase in financial losses (CSI 1998). Computer cracking has become such a problem that it is considered to be a national security risk by many developing countries.

This chapter discusses how to investigate computer crackers and presents ways to determine a cracker's intent, motivations and skill level.

HOW COMPUTER CRACKERS OPERATE

Boulanger (1998) lists several steps that a cracker would have to take to fully compromise a computer network without getting caught. Most crackers do not require all of these steps but Boulanger's analysis is useful for understanding how crackers who do not have inside access to or knowledge of the system operate:

Reconnaissance – gather information about the target system or network.

Probe and attack – probe the system for weaknesses and deploy the tools.

Toehold – exploit security weakness and gain entry into the system.

Advancement – advance from an unprivileged account to a privileged account.

Stealth – hide tracks; install a backdoor.

Listening post—establish a listening post.

Takeover – expand control from a single host to other hosts on network.

Of course, the most straightforward way to break into a computer is to steal or guess a password. However, if this is not a viable option, a cracker can usually gather enough information about a system to gain access to it. Knowing the operating system and services that are running on a computer is often all that is required – because certain services on certain operating systems are known to be vulnerable. As mentioned before, anyone can obtain programs from the Internet that exploit these vulnerabilities and can break into a computer without knowing any programming.

When crackers cannot access a system through known security holes, they use less technical methods to gain access. Crackers sometimes even dig through garbage for useful information. Crackers also try to get information using *social engineering* and *reverse social engineering*. Social engineering refers to any attempt to contact legitimate users of the target system and trick them into giving out information that can be used by the cracker to break into the system. For example, calling someone and pretending to be a new employee who is having trouble getting started can result in useful information like computer names, operating systems, and even some information about employee accounts. Alternately, pretending to be a computer technician who is trying to fix a problem can also lead to useful information.

Reverse social engineering is any attempt to have someone in the target organization contact you for assistance. Instead of contacting them, they contact you. For example, sending a memo with a "new" technical support e-mail can result in a flood of information. Reverse social engineering raises fewer suspicions than straight social engineering. When people contact you and you resolve their problems, they are unlikely to be suspicious of you and are unlikely to have any reason to report the incident to anyone.

After crackers gain access to a computer, they may be able to compromise the administrator account (known as "root" on Unix systems) thus getting unrestricted access to the entire system. In fact, certain security holes allow computer crackers to break into a computer and get root access in one step. With unlimited access to the system, it is possible for a cracker to modify any information on the computer, thus removing all traces of an intrusion. There are specific computer programs, often called root kits, that automate this process of hiding a break-in. These root kits replace programs and/or modify logs used to investigate an intrusion, making it more difficult to detect the intruder.

> **CASE EXAMPLE**
> Many crackers use toolkits that contain modified copies of common Unix commands. For example, a modified "ls" command might list all files and directories except for one directory called "stolenfiles," thus hiding a specific directory that contains incriminating evidence. Also, a modified "who" command might show all of the individuals who are logged into the computer except for the cracker. If investigators never compare these modified commands with original copies of the commands they will not notice that the times or message digests are different and they will miss valuable evidence. This situation is not uncommon and is a bit unnerving when it is encountered. However, with planning, this type of situation is not difficult to handle. Simply bring trusted copies of important commands that are needed to investigate an intrusion. Keep in mind that these commands are operating system specific. So, bring commands that are specifically for the operating system that you are investigating.

As the administrator of the machine, a cracker can run a sniffer to monitor traffic on the network. From an established listening post, a cracker could conceivably gain access to any other computer on the network or obtain sensitive information traveling over the wires.

INVESTIGATING COMPUTER INTRUSIONS

When a cracker targets a computer, the occurrence is usually referred to as an *incident*. The first step when investigating an incident is to determine if there actually was one – there must be a *corpus delicti*. Every network has its quirks, and individuals often mistake these quirks for an intruder. Detecting an intruder requires a familiarity with the type of computer and network involved and can be difficult if the cracker is skilled and experienced. In addition to examining log files and state tables, it is sometimes necessary to use computer cracking tools to determine how the cracker got in. For instance, probing the machine for known vulnerabilities and weak passwords can highlight holes through which the intruder could have gained access. There are many excellent guidelines for detecting intrusions that are referenced at the end of this chapter (CERT, 1997; ISS).

If an intrusion is detected, an investigator might decide to monitor the intruder. Be warned that monitoring an intruder is time-consuming and is only done in extreme situations, when it is the only option (Stoll 1990) or by researchers (Cheswick 1991). Monitoring is also quite risky because a cracker might notice the monitoring and take some action to make the investigation more difficult.

With or without monitoring, investigating computer intrusions involves a large amount of digital evidence. Investigators must search large log files for relevant entries, examine programs to determine their purpose closely, and explore the network for additional clues. In addition to being technically challenging, there is often pressure on an investigator to resolve the problem quickly. Relevant log files and state tables might be erased at any moment and the system owners/users want to gain access to the information on the system. It is often necessary to interpret digital evidence instantaneously to determine where additional evidence might be found.

Under such conditions, especially when several computers are involved, it is easy to overlook important digital evidence, neglect to collect digital evidence properly and document the investigation inadequately. The most effective approach to managing this kind of complex, high-pressure, error-prone investigation makes use of procedures and equipment for collecting the most common sources of digital evidence. Having a routine method for quickly preserving digital evidence for future examination leaves investigators with more time to deal with the nuances and peculiarities of individual incidents.

After collecting, documenting and preserving all of the digital evidence, investigators should perform an equivocal forensic analysis of the evidence, ultimately developing a detailed reconstruction of the crime. Using this base of evidence, investigators can begin to interpret the significance of specific aspects of the crime (e.g. victim and target selection, choice of technology, method of attack).

VICTIMOLOGY

One of the most important things to establish when a computer is directly involved in the commission of a crime is who or what was the intended target or victim? Who or what was meant to suffer as a result of the offender's actions? When a computer is used to acquire a victim (e.g. on the Internet) the computer is not a target; it is simply a tool. However, when a computer or information on a computer is destroyed to harm an individual, the computer/information is the target and the individual is the intended victim.

In this context, a *target* is defined as the object of an attack from the offender's point of view. The *intended victim* is the term for the person, group or institution that was meant to suffer loss or harm (Turvey 1999). The intended victim and the target may be one and the same. There may also be more than one intended victim. Because of the closely linked nature of computer networks, there may also be *collateral victims*. This term refers to victims that an offender causes to suffer loss or harm in the pursuit of another victim (usually because of proximity). When an arsonist burns down a building to victimize an individual or group, innocent individuals can get hurt. Similarly, when a cracker destroys a computer system to victimize an individual or group, unconnected individuals can lose data.

It is important to note that victims and targets can be symbolic. In this context, a *symbol* is any person or thing that represents as an idea, a belief, a group or even another person. For example, to a particular offender, parents can symbolize oppression, or computers can symbolize authority, or an ex-spouse can symbolize failure, or children can symbolize innocence, or supervisors or a CEO can symbolize an organization, or the Pope can symbolize the Catholic religion or God.

RISK ASSESSMENT

Although a computer is not a person, the underlying question when developing a target risk assessment is the same – why did the offender choose the target computer and what was the risk the offender was willing to take? Computer security professionals often make risk assessments of computer networks. Therefore, an organization might already have information that is useful for developing a risk assessment in an investigation.

To determine the risk of a given target, you need detailed information about it, including: the operating system, where it was located, how it was configured, what it contained, who had access to it, what other computers it regularly connected to and how difficult it was to break into. Some operating systems are more vulnerable than others but any operating system can be configured to be more secure. Investigators should ask themselves, did the offender need a high level of skill to gain access to the computer? If so, who possesses such talents?

In addition to considering the general characteristics of the target, investigators should consider the target's recent history. Determine whether there were any previous unsuccessful attempts to access the computer. A 24-hour timeline is just as useful when computers are concerned but they can contain an overwhelming amount of information. A computer does many things in 24 hours, sometimes doing several things at once, and copiously logs activities (creating voluminous logs). Creating a time line helps organize the events into a more manageable form.

In some cases it is also fruitful to look further back in time to determine if the computer has been probed for the information necessary to gain access to the target. Signs of probing and failed attempts to access the computer suggest that the offender is not very familiar with the computer. A lack of probing indicates that the cracker either knows the system intimately or is very good at removing signs of probing and intrusion.

All of this information about the target can be used to develop a risk assessment which can in turn be used to understand the offender–victim relationship and provide an investigative direction.

CRIME SCENE CHARACTERISTICS

When computer crackers make no effort to conceal their activities, investigators can obtain information about the offender's behavior from log files and other available digital evidence. However, if significant evidence has been destroyed, it is more difficult to determine what the cracker intended and investigators must rely more heavily on crime scene characteristics and victimology to understand the incident. Arson investigators are familiar with this type of situation. To help investigators understand computer crackers who destroy information, some of the crime scene characteristics that are used in arson investigations have been adapted here: point of origin, method of initiation, offender skill, and nature and intent (Turvey 1999).

POINT OF ORIGIN

The *point of origin* is a term used to refer to the specific location at which damage was initiated. The point of origin is highly revealing about the offender's intended target, and the intended victim. For instance, a computer cracker might only delete one person's files – in which case the victim is fairly obvious. A computer cracker might delete information that is important to the entire organization, targeting the entire organization or what it represents. Also, many crackers delete or modify log files to hide their presence, in which case the victim might not be obvious but the intent will be clear – the destructive act was intended to hide the intruder's identity.

METHOD OF INITIATION

The way that an offender chooses to start, or prolong, destructive activities is dependent upon the types of programs used, the amount of delay time that is desired, and the skill of the offender.

Methods of initiation for destroying information on a computer include but are not limited to:

- straightforward deletion of files;
- formatting a disk to destroy everything on it;
- delayed destruction (e.g. programming the destruction to occur at a specific time);
- repeated destruction (e.g. programming the destruction to occur at regular intervals);
- destruction triggered by an action or event (e.g. the use of a certain command to trigger a destructive program).

OFFENDER SKILL LEVEL

An effort should be made to determine if the offender created the destructive programs that were used, or if the offender used programs that already existed on the computer. The skill level and experience of a cracker is usually evident in the methods and programs used to break into and damage a system. For instance, a cracker who uses readily available software and chooses weak targets for little gain, is generally less skilled and experienced than a cracker who writes customized programs to target strong installations. Having said this, a skilled cracker can successfully achieve specific goals using programs that exist on the system. Therefore, what is known about point of origin, method of initiation, and nature and intent of the destructive act should all be taken into account when assessing the offender's skill level. The key question is, "Did the cracker achieve his/her objective?" (Did the actual damage match the intended damage?)

NATURE AND INTENT

In an investigation of a computer intrusion, it is important to determine why a cracker targeted a computer i.e. their intent and, if the system was purposefully damaged, why it was damaged. Crackers break into computers for several reasons:

- To commit other crimes – the main aim is to hide their identity while committing other crimes. For example, some crackers distribute illegal information (e.g. copyrighted software) from a compromised system. Other crackers use a compromised computer to hide their identities while they harass people.

- Jump-off point – crackers use jump-off points to hide their identities while they crack other computers. Also, crackers often use a jump-off point when the target computer is difficult to compromise from outside a network but can be compromised from another computer on the same network.

- Safe haven or listening post – crackers store incriminating evidence on these safe havens and look for other likely targets using scanners and/or sniffers.

- Exploration and excitement – the main aim is to try out new techniques, gaining experience and perhaps causing some mischief in the process.

- Theft – to steal information or services (e.g. industrial espionage, stealing credit card numbers).

- To damage or destroy information on the target computer.

Some crackers compromise a single computer for multiple purposes. For example, the computer might initially be used as a safe haven or listening post but then might be used as a jump-off point. After using the computer as a jump-off point, the cracker might decide to cover his tracks by destroying all evidence on the computer, possibly damaging the computer in the process.

An important element to bear in mind when considering the nature and intent of any destructive act is the targeting. In short, what was the destructive act intended to inflict damage upon? Was it intended to harm damage or destroy a narrow target selection or a broad target selection? *Narrow targeting* refers to any destruction that is designed to inflict specific, focused and calculated amounts of damage on a specific target. *Broad targeting* refers to destruction that is designed to inflict damage in a wide-reaching fashion. In cases involving broad targeting, there may be an intended target near the point of origin, but it may also be designed to reach beyond that primary target for other victims in the environment. For instance, if many people share a computer that is targeted, there may only be one intended victim but a broad targeting can result in many collateral victims.

To determine if the targeting was narrow or broad, it is helpful to determine intentional vs. actual damage. This means learning as much about the configuration of the target computer as possible and the amount of damage incurred by the target. For example, programs like "chroot" limit the damage that can be done if one application (e.g. a Web server) is compromised. An intruder who is hoping to damage a wide area of the computer will be thwarted by such restrictions. If the intruder destroys everything in the restricted area, this is likely evidence of broad targeting and the cracker may not have achieved his/her goal of destroying everything on the computer. On the other hand, if the intruder deletes a few files in the restricted area, this is evidence of narrow targeting and the intruder has probably achieved his/her goal.

MOTIVATIONAL ASPECTS OF COMPUTER CRACKERS

The typologies detailed in Chapter 3 are more than adequate to the task of classifying the behaviors associated with damaging computers and the information they contain, with the single addition of *precautionary-oriented* behaviors (Turvey 1999).

> A precautionary act is any behavior committed by an offender before, during, or after an offense that is consciously intended to confuse, hamper, or defeat investigative or forensic efforts for the purposes of concealing their identity, their connection to the crime, or the crime itself.

Precautionary-oriented computer cracking refers to the destruction of information stored on a computer as a precautionary act, i.e. to conceal, damage or destroy any items of evidentiary value. It should be noted that these types of precautionary acts are not always very thorough. Items that an intruder intended to destroy can be examined by forensic scientists to exploit them for their full evidentiary potential, no matter how little debris is left behind. For example, if a small portion of a deleted file remains on a disk, this remaining digital evidence should be carefully reconstructed and examined to determine why the offender tried to destroy it.

Examples of precautionary-oriented behavior include:

- formatting a hard drive or physically damaging a computer to cover tracks;
- deleting startup files so that the computer cannot be rebooted;
- deleting log files to erase links between the cracker and the computer;
- destroying personal items that link the cracker to the target or victim (e.g. notes created while planning the crime or programs used to commit the crime).

Remember that even when computer crackers are careful to hide their identities, they often have quite distinct MO and signature behaviors that distinguish them. The items a cracker takes or leaves behind are significant when understanding MO and signature, and what a criminal tries to destroy is often the most telling.

CASE EXAMPLE

A scenario can help investigators comprehend the basic process of investigating a computer intrusion[1]. Imagine that you are called in to investigate a possible intrusion of a computer called "forensic-science.com" running the Linux operating system. The machine is critical to the operation of the organization and many people use it for a variety of purposes. The priorities are to gather evidence of the break-in and to restore the integrity of the machine as quickly as possible. Therefore, it is not feasible to monitor the cracker or disconnect the computer for a leisurely examination. Before you begin, you ask everyone to log out of the computers that might be compromised while you conduct your investigation. You also obtain the administrator (root) password so that you can move around and examine the entire computer without restrictions.

To begin your examination, you note the current date and time, documenting any discrepancy, and you type the "script evidence" command. This command opens a log file called "evidence" that will store a complete record of your activities until you type "exit" to stop the logging process. You then type "who" to obtain a list of currently logged in users[2].

```
# /bin/script evidence
Script started, file is evidence
# date
Sat Mar 6 20:03:34 EDT 1999
# /bin/who
```

[1] This scenario is fabricated to demonstrate key aspects of investigating a computer intrusion. Some knowledge of Unix is assumed in this scenario. For additional information about Unix see the references at the end of this chapter.

[2] Although operating the computer can overwrite evidence, not examining the system and simply rebooting the computer can destroy much more evidence. For example, processes that are running in RAM will be lost and connections from remote computers will be lost.

| root console | Mar 6 16:00 | |
| rewt pts/26 | Mar 6 15:45 | (174-16-52.world.com) |

The "who" command shows that only you (root) and *rewt* are connected. Since you asked everyone to log out of the machine, you suspect that the cracker is using the *rewt* account to connect from an ISP called World.com. To obtain additional evidence of this connection, you also type "netstat -a" (remembering to take a print screen, of course) to display all recent and current TCP/IP connections to the computer.

```
# /bin/netstat -a

cases.forensic-science.com.telnet 174-16-52.world.com.1171  8235    0 64240    0
ESTABLISHED
```

The results of the "netstat" command confirm that there is a Telnet connection between cases.forensic-science.com and 174-16-52.world.com.

You then type "last rewt" to obtain a list of recent logins.

```
# /bin/last rewt
```

| rewt | pts/26 | 174-16-52.world.com | Sat Mar 6 | 15:45 still logged in |
| rewt | pts/5 | 214-72-229.world.com | Sat Mar 6 | 00:13 - 00:27 (00:13) |

The output of the "last rewt" command indicates that the intruder logged in earlier in the day and is still logged in (remember that this redundancy of evidence is desirable). You then list all of the processes that *rewt* is running at that moment using the "ps -auxwww | grep rewt" command combination and you detect a sniffer and a destructive program running. Notice that each process has a number associated with it in the second column. Also note that the first line shows a program called "/tmp/.hidden/destroy" being run on a remote computer (www.corpus-delicti.com) using the remote shell command "rsh"[3]:

[3]STIME is the starting time of the process, given in hours, minutes and seconds. A process begun more than twenty-four hours before the "ps" inquiry is executed is given in months and days. TIME is the cumulative execution time for the process.

```
# /bin/ps -auxwww | grep rewt
```

UID	PID	PPID	C	STIME TTY	TIME CMD
rewt	2198	2191	0	Mar 6 ?	378:50 rsh www.corpus-delicti.com exec/tmp/.hidden/destroy
rewt	2186	1993	0	Mar 6 ?	295:31 sniffer
root	4094	3155	0	16:02:14 ?	0:00 grep rewt

```
rewt           1993   1946   0        15:46:57 pts/24    0:01 -csh
# kill -9 2198
# kill -9 2186
# kill -9 1993
```

You are now certain *rewt* is your cracker and you notify the owner of the machine that her system has been compromised. The owner has no interest in monitoring the intruder and instructs you to prevent the intruder from doing more damage. To get rid of the intruder you kill all of his processes using the "kill" command, automatically logging him off the machine. The "kill" command terminates the process that is associated with the given number. At this point you decide to reboot the computer and make a bitstream copy of the hard drive.

With the cracker gone and the damage contained, it is time to examine the evidence and reconstruct the crime. At this point, the owner is observing over your shoulder so you take the opportunity to explain what the intruder has done to her system. You look through the syslog file and find that the intruder gained access to the computer through a vulnerable version of mountd.

```
Mar 5 23:43:13 cases.forensic-science.com mountd[513]: Unauthorized access by
NFS client 174-16-65.world.com.

Mar 5 23:43:13 cases.forensic-science.com syslogd: Cannot glue message parts
together

Mar 5 23:43:13 cases.forensic-science.com mountd[513]: Blocked attempt of 174-
16-65.world.com to mount

~P~P~P~P~P~P~P~P~P~P~P~P~P~P~P~P~P~P~P~P~P~P~P~P~P~P~P~P~P~P~P~P
~P~P~P~P~P~P~P~P~P~P~P~P~P~P~P~P~P~P~P~P~P~P~P~P~P~P~P~P~P~P~P~P
~P~P~P~P~P~P~P~P~P~P~P~P~P~P~P~P~P~P~P~P~P~P~P~P~P~P~P~P~P~P~P~P
~P~P~P~P~P~P~P~P~P~P~P~P~P~P~P~P~P~P~P~P~P~P~P~P~P~P~P~P~P~P~P~P
~P~P~P~P~P~P~P~P~P~P~P~P~P~P~P~P~P~P~P~P~P~P~P~P~P~P~P~P~P~P~P~P
~P~P~P~P~P~P~P~P~P~P~P~P~P~P~P~P~P~P~P~P~P~P~P~P~P~P~P~P~P~P~P~P
~P~P~P~P~P~P~P~P~P~P~P~P~P~P~P~P~P~P~P~P~P~P~P~P~P~P~P~P~P~P~P~P
~P~P~P~P~P~P~P~P~P~P~P~P~P~P~P~P~P~P~P~P~P~P~P~P~P~P~P~P~P~P~P~P
~P~P~P~P~P~P~P~P~P~P~P~P~P~P~P~P~P~P~P~P~P~P~P~P~P~P~P~P~P~P~P~P
~P~P~P~P~P~P~P~P~P~P~P~P~P~P~P~P~P~P~P~P~P~P~P~P~P~P~P~P~P~P~P~P
~P~P~P~P~P~P~P~P~P~P~P~P~P~P~P~P~P~P~P~P~P~P~P~P~P~P~P~P~P~P~P~P
~P~P~P~P~P~P~P~P~P~P~P~P~P~P~P~P~P~P~P~P~P~P~P~P~P~P~P~P~P~P~P~P
~P~P~P~P~P~P~P~P~P~P~P~P~P~P~P~P~P~P~P~P~P~P~P~P~P~P~P~P~P~P~P~P
~P~P~P~P~P~P~P~P~P~P~P~P~P~P~P~P~P~P~P~P~P~P~P~P~P~P~P~P~P~P~P~P
~P~P~P~P~P~P~P~P~P~P~P~P~P~P~P~P~P~P~P~P~P~P~P~P~P~P~P~P~P~P~P~P
~P~P~P~P~P~P~P~P~P~P~P~P~P~P~P~P~P~P~P~P~P~P~P~P~P~P~P~P~P~P~P~P
~P~P~P~P~P~P~P~P~P~P~P~P~P~P~P~P~P~P~P~P~P~P~P~P~P~P~P~P~P~P~P~P
~P~P~P~P~P~P~P~P~P~P~P~P~P~P~P~P~P~P~P~P-P3Û3À˚˚[Í~@3Ò3À~KÚ˚FÍ~@ρ
```

```
Âuô1À˜¨BÍ~@~EÀubëb˘V~<ýt˚fρÀt˚Këõ˚0ρÈ~HFÿëì˜˜˜B~I˚FρÉ~IF˚D˚¨F~IF˚H˚flÛρÃ~Iñí~
@I˚F˚¨Bf~IF˚L˚*f~IF˚N~MF˚L~IF˚D1À~IF˚P˚¨P~IF˚H˚fρÁÍ~@˚¨A~IF˚D˚f˚DÍ~@ë˚DëLëR1À~I
F˚D~IF˚H˚fρÁÍ~@~HÃ˚?ÉÍ~@˚?ρÁÍ~@˚?ρÁÍ~@,.bin@~I˚F,.sh!@~IF˚DIÀ~HF˚G~Iv˚H~IF˚L˚¨
K~Ió~MN˚H~MV˚LÍ~@IÀ˚¨AIÛÍ~@èEÿÿÿÿÿÿÿPrivet ADMcrcw~P(~˚Ë˚H(~˚Ë˚H(~˚Ë˚H(~˚Ë˚H(~
˚Ë˚H(~˚Ë˚H(~˚Ë˚H(~˚Ë˚H(Mar 5 23:43:13 cases.forensic.science.com˚H(~˚Ë˚H(~˚Ë˚H(~
˚Ë˚H(~˚Ë˚H(~˚Ë˚H(~˚Ë˚H(~˚Ë˚H(~˚Ë˚H(~˚Ë˚H(~˚Ë˚H(~˚Ë˚H-˚Ë˚H(~˚Ë˚H(~˚Ë˚H(~˚Ë˚H(~
˚Ë˚H(~˚Ë˚H(~˚Ë˚H(~˚Ë˚H(~˚Ë˚H(~˚Ë˚H(~˚Ë˚H(~˚Ë˚H-˚Ë˚H(~˚Ë˚H(~˚Ë˚H(~˚Ë˚H(~˚Ë˚H(~
˚Ë˚H(~˚Ë˚H(~˚Ë˚H(~˚Ë˚H(~˚Ë˚H(~˚Ë˚H(~˚Ë
```

You also find that the user logged in using an account created by the above overflow data called *doomed* and then switch to another newly created account called *rewt*.

```
Mar 5 23:46:54 cases.forensic-science.com PAM_pwdb[3122]: (login) session
opened for user doomed by (uid=0)

Mar 5 23:46:54 cases.forensic-science.com login[3122]: LOGIN ON ttyp0 BY crak0
FROM 174-16-65.world.com

Mar 5 23:50:03 cases.forensic-science.com PAM_pwdb[3130]: (su) session opened
for user rewt by doomed(uid=0)
```

You then go to /tmp to look at the "hidden" directory you noticed in the process list. However, the "hidden" directory does not turn up when you list the contents of the /tmp directory using the "ls" command.

```
#/bin/cd      /tmp
#/bin/ls      -altc
drwx------   2 root       root   512        Mar 6 Jan 1 15:33   ./
drwx------   8 root       root   512        Jan 1 15:33         ../
```

This leads you to suspect that the intruder brought a rootkit to facilitate the intrusion process. The intruder would have installed the rootkit as follows:

```
mkdir .hidden
mv rootkit.tar.gz .hidden
cd .hidden
tar zvf rootkit.tar.gz
ls
cd rootkit
./install
exit
```

To determine if the "hidden" directory is still present, you use the "du" command to list all of the subdirectories.

```
#/bin/du
10273 ./.hidden
10273
```

Sure enough, the hidden directory did not show up using the standard "ls" command, indicating that the "ls" command has been replaced with a modified version that purposefully does not list this hidden directory[4]. So, you go directly to the hidden directory and list its contents and find that the intruder was gathering information.

```
#/bin/cd    /tmp/.hidden
#/bin/ls -altc
-rw-r--r--   1   rewt   rewt   3925716   Mar 6 21:21   information3
-rw-r--r--   1   rewt   rewt   108133    Mar 6 16:48   information2
-rw-r--r--   1   rewt   rewt   1818708   Mar 6 16:03   information 1
-rw-r--r--   1   rewt   rewt   4414846   Mar 6 15:54   destroy
drwxr-xr-x   2   rewt   rewt   512       Mar 6 00:22   sniffer
drwxr-xr-x   3   rewt   rewt   512       Mar 6 00:20
drwxr-xr-x   393 root   root   7168      Jan 1 15:33
```

The fact that the "ls" command has been changed and that there was a sniffer running confirms that the cracker gained root access to the machine. This implies that anything on the system could have been modified and that the data on the computer should be backed up, the disk should be formatted, and the operating system should be reinstalled. It also means that the cracker could have obtained everyone's passwords either by using the sniffer or by taking the file that contains everyone's passwords and running a specialized program to crack them. Thus, every password should be changed after the operating system has been reinstalled and the data has been restored from the backup.

In summary, a careful review of the log files shows that the cracker obtained unauthorized and privileged access to the machine using a well-publicized vulnerability. The cracker initially obtained access to the computer from a dialup account at World.com, modified the system using a rootkit, and created a hidden directory that the modified "ls" command would not list. The hidden directory contains various tools that the cracker used, including the sniffer. You also recall from the process list that the cracker was running a destructive program on a remote machine (www.corpus-delicti.com). Unfortunately, almost all of the data on this second machine has been lost, destroying several months' work. The head of the organization is turning pale

[4] *The RedHat Package Manager (RPM) provides a convenient way to determine if files like "ls" have been modified. The command "rpm -Va" verifies all of the important files on a system - the system manuals describe how to interpret the results. Although this method can be useful, it is not failsafe because a sophisticated intruder can modify the RPM database, thus hiding any changes that were made to the system.*

as she watches over your shoulder and clearly indicates that she wants to press charges immediately. You suggest that she contact her lawyer as soon as possible and work with World.com to determine the identity of their customer whose account was used to connect to her computer.

Finally, you type "exit" to close your automatically generated evidence log file (originally opened using the "script evidence" command), and you print any evidence that you can, signing and dating each page. Also, to be safe, you make a regular copy all of the evidence to a disk in a way that preserves the timestamps and other file attributes (e.g. using "tar" rather than "cp"), making certain to inventory and note the message digest of each file. Then you make a duplicate disk of the evidence for safekeeping and you check both disks on another computer to verify that you can read them. You label, date and initial both disks, and also note the type of computer and operating system (e.g. Redhat Linux 5.2), what program(s) and/or command(s) you used to copy the files, and the information believed to be contained in the files.

You then work with the system administrators to obtain log files from the main routers that the intruder needed to go through to gain access to the machine. You find a large number of error messages on the router that joins the organization's network to the Internet. These log files indicate that an intruder tried to break into the organization in a number of ways before gaining access. All of these log entries show that the intruder used the World.com ISP.

A few days later, when the World.com ISP divulges the identity of their customer, it turns out to be an employee of a competitor that wanted to obtain information about the organization and disrupt their work. You have gathered enough digital evidence to demonstrate the intruder's intent and the amount of damage that he has done. When faced with this evidence, the competitor agrees to pay a large settlement. Additionally, the media get wind of the incident and publicize the case, causing significant damage to the competitor's reputation.

SUMMARY

Computer cracking is the most challenging type of cybercrime from a digital evidence perspective. Every computer and network is different, configured by the owner in a very personal way. Some systems are highly customized, fitting the specific needs of a skilled computer user while other systems are highly disorganized. In many ways, investigating a computer intrusion is like going into someone's kitchen and trying to determine what is out of place. In some cases, anomalies are obvious, like seeing plates in a cutlery drawer.

In other cases investigators must interview system owners/users and examine backup tapes and log files to determine what has been changed by the computer cracker.

Additionally, every computer cracker is different – choosing targets/victims for different reasons, using different methods of approach and attack and exhibiting different needs and intents. Ex-employees break into computers, damaging them in retaliation for some perceived wrong. Technically proficient individuals break into opportune targets to feel more powerful. Thieves and spies break into computers to obtain valuable information. Malicious individuals break into medical databases, changing prescriptions to overdose an intended victim. These types of crime are becoming more prevalent and are creating a need for skilled investigators equipped with procedures and tools to help them collect, process and interpret digital evidence.

REFERENCES

Boulanger, A. (1998) "Catapults and grappling hooks: The tools and techniques of information warfare," *IBM Systems Journal*, 37 (1) [http://www.research.ibm.com/journals/sj/371/boulanger html].

Carter, D.L. and Katz, A.J. (1996) "Computer Crime: An Emerging Challenge for Law Enforcement," *FBI Law Enforcement Bulletin* (December).

CERT (1997) *CERT Coordination Center Intruder Detection Checklist*; available at http://www.cert.org/ftp/tech_tips/intruder_detection_checklist.

Cheswick, B. (1991) *An Evening with Berferd: In Which a Cracker is Lured, Endured and Studied*, AT&T Bell Laboratories [ftp://research.att.com/dist/internet_security/berferd.ps].

CSI/FBI (1998) *1998 CSI/FBI Computer Crime and Security Survey* [http://www.gocsi.com].

Garfinkel, S. and Spafford, G. (1996) *Practical Unix and Internet Security*, 2nd edn, Cambridge, MA: O'Reilly & Associates, Inc.

National Computer Security Association (1997) *Internet Security Professional Reference*, Indianapolis, IN: New Riders Publishing.

Stoll, C. (1990) *The Cuckoo's Egg: Tracking a Spy Through the Maze of Computer Espionage*, New York, NY: Pocket Books.

Stoll, C. (1984) "Stalking the Wily Hacker," *Communications of the ACM*, 27 (4) (April).

Turvey, B. (1999) *Criminal Profiling: An Introduction to Behavioral Evidence Analysis*, London: Academic Press.

RESOURCES

Rootshell [http://www.rootshell.com]

Internet Security Systems [http://www.iss.net]

L0pht [http://www.l0pht.com]

## CHAPTER 11

CYBERSTALKING

In 1990, after five women were murdered by stalkers, California became the first state in the US to enact a law to deal with this specific problem. Then, in 1998, California explicitly included electronic communications in their anti-stalking law. The relevant sections of the California Penal Code have strongly influenced all subsequent anti-stalking laws in the US, clearly defining stalking and related terms[1].

[1]*The equivalent law in the UK is the Protection from Harassment Act 1997 (Chapter 40).*

> Any person who willfully, maliciously, and repeatedly follows or harasses another person and who makes a credible threat with the intent to place that person in reasonable fear of death or great bodily injury is guilty of the crime of stalking ... "harasses" means a knowing and willful course of conduct directed at a specific person that seriously alarms, annoys, torments, or terrorizes the person, and that serves no legitimate purpose. This course of conduct must be such as would cause a reasonable person to suffer substantial emotional distress, and must actually cause substantial emotional distress to the person.
>
> ... "course of conduct" means a pattern of conduct composed of a series of acts over a period of time, however short, evidencing a continuity of purpose ... "credible threat" means a verbal or written threat, including that performed through the use of an electronic communication device, or a threat implied by a pattern of conduct or a combination of verbal, written, or electronically communicated statements and conduct made with the intent to place the person that is the target of the threat in reasonable fear for his or her safety or the safety of his or her family and made with the apparent ability to carry out the threat so as to cause the person who is the target of the threat to reasonably fear for his or her safety or the safety of his or her family. It is not necessary to prove that the defendant had the intent to actually carry out the threat ... "electronic communication device" includes, but is not limited to, telephones, cellular phones, computers, video recorders, fax machines, or pagers. (California Penal Code 646.9)

Note that persistence is one of the operative concepts when dealing with stalking. A single upsetting e-mail message is not considered harassment because it is not a pattern of behavior. Remember that anti-stalking laws were enacted to protect individuals against persistent terrorism and physical danger, not against annoyance or vague threats.

The distinction between annoyance and harassment is not easily defined. It is usually enough to demonstrate that the victim suffered substantial emotional distress. However, there is always the argument that the victim overreacted to the situation. If a victim is not found to be a "reasonable person" as described in the law a court might hold that no harassment took place. Therefore, when investigating a stalking case, it is important to gather as much evidence as possible to demonstrate that harassment took place and that the victim reacted to the credible threat in a reasonable manner.

The explicit inclusion of electronic communication devices in California's anti-stalking law is a clear acknowledgement of the fact that stalkers are making increasing use of new technology to further their ends. In addition to using voice mail, fax machines, cellular phones and pagers, stalkers use computer networks to harass their victims. The term *cyberstalking* refers to stalking that involves the Internet. This chapter briefly describes how cyberstalkers operate, what motivates them, and what investigators can do to apprehend them. Additional resources that relate to various aspects of stalking are presented at the end of this chapter.

HOW CYBERSTALKERS OPERATE

Cyberstalking works in much the same way as stalking in the physical world. In fact, many offenders combine their online activities with more traditional forms of stalking and harassment such as telephoning the victim and going to the victim's home. Some cyberstalkers obtain victims over the Internet and others put personal information about their victims on the Internet, encouraging others to contact the victim, or even harm them.

> CASE EXAMPLE (Associated Press, 1997)
> Cynthia Armistead-Smathers of Atlanta believes she became a target during an e-mail discussion of advertising in June 1996. First she received nasty e-mails from the account of Richard Hillyard of Norcross, Ga. Then she began receiving messages sent through an "anonymous remailer," an online service that masks the sender's identity.
>
> After Hillyard's Internet service provider canceled his account, Ms Armistead-Smathers began getting messages from the Centers for Disease Control and Prevention in Atlanta, where he worked. Then she got thousands of messages from men who had seen a posting of a nude woman, listing her e-mail address and offering sex during the Atlanta Olympics.
>
> But police said there was little they could do – until she got an anonymous message from someone saying he had followed Ms Armistead-Smathers and her five-year-old daughter from their post office box to her home.
>
> "People say 'It's online. Who cares? It isn't real.' Well this is real," Ms Armistead-Smathers said. "It's a matter of the same kind of small-minded bullies who maybe

wouldn't have done things in real life, but they have the power of anonymity from behind a keyboard, where they think no one will find them."

In general, stalkers want to exert power over their victims in some way, primarily through fear. The crux of a stalker's power is information about and knowledge of the victim. A stalker's ability to frighten and control a victim increases with the amount of information that he can gather about the victim. Stalkers use information like telephone numbers, addresses and personal preferences to impinge upon their victims' lives. Also, over time cyberstalkers can learn what sorts of things upset their victims and can use this knowledge to harass the victims further.

Since they depend heavily on information, it is no surprise that stalkers have taken to the Internet. After all, the Internet contains a vast amount of personal information about people and makes it relatively easy to search for specific items. As well as containing people's addresses and phone numbers, the Internet records many of our actions, choices, interests and desires. Databases containing social security numbers, credit card numbers, medical history, criminal records, and much more can also be accessed using the Internet. Additionally, cyberstalkers can use the Internet to harass specific individuals or acquire new victims from a large pool of potential targets.

ACQUIRING VICTIMS

Past studies indicate that many stalkers had a prior acquaintance with their victims before the stalking behavior began (Harmon *et al.* 1995). The implication of these studies is that investigators should pay particular attention to acquaintances of the victim. However, these studies are limited because many stalking cases are unsolved or unreported. Additionally, it is not clear if these studies apply to the Internet. After all, it is uncertain what constitutes an acquaintance on the Internet and the Internet makes it easier for cyberstalkers to find victims of opportunity[2]. Cyberstalkers can search the Web, browse through ICQ and AOL profiles, and lurk in IRC and AOL chat rooms looking for likely targets – vulnerable, under-confident individuals who will be easy to intimidate.

[2]A victim of opportunity is a victim whom a stalker was not acquainted with before the stalking began.

CASE EXAMPLE
One stalker repeatedly acquired victims of opportunity on AOL and used AOL's Instant Messenger to contact and harass them. The stalker also used online telephone directories to find victims' numbers, harassing them further by calling their homes. This approach left very little digital evidence because none of the victims recorded the Instant Messenger sessions, they did not know how to find the stalker's IP address, and they did not contact AOL in time to track the stalker[3].

Of course, the victims were distressed by this harassment, feeling powerless to stop the instant messages and phone calls. This sense of powerlessness was the primary goal of the cyberstalker. This stalker may have picked AOL as his stalking

[3]Recall from Chapter 7 that netstat can be used to view current and recent TCP/IP connections to a computer. Investigators can use an IP address to track down a cyberstalker.

territory because of the high number of inexperienced Internet users and the anonymity that it affords.

As a rule, investigators should rely more on evidence than on general studies. Although research can be useful to a certain degree, evidence is the most reliable source of information about a specific case and it is what the courts will use to make a decision.

ANONYMITY AND SURREPTITIOUS MONITORING

The Internet has the added advantage of protecting a stalker's identity and allowing a stalker to monitor a victim's activities. For example, stalkers acquainted with their victims use the Internet to hide their identity, sending forged or anonymous e-mail and using ICQ or AOL Instant Messenger to harass their victims. Also, stalkers can utilize ICQ, AOL Instant Messenger, and other applications (e.g. finger) to determine when a victim is online. Most disturbing of all, stalkers can use the Internet to spy on a victim. Although few cyberstalkers are skilled enough to break into a victim's e-mail account or intercept e-mail in transit, a cyberstalker can easily observe a conversation in a live chat room. This type of pre-surveillance of victims and amassing of information about potential victims might suggest intent to commit a crime but it is not a crime in itself, and is not stalking as defined by the law.

ESCALATION AND VIOLENCE

It is often suggested that stalkers will cease harassing their victims once they cease to provoke the desired response. However, some stalkers become aggravated when they do not get what they want and become increasingly threatening. As was mentioned at the beginning of this chapter, stalkers have resorted to violence and murder. Therefore, it is important for investigators to be extremely cautious when dealing with a stalking case. Investigators should examine the available evidence closely, protect the victim against further harm as much as possible, and consult with experts when in doubt. Most importantly, investigators should not make hurried judgements that are based primarily on studies of past cases.

INVESTIGATING CYBERSTALKING

There are several stages to investigating a cyberstalking case[4]:

- *Interview victim*: determine what evidence the victim has of cyberstalking and obtain details about the victim that can be used to develop victimology. The aim of this initial information-gathering stage is to confirm that a crime has been committed and to obtain enough information to move forward with the investigation.

[4]*These stages assume that the identity of the cyberstalker is unknown. Even if the victim suspects an individual, investigators are advised to explore alternative possibilities and suspects – question everything and assume nothing.*

- *Interview others*: if there are other people involved, interview them to compile a more complete picture of what occurred.

- *Victimology and risk assessment*: determine why an offender chose a specific victim and what risks the offender was willing to take to acquire that victim. The primary aim of this stage of the investigation is to understand the victim–offender relationship and determine where additional digital evidence might be found.

- *Search for additional digital evidence*: use what is known about the victim and cyberstalker to perform a thorough search of the Internet. Victimology is key at this stage, guiding investigators to locations that might interest the victim or individuals like the victim. The cyberstalker initially observed or encountered the victim somewhere and investigators should try to determine where. Consider the possibility that the cyberstalker encountered the victim in the physical world. The aim of this stage is to gather more information about the crime, the victim and the cyberstalker.

- *Crime scene characteristics*: examine crime scenes and cybertrails for distinguishing features (e.g. location, time, method of approach, choice of tools) and try to determine their significance to the cyberstalker. The aim of this stage is to gain a better understanding of the choices that the cyberstalker made and the needs that were fulfilled by these choices.

- *Motivation*: determine what personal needs the cyberstalking was fulfilling. Be careful to distinguish between intent (e.g. to exert power over the victim, to frighten the victim) and the personal needs that the cyberstalker's behavior satisfied (e.g. to feel powerful, to retaliate against the victim for a perceived wrong). The aim of this stage is to understand the cyberstalker well enough to reiterate.

If the identity of the cyberstalker is still not known, interview the victim again. The information that investigators have gathered might help the victim recall additional details or might suggest a likely suspect to the victim.

To assist investigators carry out each of these stages in an investigation, additional details are provided here.

INTERVIEWS

Investigators should interview the victim and other individuals with knowledge of the case to obtain details about the inception of the cyberstalking and the sorts of harassment the victim has been subjected to. In addition to collecting all of the evidence that the victim has of the cyberstalking, investigators should gather all of the details that are required to develop a thorough victimology as described in the next section.

While interviewing the victim, investigators should be sensitive to be as tactful as possible while questioning everything and assuming nothing. Keep in mind that victims tend to blame themselves, imagining that they encouraged the stalker in some way (e.g. by accepting initial advances or by making too much personal information available on the Internet) (Pathe 1997). It is therefore important for everyone involved in a cyberstalking investigation to help the victim regain confidence by acknowledging that the victim is not to blame. It is also crucial to help victims protect themselves from potential attacks. The National Center for Victims of Crime has an excellent set of guidelines developed specifically for victims of stalking (NCVC 1995).

VICTIMOLOGY

In addition to helping victims protect themselves against further harassment, investigators should try to determine how and why the offender selected a specific victim. To this end, investigators should determine whether the cyberstalker knew the victim, learned about the victim through a personal Web page, saw a Usenet message written by the victim, or noticed the victim in a chat room.

It is also useful to know why a victim made certain choices to help investigators make a risk assessment. For example, individuals who use the Internet to meet new people are at higher risk than individuals who make an effort to remain anonymous. In some instances, it may be quite evident why the cyberstalker has chosen a victim but if a cyberstalker chooses a low risk victim, investigators should try to determine which particular characteristics the victim possesses that might have attracted the cyberstalker's attention (e.g. residence, work place, hobby, personal interest, demeanor). These characteristics can be quite revealing about a cyberstalker and can direct investigators' attention to certain areas or individuals.

Questions to ask at this stage include:

- Does the victim know or suspect why, how and/or when the cyberstalking began?
- What Internet Service Provider(s) do(es) the victim use and why?
- What online services does the victim use and why (e.g. Web, free e-mail services, Usenet, IRC)?
- When does the victim use the Internet and the various Internet services (does the harassment occur at specific times, suggesting that the cyberstalker has a schedule or is aware of the victim's schedule)?
- What does the victim do on the Internet and why?
- Does the victim have personal Web pages or other personal information on the Internet (e.g. AOL profile, ICQ Web page, customized finger output)? What information do these items contain?

In addition to the victim's Internet activities, investigators should examine the victim's physical surroundings and real world activities.

When the identity of the cyberstalker is known or suspected, it might not seem necessary to develop a complete victimology. Although it is crucial to investigate suspects, this should not be done at the expense of all else. Time spent trying to understand the victim–offender relationship can help investigators understand the offender, protect the victim, locate additional evidence, and discover additional victims. Furthermore, there is always the chance that the suspect is innocent, in which case investigators can use the victimology that they have developed to find other likely suspects.

RISK ASSESSMENT

A key aspect of developing victimology is determining victim and offender risk. Generally, women are at greater risk than men of being cyberstalked and new Internet users are at greater risk than experienced Internet users. Individuals who frequent the equivalent of singles bars on the Internet are at greater risk than those who just use the Internet to search for information. A woman who puts her picture on a Web page with some biographical information, an address and phone number is at high risk because cyberstalkers can fixate on the picture, obtain personal information about the woman from the Web page, and start harassing her over the phone or in person.

Bear in mind that victim risk is not an absolute thing – it depends on the circumstances. A careful individual who avoids high risk situations in the physical world might be less cautious on the Internet. For example, individuals who are not famous in the world at large might have celebrity status in a certain area of the Internet, putting them at high risk of being stalked by someone familiar with that area. Individuals who are sexually reserved in the physical world might partake in extensive sexual role-playing on the Internet, putting them at high risk of being cyberstalked.

If a cyberstalker selects a low risk victim, investigators should try to determine what attracted the offender to the victim. Also, investigators should determine what the offender was willing to risk when harassing the victim. Remember that offender risk is the risk as an offender perceives it – investigators should not try to interpret an offender's behavior based on the risks they perceive. An offender will not necessarily be concerned by the risks that others perceive. For example, some cyberstalkers do not perceive apprehension as a great risk, only an inconvenience that would temporarily interfere with his ability to achieve his goal (to harass the victim) and will continue to harass their victims, even when they are under investigation.

SEARCH

Investigators should perform a thorough search of the Internet using what is known about the victim and the offender and should examine personal computers, log files on servers, and all other available sources of digital evidence as described in this text. For example, when a cyberstalker uses e-mail to harass a victim, the messages should be collected and examined. Also, other e-mail that the victim has received should be examined to determine if the stalker sent forged messages to deceive the victim. Log files of the e-mail server that was used to send and receive the e-mail should be examined to confirm the events in question. Log files sometimes reveal other things that the cyberstalker was doing (e.g. masquerading as the victim, harassing other victims) and can contain information that leads directly to the cyberstalker.

CASE EXAMPLE

Gary Steven Dellapenta became the first person to be convicted under the new section of California's stalking law that specifically includes electronic communications. After being turned down by a woman named Randi Barber, Dellapenta retaliated by impersonating her on the Internet and claiming she fantasized about being raped.

Using nicknames such as "playfulkitty4U" and "kinkygal30," Dellapenta placed online personal ads and sent messages saying such things as "I'm into the rape fantasy and gang-bang fantasy too." He gave respondents Barber's address and telephone number, directions to her home, details of her social plans and even advice on how to short-circuit her alarm system.

Barber became alarmed when men began leaving messages on her answer machine and turning up at her apartment. In an interview (Newsweek 1999), Barber recalled that one of the visitors left after she hid silently for a few minutes, but phoned her apartment later. "What do you want?" she pleaded. "Why are you doing this?" The man explained that he was responding to the sexy ad she had placed on the Internet.

"What ad? What did it say?" Barber asked. "Am I in big trouble?"

"Let me put it to you this way," the caller said. "You could get raped."

When Barber put a note on her door to discourage the men who were responding to the personal ads, Dellapenta put new information on the Internet claiming that the note was just part of the fantasy.

In an effort to gather evidence against Dellapenta, Barber kept recordings of messages that were left on her machine and contacted each caller, asking for any information that about the cyberstalker. Two men cooperated with her request for help, but it was ultimately her father who gathered the evidence that was necessary to identify Dellapenta.

Barber's father helped to uncover Dellapenta's identity by posing as an ad respondent and turning the e-mails he received over to investigators.

[Investigators] traced the e-mails from the Web sites at which they were posted to the servers used to access the sites. Search warrants compelled the Internet companies to identify the user. All the paths led police back to Dellapenta. "When you go on the Internet, you leave fingerprints – we can tell exactly where you've been," says sheriff's investigator Mike Gurzi, who would eventually verify that all the e-mails originated from Dellapenta's computer after studying his hard drive. The alleged stalker's MO was tellingly simple: police say he opened up a number of free Internet e-mail accounts pretending to be the victim, posted the crude ads under a salacious log-on name and started e-mailing the men who responded. (Newsweek 1999)

Dellapenta admitted to authorities that he had an "inner rage" against Barber and pleaded guilty to one count of stalking and three counts of solicitation of sexual assault.

When searching for evidence of cyberstalking it is useful to distinguish between the offender's harassing behaviors and surreptitious monitoring behaviors. A victim is usually only aware of the harassment component of cyberstalking. However, cyberstalkers often engage in additional activities that the victim is not aware of. Therefore, investigators should not limit their search to the evidence of harassment that the victim is already aware of but should look for evidence of both harassment and surreptitious monitoring.

If the victim frequented certain areas, investigators should comb those areas for information and should attempt to see them from the cyberstalker's perspective. Could the cyberstalker have monitored the victim's activities in those areas? If so, would this monitoring have generated any digital evidence? For example, if the victim maintains a Web page, the cyberstalker might have monitored its development in which case the Web server log would contain the cyberstalker's IP address (with associated times) and the cyberstalker's personal computer would indicate that the page had been viewed (and when it was viewed). If the cyberstalker monitored the victim in IRC, he might have kept log files of the chat sessions. If the cyberstalker broke into the victim's e-mail account the log files on the e-mail server should reflect this.

Keep in mind that the evidence search and seizure stage of an investigation forms the foundation of the case – incomplete searches and poorly collected digital evidence will result in a weak case. It is therefore crucial to apply the forensic science concepts presented in this text diligently. Investigators should collect, document and preserve digital evidence in a way that will facilitate the reconstruction and prosecution processes. Also investigators should become intimately familiar with available digital evidence, looking for class and individualizing characteristics in an effort to maximize its potential.

CRIME SCENE CHARACTERISTICS

When investigating cyberstalking, investigators might not be able to define the primary crime scene clearly because digital evidence is often spread all over the Internet. However, the same principle of behavioral evidence analysis applies – aspects of a cyberstalker's behavior can be determined from choices and decisions that a cyberstalker made and the evidence that was left behind, destroyed, or taken away. Therefore, investigators should thoroughly examine the point of contact and cybertrails (e.g. the Web, Usenet, personal computers) for digital evidence that exposes the offender's behavior.

To begin with, investigators should ask themselves why a particular cyberstalker used the Internet – what need did this fulfill? Was the cyberstalker using the Internet to obtain victims, to remain anonymous or both? Investigators should also ask why a cyberstalker used particular areas of the Internet – what affordances did the Internet provide? MO and signature behaviors can usually be discerned from the way a cyberstalker approaches and harasses victims on the Internet.

How cyberstalkers use the Internet can say a lot about their skill level, goals and motivations. Using IRC rather than e-mail to harass victims suggests a higher skill level and a desire to gain instantaneous access to the victim while remaining anonymous. The choice of technology will also determine what digital evidence is available. Unless a victim keeps a log, harassment on IRC leaves very little evidence whereas harassing e-mail messages are enduring and can be used to track down the sender.

Additionally, investigators can learn a great deal about offenders' needs and choices by carefully examining their words, actions and reactions. Increases and decreases in intensity in reaction to unexpected occurrences are particularly revealing. For example, when a cyberstalker's primary mode of contact with a victim is blocked the cyberstalker might be discouraged, unperturbed or aggravated. How cyberstalkers choose to react to setbacks indicates how determined they are to harass specific victims and what they hope to achieve through the harassment. Also, a cyberstalker's intelligence, skill level and identity can be revealed when he modifies his behavior and use of technology to overcome obstacles.

MOTIVATIONAL ASPECTS OF CYBERSTALKING

There have been a number of attempts to categorize stalking behavior and develop specialized typologies (Meloy 1998). However, these typologies were not developed with investigations in mind and are primarily used by clinicians to diagnose mental illnesses and administer appropriate treatments.

When investigating cyberstalking, the motivational typologies discussed in Chapter 3 can be used as a sounding board to gain a greater understanding of stalkers' motivations. Recall the case example in Chapter 3 describing Andrew Archameau's power reassurance behaviors. Also, as described earlier in this chapter, some stalkers pick their victims opportunistically and get satisfaction by intimidating them, fitting into the power-assertive typology.

Other stalkers are driven by a need to retaliate against their victims for perceived wrongs, exhibiting many of the behaviors described in the anger retaliatory typology. For instance, Dellapenta, the Californian cyberstalker who went to great lengths to terrify Randi Barber, stated that he has an "inner rage" directed at Barber that he could not control. Dellapenta's behavior confirms this statement, indicating that he was retaliating against Barber for a perceived wrong. His messages were degrading and were designed to bring harm to Barber. Furthermore, Dellapenta tried to arrange for other people to harm Barber, indicating that he did feel the need to hurt her himself. Although it is possible that Dellapenta felt some desire to assert power over Barber, his behavior indicates that he was primarily driven by a desire to bring harm to her.

SUMMARY

Cyberstalking is not different from regular stalking – the Internet is just another tool that facilitates the act of stalking. In fact, many cyberstalkers also use the telephone and their physical presence to achieve their goals. Stalkers use the Internet to acquire victims, gather information, monitor victims, hide their identities and avoid capture. Although cyberstalkers can become quite adept at using the Internet, investigators with a solid understanding of the Internet and a strong investigative methodology will usually be able to discover the identity of a cyberstalker.

With regard to a strong investigative methodology, investigators should get into the habit of following the steps described in this chapter (interviewing victims, developing victimology, searching for additional evidence, analyzing crime scenes, and understanding motivation).

The type of digital evidence that is available in a cyberstalking case depends on the technologies that the stalker uses. However, a cyberstalker's personal computer usually contains the most digital evidence, including messages sent to the victim, information gathered about the victim, and even information about other victims.

It is difficult to make accurate generalizations about cyberstalkers because a wide variety of circumstances can lead to cyberstalking. A love interest turned sour can result in obsessive and retaliatory behavior. An individual's desire for power can drive him to select and harass vulnerable victims opportunistically. The list goes on, and any attempt to generalize or categorize necessarily excludes some of the complexity and nuances of the problem. Therefore, investigators who hope to address this problem thoroughly should be wary of generalizations and categorizations, only using them to understand available evidence further.

REFERENCES

Associated Press (1997) "As online harassment grows, calls for new laws follow,"
1 April.

Foote, D. (1999) "You Could Get Raped," *Newsweek 8* February.

Harmon, R., Rosner, R. and Owens, H. (1995) "Obsessional Harassment and Erotomania
in a Criminal Court Population," *Journal of Forensic Science*, JFSCA, 40 (20): 188–96.

Meloy, J. R. (ed.) (1998) *The Psychology of Stalking: Clinical and Forensic Perspectives*,
Academic Press.

Meloy, J. R. (1999) "Stalking: An Old Behavior, A New Crime," in Meloy, J.R. (ed.)
Psychiatric Clinics of North America.

National Center for Victims of Crime (1995) *Safety* [available at
http://www.ncvc.org/infolink/svsafety.htm].

Pathe, M. and Mullen, P. E. (1997) The Impact of Stalkers on their Victims," *British
Journal of Psychiatry*, 170:12–17.

RESOURCES

Safe Internet [http://www.safeinternet.com/stalking.html]

Cyber Angels [http://www.cyberangels.org/stalking.html]

National Center for Victims of Crime [http://www.ncvc.org/infolink/info46.htm]

The Anti Stalking Website [http://www.antistalking.com/aboutstalkers.htm]

Stalking Victim's Sanctuary [http://www.stalkingvictims.com]

Victim-Assistance Online [http://www.vaonline.org]

## CHAPTER 12

DIGITAL EVIDENCE AS ALIBI

The key pieces of information in an alibi are time and location. When an individual does anything involving a computer or network, the time and location is often noted, generating digital evidence that can be used to support or refute an alibi. For example, telephone calls, credit card purchases and ATM transactions are all supported by computer networks that keep detailed logs of activities. Telephone companies keep an archive of the number dialed, the time and duration of the call, and sometimes the caller's number. Credit card companies keep records of the dates, times and locations of all purchases. Similarly, banks keep track of the dates, times and locations of all deposits and withdrawals. These dates, times and locations reside on computers for an indefinite period of time and individuals receive a report of this information each month in the form of a bill or financial statement.

Other computer networks, like the Internet, also contain a large amount of information about times and locations. When an e-mail message is sent, the time and originating IP addresses are noted in the header. Log files that contain information about activities on a network are especially useful when investigating an alibi because they contain times, IP addresses, a brief description of what occurred, and sometimes even the individual computer account that was involved. However, computer times and IP addresses can be manipulated, allowing a criminal to create a false alibi.

On many computers it requires minimal skill to change the clock or the creation time of a file. Also, people can program a computer to perform an action, like sending an e-mail message, at a specific time. In many cases, scheduling events does not require any programming skill – it is a simple feature of the operating system. Similarly, IP addresses can be changed, allowing individuals to pretend that they are connected to a network from another location. Therefore, investigators should not rely on one piece of digital evidence when examining an alibi – they should look for an associated cybertrail. This chapter discusses the process of investigating an alibi when digital evidence is involved, and uses scenarios to demonstrate the strengths and weaknesses of digital evidence as an alibi.

INVESTIGATING AN ALIBI

When investigating an alibi that depends on digital evidence, the first step is to assess the reliability of the information on the computers and networks involved. Some computers are configured to synchronize their clocks regularly with very accurate time satellites and make a log of any discrepancies. Other computers allow anyone to change their clocks and do not keep logs of time changes. Some computer networks control and monitor which computers are assigned specific IP addresses using protocols like BOOTP and DHCP. Other networks do not strictly control IP address assignments, allowing anyone to change the IP address on a computer.

In some situations, interviewing several individuals who are familiar with the computer or network involved will be sufficient to determine if an alibi is solid. These individuals should be able to explain how easy or difficult it is to change information on their system. For example, a system administrator can usually illustrate how the time on a specific computer can be altered and the effects of such a change. If log files are generated when the time is changed, these log files should be examined for digital evidence related to the alibi.

In other situations, especially when an obscure piece of equipment is involved, it might be necessary to perform extensive research – reading through documentation, searching the Internet for related information, and even contacting manufacturers with specific questions about how their products function. The aim of this research is to determine the reliability of the information on the computer system, to confirm the existence of logs that could be used to support or refute an alibi and to determine if events that support or refute an alibi were physically possible. If no documentation is available, the manufacturer is no longer in business, or the equipment/network is so complicated that nobody fully understands how it works, it might be necessary to recreate the events surrounding the alibi to determine the reliability of the associated digital evidence.

By performing the same actions that resulted in an alibi, an investigator can determine what digital evidence should exist. The digital data that is created when investigators recreate the events surrounding an alibi can be compared with the original digital evidence. If the alibi is false, there should be some discrepancies. Ideally, this recreation process should be performed using a test system rather than the actual system to avoid destroying important digital evidence. A test system should resemble the actual system closely enough to enable investigators to recreate the alibi that they are trying to verify. If a test system is not available it is crucial to back up all potential digital evidence before attempting to recreate an alibi.

It is quite difficult to fabricate an alibi on a network successfully because an individual rarely has the ability to falsify digital evidence on all of the computers that are involved. If an alibi is false, a thorough examination of the computers involved will usually turn up some obvious inconsistencies. The most challenging situations arise when investigators cannot find any evidence to support or refute an alibi. When this situation arises, it is important to remember an axiom from forensic science – absence of evidence is not evidence of absence. If a person claims to have checked e-mail on a given day from a specific location and there is no evidence to support this assertion, that does not mean that the person is lying. No amount of research into the reliability of the logging process will change the fact that an absence of evidence is not evidence of absence. It is crucial to base all assertions on solid supporting evidence, not on an absence of evidence. To demonstrate that someone is lying about an alibi, it is necessary to find evidence that clearly demonstrates the lie.

CASE EXAMPLE
A suspect claims to have been at work during the weekend at the time of a homicide, fixing a network problem, and checking e-mail. The investigators were not familiar with computer networks and depended heavily on the system administrators at the organization where the suspect worked. Unfortunately, the system administrators were not fully briefed on the details of the case and did not have all of the information necessary to examine their log files thoroughly[1].

As a result, one of the most important IP addresses involved was not included in the search and the investigators could not find any indication that the suspect checked his e-mail. The investigators jumped to the conclusion that the suspect was lying about his alibi based on this absence of evidence.

A few days later, the suspect was at work and noticed a timestamp that was created when he fixed the network problem on the day of the crime. The suspect prudently asked his coworkers to witness and document the evidence. However, when the suspect presented this evidence to the investigators, they were incredulous, assuming that he had fabricated the timestamp after the fact. However, the truth of the matter was that the investigators did not research the network components involved and did not recognize an important source of digital evidence. Their negligence led them to suspect the wrong man, causing over two years of disruption in his life, costing him his job, costing the state and organization untold amounts of money, and worst of all, letting the actual murderer go free.

[1]*The oversight was noticed several years later when the case was being tried.*

An interesting aspect of investigating an alibi is that no amount of supporting evidence can prove conclusively that an individual was in a specific place at a specific time. With enough knowledge and resources, any amount of physical and digital evidence can be falsified to fabricate an alibi. Therefore, a large amount of supporting evidence indicates that the alibi is probably true, but not definitely true. For this reason, it rarely makes sense for a defense attorney to spend time and resources searching for digital evidence that supports a client's alibi. No amount of evidence will prove that the alibi is true and the more the alibi is examined, the more likely it is that an inconsistency will be found that could weaken the attorney's ability to defend the client.

TIME AS ALIBI

Suppose that, on 19 March 1999, an individual broke into the Museum of Fine Arts in Boston and stole a precious object. Security cameras show a masked burglar entering the museum at 8 pm and leaving at 8:30. The prime suspect claims to have been at home in New York, hundreds of miles away from Boston, when the crime was committed. According to the suspect, the only noteworthy thing he did that evening was to send an e-mail to a friend. The friend is very cooperative and provides investigators with the following e-mail.

> From: suspect@newyork.net
>
> Date: Fri, 19 Mar 1999 20:10:05 EST
>
> Subject: A quick hello
>
> To: witness@miami.net
>
> I am sitting innocently at home with nothing to do and I thought I would drop a line to say hello.

The e-mail does suggest that the suspect sent the message at the time of the burglary. However, the investigators are familiar enough with e-mail to know that the header will contain dates and times of all of the computers that handled the message. They obtain the full header and examine it for any discrepancies.

> Received: from mail.newyork.net by mail.miami.net (8.8.5/8.8.5) with ESMTP id
>
>   NAA23905 for <witness@miami.net>; Sat, 20 Mar 1999 13:49:19 -0500 (EST)
>
> Received: from suspectshome.newyork.net by mail.newyork.net (PMDF V5.1-10
>
>   #20971) with SMTP id <01J9206HG9T400NWE6@newyork.net> for
>   witness@miami.net; Sat, 20 Mar 1999 13:49:22 EST
>
> From: suspect@newyork.net
>
> Date: Fri, 19 Mar 1999 20:10:05 EST
>
> Subject: A quick hello
>
> To: witness@miami.net
>
> Message-id: <01J9206VTW2E00NWE6@newyork.net>
>
> I am sitting innocently at home with nothing to do and I thought I would drop a line to say hello.

Sure enough, the dates and times in the header do not match, indicating that the e-mail message was forged on the afternoon of 20 March. The suspect's alibi is refuted. The investigators obtain the related log entries from the two mail servers that handled the message (mail.newyork.net and mail.miami.net) as further proof that the message was sent on 20 March rather than on the night of the crime. Additionally, the investigators search the suspect's e-mail and discover messages that he sent to himself earlier in the week, testing and refining his forging skills. Finally, to demonstrate how the suspect sent the forged e-mail, the investigators perform the following e-mail forgery steps, inserting the false date (Fri, 19 Mar 1999 20:10:05 EST) just as the suspect did:

```
% telnet mail.newyork.net 25

Trying 10.232.19.48...

Connected to mail.newyork.net.

Escape character is '^]'.

220 mail.newyork.net — Server ESMTP (PMDF V5.1-10 #20971)

helo suspectshome.newyork.net

250 mail.newyork.net OK, suspectshome.newyork.net.

mail from: suspect@newyork.net

250 2.5.0 Address Ok.

rcpt to: witness@miami.net

250 2.1.5 witness@miami.net OK.

data

354 Enter mail, end with a single ".".

Subject: A quick hello

Date: Fri, 19 Mar 1999 20:10:05 EST

I am sitting innocently at home with nothing to do and I thought I would drop a
line to say hello.

.

250 2.5.0 Ok.

quit
```

After being presented with this evidence, the suspect admits to stealing the precious object and selling it on the black market. The suspect identifies the buyer and the object is recovered.

LOCATION AS ALIBI

Suppose that the same precious object was stolen again when the burglar from the previous scenario was released from prison a few months later. This time, however, the burglar claims to have been in California, thousands of miles away, starting a new life. The burglar's parole officer does not think that the suspect left California but cannot be certain. The only evidence that supports the suspect's alibi is an e-mail message to his friend in Miami. Though the suspect's friend is irritated at being involved again, she gives the investigators the following e-mail.

> Received: from mail.california.net by mail.miami.net (8.8.5/8.8.5) with ESMTP id
>
> NAA23905 for <witness@miami.net>; Fri, 21 May 1999 22:03:46 EST -0500 (EST)
>
> Received: from suspectshome.california.net by mail.california.(InterMail v03.02.07
>
> 118 124) with SMTP id <19990521220346.CBJN9925@california.net> for
> <witness@miami.net>; Fri, 21 May 1999 22:03:46 +0000
>
> From: suspect@california.net
>
> Date: Fri, 21 May 1999 22:03:46 EST
>
> Subject: New E-mail Address
>
> To: witness@miami.net
>
> Message-id: < 001801be724c$dc842000$1f02480c@california.net>
>
> I have moved to California to start afresh. You can send e-mail to me at this address.

The investigators examine the e-mail header, determine that it was sent while the burglar was in the museum, and find no indication that the e-mail was forged. The suspect claims that someone is trying to frame him and assures the investigators that he has no knowledge of the crime. The following month, when the Museum of Fine Arts received its phone bill, an administrator finds an unusual telephone call to California on the night of the burglary. The investigators are notified and they determine that the number belongs to an ISP in California (california.net). Unfortunately, the ISP's dialup logs were deleted several weeks earlier and there is not enough evidence to link the suspect to the telephone call. The investigators search the suspect's computer but do not find any incriminating evidence.

Investigators are stumped until it occurs to them to investigate the suspect's friend in Miami more thoroughly. By examining the friend's credit card records, the investigators determine that she bought a plane ticket to Boston on the day of the burglary. Also, the investigators find that her laptop is configured to connect to california.net and her telephone records show that she made several calls from Miami to the ISP while planning the robbery. Finally, investigators search the slack space on her hard drive and find remnants of the e-mail message that she sent from the Museum of Fine Arts during the robbery. When presented with all of this digital evidence, the woman admits to stealing the precious object and implicating the original suspect. This time a different buyer is identified and the object is recovered once again.

SUMMARY

As investigators learn about new technologies, it is useful to think about how they will affect routine aspects of investigations such as alibis. With people spending an increasing amount of time using computers and networks, there are bound to be more alibis that depend on digital evidence. Computers contain information about times and locations that can be used to confirm or refute an alibi. However, digital evidence can rarely prove conclusively that someone was in a specific place at a specific time. Remember that IP addresses are associated with computers – not individuals. Therefore, an accomplice could help a criminal fabricate an alibi using the criminal's computer. Also, some computer times can be changed to corroborate an alibi. By following cybertrails, investigators might find a computer program that simulated an alibi or they might learn that the computer clock was changed at the time in question.

Though it is easy to change the time of a personal computer, many computers keep a log of time changes. Also, when dealing with computers on a network, it becomes more difficult to change computer times. When multiple computers are involved, changing the time on one will result in a notable inconsistency with others. Therefore, when examining an alibi that involves a computer or network, investigators should search log files for time inconsistencies.

Finally, it is important to examine the computer equipment closely. How a component was configured or how it was used can make certain scenarios impossible. Knowing what was possible and what was impossible can make it easier to support or refute an alibi.

## CHAPTER 13

LAWS, JURISDICTION, SEARCH AND SEIZURE

Many cybercrimes can be addressed using existing laws. After all, cybercrime is just a new manifestation of age-old crimes – the only difference is that a new technology is involved. At least one attorney realized this fact in making use of an old legal precedent when dealing with new problems in cyberspace.

> Trespass to property or chattels (Compuserve Incorporated v. Cyber Promotions, Inc., 962 F. Supp. 1015 [S.D. Ohio 1997]):
> In 1997, Compuserve, a large online service provider, brought action against Cyber Promotions, Inc. and Sanford Wallace for sending large amounts of unsolicited, e-mail advertisements (SPAM) to Compuserve subscribers. This legal action arose after Cyberpromotions responded to Compuserve's initial complaints by sending even more SPAM than before. Compuserve attempted to filter out the SPAM but Cyberpromotions took measures to avoid the e-mail filtering. In court, Cyberpromotions argued that they had every right to send SPAM to Compuserve customers because, by connecting to the Internet, Compuserve had essentially invited the public to enter their establishment for business purposes. A clever and well-read attorney countered, claiming "trespass to property or chattels," citing a legal precedent from the 1800s. Based on the strength (and probably the cleverness) of this argument, Cyberpromotions was prohibited from sending SPAM to any Compuserve e-mail address.

Rather than count on the ingenuity of individual attorneys to adapt existing laws to cybercrime, several laws have been amended to include computer technology specifically. For instance, laws prohibiting the creation and distribution of child pornography have been amended to include the use of computers and networks (Child Pornography and Prevention Act of 1996 – 18 USC §2251(c)(2)(A) & (B)). Also, existing stalking laws have been modified to include cyberstalking (California Penal Code 646.9).

Although existing laws can be applied to most forms of cybercrime, lawmakers perceived a need for separate statutes to deal unambiguously with certain forms of computer abuse. This is stated most explicitly in Florida's computer crime statute:

> While various forms of computer crime might possibly be the subject of criminal charges based on other provisions of law, it is appropriate and desirable that a

supplemental and additional statute be provided which proscribes various forms of computer abuse. (Fla. Stat. 815.02)

This chapter describes how these new laws evolved in various countries and presents two US laws that were enacted with cybercrime in mind: the Computer Fraud and Abuse Act (CFAA) and the Electronic Communications and Privacy Act (ECPA). This chapter also discusses jurisdiction, search and seizure.

TIMELINE OF COMPUTER CRIME LAW

Besides component theft, some of the earliest recorded computer crimes occurred in 1969 and 1970 when student protestors burned computers at various universities. At about the same time, individuals were discovering methods for gaining unauthorized access to large time-shared computers (essentially stealing time on the computers), an act that was not illegal at the time. In the 1970s many crimes involving computers were dealt with using existing laws. However, there were some legal struggles because digital property was seen as intangible and therefore outside of the laws protecting physical property. Since then, the distinction between digital and physical property has become less pronounced and the same laws are often used to protect both.

Computer intrusion and fraud committed with the help of computers were the first crimes to be widely recognized as a new type of crime. The first computer crime law to address computer fraud and intrusion, the Florida Computer Crimes Act, was enacted in Florida in 1978 after a highly publicized incident at the Flagler Dog Track. Employees at the track used a computer to print fraudulent winning tickets. The Florida Computer Crimes Act also defined all unauthorized access to a computer as a crime, even if there was no maliciousness in the act. This stringent view of computer intrusion was radical at the time but has since been adopted by every US state except Vermont. This change of heart about computer cracking was largely in reaction to the growing publicity received by computer crackers in the early 1980s. It was during this time that governments around the world started enacting similar laws. Canada was the first country to enact a federal law to address computer crime specifically in amending their Criminal Code in 1983. The US Federal Computer Fraud and Abuse Act was passed in 1984 and amended in 1986, 1988, 1989 and 1990. The Australian Crimes Act was amended in 1989 to include Offenses Relating to Computers (section 76) and the Australian states enacted similar laws at around the same time. In Britain, the Computer Abuse Act was passed in 1990 to criminalize computer cracking specifically. Many other countries have also enacted new laws to deal with computer crime but there are still many that have not.

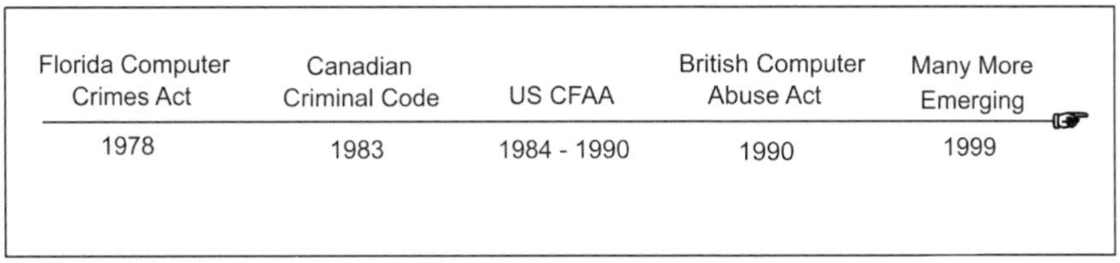

Florida Computer Crimes Act	Canadian Criminal Code	US CFAA	British Computer Abuse Act	Many More Emerging
1978	1983	1984 - 1990	1990	1999

Figure 13.1

Time line of key events in the development of computer crime laws.

In the 1990s, the commercialization of the Internet and the development of the World Wide Web popularized the Internet, making it accessible to millions. Crime on the global network diversified and the focus moved away from computer crackers. As a result, new laws to deal with copyright, child pornography, and privacy were enacted. A more detailed view of the history of computer crime can be found in *Crime, Deviance and the Computer* (Hollinger 1997)[1].

THE COMPUTER FRAUD AND ABUSE ACT OF 1986 (CFAA)

The Computer Fraud and Abuse Act (CFAA) was enacted in 1984 and was amended by the Computer Fraud and Abuse Act of 1986 (this act has been amended several times since). Unfortunately, the CFAA has not been very useful – it has only been used a few times since its enactment. Richard Morris is one of the few individuals to be prosecuted under the CFAA for releasing his infamous Internet worm.

[1] *Crime, Deviance and the Computer consists of a collection of articles from various authors and is separated into four sections: The Discovery of Computer Abuse (1946–76), The Criminalization of Computer Crime (1977–87), The Demonization of Hackers (1988–92), and The Censorship Period (1993–present).*

> The Internet worm (US v. Morris, 928 F.2d 504 [2d Cir., 1991]):
> In 1988, Robert Morris, a graduate student at Cornell University and the son of the National Computer Security Center's chief scientist, made history by creating and letting loose a computer program that replicated itself repeatedly on thousands of machines on the Internet. This program, called a worm, exploited vulnerabilities in a widely used operating system called BSD UNIX. Although this worm automatically broke into computers and made efforts to hide itself, it made no explicit attempt to steal from or damage the computers it infected. In essence, its only purpose was to break into as many computers as it could. Morris later claimed that he was simply experimenting, trying to add to his already formidable knowledge of computers. Unfortunately, the experiment went terribly wrong. The worm was so successful at replicating itself that it overloaded the Internet, bringing more than 6000 installations to a grinding halt (Spafford 1989).
>
> After a few days, the worm was eradicated, but the aftermath was even more dramatic than the event itself. The worm had demonstrated, more than any other single event, that the Internet was not secure and that trust alone was not sufficient protection against attack. Anger and fear overshadowed the trust that had made the Internet possible. People were out for blood and Morris made history once again by being the first person to be convicted by jury under the Computer Fraud and Abuse Act (CFAA) of 1986 (two others had been convicted

under the CFAA but not by a jury). He was required to pay the maximum allowable under the CFAA ($10,000), serve three years' probation, and contribute 400 hours of community service.

The CFAA was primarily designed to protect national security, financial and commercial information, medical treatment and interstate communication systems. The CFAA protects these systems against a wide range of malicious acts including unauthorized access. In this statute, access to a computer is considered to be unauthorized if it is without permission or if it exceeds the permission originally granted. Therefore, authorized users can be liable under this statute if they do something that they were not permitted to do. In addition to addressing intrusion and damage, this statute prohibits denial of service attacks that cause a loss of $1000 or more. Additionally, the CFAA allows any person who suffers a loss as a result of one of the actions covered by the Act to bring a civil action against the violator to obtain compensation.

An overview of this statute is provided in Table 13.1 with a summary of the most interesting portions.

Table 13.1

Summary of the Computer Fraud and Abuse Act of 1986.

SECTION	SUMMARY	PENALTIES
Section (a)(1)	Obtaining unauthorized access to information regarding national defense, foreign relations, and atomic energy	A fine and/or up to 10 years' imprisonment for a first offense and up to 20 years for subsequent offenses
Section (a)(2)	Obtaining unauthorized access to records from a financial institution, credit card issuer, or consumer-reporting agency	A fine and/or up to 1 year's imprisonment for a first offense and up to 10 years for subsequent offenses
Section (a)(3)	Interfering with government operations by obtaining unauthorized access to their computers or computers that they use	A fine and/or up to 1 year's imprisonment for a first offense and up to 10 years for subsequent offenses
Section (a)(4)	Obtaining unauthorized access to a Federal interest computer[2] to commit fraud or theft unless the object of the fraud and the thing obtained consists only of the use of the computer	A fine and/or up to 5 years' imprisonment for a first offense and up to 10 years for subsequent offenses
Section (a)(5)(A)	"Whoever … through means of a computer used in interstate commerce or communications, knowingly causes the transmission of a program, information, code, or command to a computer or computer system if the person causing the transmission intends that such transmission will damage, or cause damage to, a computer, computer system, network, information, data, or program; or withhold or deny, or cause the withholding or denial, of the use of a computer, computer services, system or network, information, data, or program" provided the	A fine and/or up to 5 years' imprisonment for a first offense and up to 10 years for subsequent offenses

[2] *A Federal interest computer is a computer used exclusively by a financial institution or the United States Government, used on a nonexclusive basis but where the conduct affects use by the financial institution or government or which is one of two or more computers used in committing the offense, not all of which are located in the same state.*

Table 13.1 (cont'd).

	access is unauthorized and causes loss or damage of $1000 or more over a one year period or "modifies or impairs, or potentially modifies or impairs, the medical examination, medical diagnosis, medical treatment, or medical care of one or more individuals."	
Section (a)(5)(B)	"Whoever ... through means of a computer used in interstate commerce or communications, knowingly causes the transmission of a program, information, code, or command to a computer or computer system with reckless disregard of a substantial and unjustifiable risk that the transmission will damage, or cause damage to, a computer, computer system, network, information, data, or program; or withhold or deny, or cause the withholding or denial, of the use of a computer, computer services, system or network, information, data, or program" provided the access is unauthorized and causes loss or damage of $1000 or more over a one year period or "modifies or impairs, or potentially modifies or impairs, the medical examination, medical diagnosis, medical treatment, or medical care of one or more individuals."	A fine and/or up to 1 year's imprisonment
Section (a)(6)	Trafficking in passwords that affect interstate commerce or involve the password to a computer that is used by or for the US government	A fine and/or up to 1 year's imprisonment for a first offense and up to 10 years for subsequent offenses

It is worth noting that the CFAA is not designed to exclude other laws. Therefore, the CFAA can be used to bring additional charges against an individual for a single crime as two members of a group called the Legion of Doom discovered.

Legion of Doom (US v. Riggs, 749 F. Supp. 414 [N.D. Ill. 1990])
In 1988, Robert Riggs gained unauthorized access to the computer system of a telephone company named Bell South and downloaded information describing an enhanced 911 system for handling emergency services in municipalities (e.g. police, fire, and ambulance calls). Riggs then gave the materials to Craig Neidorf who published them in an online newsletter called PHRACK. Riggs and Neidorf were charged under three separate laws: the CFAA; a federal wire fraud statute; and a statute prohibiting interstate transportation of stolen property. The court specifically noted that the CFAA could be used in conjunction with other laws. Riggs was convicted for breaking into the Bell South computer system. The charges against Neidorf were dropped after it transpired that the materials he published were not as private as Bell South had claimed – they were selling copies to anyone who requested them.

Another noteworthy ruling involving the CFAA occurred when a recently dismissed bank employee named Bernadette Sablan was charged with damaging her employer's records (US v. Sablan, 92 F.3d 865 [9th Cir. 1995]). Sablan claimed to be drunk at the time and argued that she did not intend to do any damage. However, Sablan was convicted after the court determined that the CFAA only requires intent to gain unauthorized access to the computer and does not require intent to do damage.

All states except Vermont have additional computer crime statutes that extend the CFAA. These state statutes apply to all computers, not just government, financial, or communication systems. Also, many of these state statutes make it illegal to break into a computer (even if no damage is done), alter or destroy data (even if the damage is recoverable), steal services, deny another person access, or use the computer with intent to commit a variety of crimes. However, as with the CFAA, these state computer crime statutes are used infrequently. Because these laws are new and are often vaguely worded, it can be difficult to find attorneys who understand the issues and procedures. Also, few organizations (including law enforcement agencies) are willing to spend the time and resources necessary to investigate a computer crime when they are uncertain of the results.

ELECTRONIC COMMUNICATIONS AND PRIVACY ACT

Investigators sometimes need to obtain the destination, origin or even the contents of certain communications. Because all of this information is normally considered private, certain procedures have been put in place to prevent anyone, particularly the government, from misusing this information. The Fourth Amendment requires that a search warrant be secured before law enforcement officers can search a person's house, person, papers and effects. As computer networks became more widely used, law makers felt that it was necessary to make more stringent privacy laws to protect information that is stored on and transmitted using computers specifically. Therefore, the Electronic Communications and Privacy Act (ECPA), presented below, was enacted in 1986 to protect all forms of electronic communications.

The ECPA prohibits anyone, not just the government, from unlawfully accessing (18 USC 2511-2521) or intercepting (18 USC 2701-2709) electronic communications. Rather than detail every aspect of these complex sections, the title of each is presented with a summary of the most interesting portions (Table 13.2)[3].

[3]This brief coverage of the ECPA necessarily excludes some important provisions of the act. The summary accurately portrays the general nature of the ECPA, but attorneys handling a specific matter that might be governed by the ECPA should thoroughly review it before discussing the matter.

SECTION AND TITLE	HIGHLIGHTS
§2511. Interception and disclosure of wire, oral, or electronic communications prohibited	Exception: An operator of a switchboard, or an officer, employee, or agent of a provider of wire or electronic communication service can intercept, disclose or use information obtained under certain conditions.
§ 2512. Manufacture, distribution, possession, and advertisement of wire, oral, or electronic communication intercepting devices prohibited	It is acceptable for a service provider or US government employee to manufacture, possess, or transport devices that can intercept wire, oral, or electronic communications.
§ 2513. Confiscation of wire, oral, or electronic communication interception devices	Interception devices may be seized and forfeited to the United States if they are in violation of the previous two sections.
§ 2515. Prohibition of use as evidence of intercepted wire or oral communications	This section explicitly states that any communications intercepted in violation of the ECPA cannot be used as evidence.
§ 2516. Authorization for interception of wire, oral, or electronic communications	Only a select few (e.g. the Attorney General) can request authorization from a Federal judge for a Federal agency (e.g. FBI) to intercept communications for a range of federal crimes. Similar conditions apply to state attorneys, agencies, and judges.
§ 2517. Authorization for disclosure and use of intercepted wire, oral, or electronic communications	If an intercepted transmission contains evidence of additional crimes this evidence can only be used if approved by a judge.
§ 2518. Procedure for interception of wire, oral, or electronic communications	Must have probable cause and have exhausted all other options (or other options are too dangerous or are unlikely to succeed). Also, the recording of evidence will be done in such a way as will protect the recording from editing or other alterations and a copy of the evidence will be made available to the judge issuing the order and sealed under his direction (to preserve the evidence).
§ 2519. Reports concerning interception of wire, oral, or electronic communications	Reports must be submitted to the Administrative Office of the US Courts describing various aspects of all interceptions approved under the ECPA.
§ 2520. Recovery of civil damages	Any individuals whose communications are intercepted, disclosed or intentionally used in violation of the ECPA may recover civil damages up to two years after the violation.
§ 2521. Injunction against illegal interception	The Attorney General may initiate a civil action in a district court to prevent an imminent or ongoing violation of the ECPA.
§ 2701. Unlawful access to stored communications	Exceptions: Several individuals can authorize access to stored communications including a person who created or received the communication and the communication service provider.
§ 2702. Disclosure of contents	A person or entity providing electronic communication or remote computing service to the public can only disclose the contents of stored communications under very specific conditions.

Table 13.2

Salient points of the Electronic Communications and Privacy Act (ECPA).

Table 13.2 (cont'd).

§ 2703. Requirements for government access	Communications that have been stored for more than 180 days are less protected than those that have been stored for less time. The subscriber or customer must be notified unless a warrant or court order specifies otherwise.
§ 2704. Backup preservation	A government entity may require that the Owner to whom the request is directed makes a copy of evidence before the subscriber or customer is notified of the subpoena or court order.
§ 2705. Delayed notice	A government entity may request that a subscriber or customer not be notified for up to ninety days.
§ 2706. Cost reimbursement	A government entity will reimburse the person or entity that provides the information if any costs are accrued in the process.
§ 2707. Civil action	Any individuals whose stored communications are accessed in violation of the ECPA may recover civil damages up to two years after the violation.
§ 2708. Exclusivity of remedies	This short section explicitly states that the remedies and sanctions described in the ECPA are the only ones for nonconstitutional violations of the ECPA.
§ 2709. Counterintelligence access to telephone toll and transaction records	A wire or electronic communication Owner must provide the Director of the FBI, or any other designated individuals in the FBI, with subscriber information, toll billing records, and electronic communication transactional records if the information is relevant to an authorized foreign counterintelligence investigation.

The ECPA stipulates that, to obtain authorization to intercept transmissions, law enforcement must follow a specific procedure and obtain a court order (or another certification in writing) that satisfies a given list of requirements. These rigid requirements make it more difficult to obtain authorization to intercept electronic communications[4].

There is more flexibility when it comes to stored electronic communications:

> 2703(1) A governmental entity may require a provider of remote computing service to disclose the contents of any electronic communication to which this paragraph is made applicable by paragraph (2) of this section –
>
> i) without required notice to the subscriber or customer, if the governmental entity obtains a search warrant issued under the Federal Rules of Criminal Procedure or equivalent State warrant; or
>
> ii) with prior notice from the governmental entity to the subscriber or customer if the government entity –
>
> > i) uses an administrative subpoena authorized by a Federal or State statute or a Federal or State grand jury subpoena; or

[4] *When dealing with intercepted transmissions, a search warrant will not satisfy the ECPA's court order requirement.*

ii) obtains a court order for such disclosure under subsection (d) of this section;

except that delayed notice may be given pursuant to section 2705 of this title.

This distinction between stored and transmitted communications was made because intercepting transmissions is potentially a greater invasion of privacy than collecting stored communications. When intercepting communications, there is a high chance that unrelated, private information will also be intercepted whereas stored communications are more discrete and the chance of collecting unrelated, private information is limited.

An interesting distinction between intercepted and stored communications arose during the Steve Jackson Games case (detailed in Chapter 4), in which the Secret Service violated the ECPA by reading and deleting e-mail that had never reached the intended recipients. Steve Jackson Games argued that the Secret Service had intercepted the e-mail because it had not been delivered to the intended recipients. However, the court argued that the e-mail had been delivered to the recipients' mailboxes and the ECPA made a clear distinction between storage and transmission so there was no way that the deleted e-mail fell into both categories. The e-mail would have to have been actively traveling through a wire or computer to qualify for the transmission clause.

There is one aspect of the ECPA that is still hotly debated. It is argued that under certain conditions (e.g. prior consent by one of the participants in a communication) an organization can search employees' communications. Therefore, many organizations have policies that allow them to monitor communications and all employees are required to agree to the policy by signature before gaining access to e-mail or a network. However, some people feel that any random monitoring of communications is not in the spirit of the law and that an employee's consent should be obtained each time the employer needs to access or intercept communications.

A more detailed description of the ECPA and other privacy laws can be found in *High-Technology Crime: Investigating Cases Involving Computers* (Rosenblatt 1995)[5].

[5]*Rosenblatt interprets the ECPA twice. One interpretation is aimed at law enforcement and the other is directed at corporate investigators.*

SEARCH AND SEIZURE CONSIDERATIONS

There are four questions that investigators must ask themselves when searching and seizing digital evidence:

1 Does the Fourth Amendment and/or ECPA apply to the situation?

2 Have the Fourth Amendment and/or ECPA requirements been met?

3 How long can investigators remain at the scene?

4 What do investigators need to re-enter?

When answering these questions, remember that the ECPA prohibits anyone, not just the government, from unlawfully accessing or intercepting electronic communications, whereas the Fourth Amendment only applies to the government. Recall that the Fourth Amendment requires that a search warrant be secured before law enforcement officers can search a person's house, person, papers and effects. To obtain a warrant, investigators must demonstrate probable cause and detail the place to be searched and the persons or things to be seized. More specifically, investigators have to convince a judge or magistrate that:

1 A crime has been committed;

2 Evidence of crime is in existence;

3 The evidence is likely to exist at the place to be to searched.

Be aware that law enforcement officers do not always require a search warrant to search and seize evidence. The main exceptions are plain view, consent and exigency. If law enforcement see evidence in plain view, they can seize it provided they obtained access to the area validly. By obtaining consent to search, investigators can perform a search without a warrant. A consent form should be used when obtaining consent to reduce the chance of the search being successfully challenged in court. The form should include the name of the person giving consent, the name of the investigator, the address of premises, date, and a general description of the search. The person giving consent and two witnesses should sign the consent form.

Regarding exigency, a warrantless search can be made for any emergency threatening life and limb. It is difficult to imagine a case in which a computer could be collected under exigent circumstances. Even in a homicide, a warrant is required for an in-depth search of the suspect's possessions. If investigators really believe that there is some urgency (that searching the contents of the computer will stop a suspect from killing again) they might be able to obtain a Mincey warrant, which can be easier to obtain than a full warrant. The Mincey warrant came about as a result of the following case:

Mincey (437 US 385 98 S. Ct. 2408 [1978])
Investigators in Tucson, Arizona forcibly entered Rufus Mincey's apartment after arranging to purchase heroin from him. Mincey shot and killed one of the investigators before he was apprehended. The first officers at the scene followed proper procedure, quickly looking for any emergency threatening life and limb. However, the homicide detectives that arrived later did not obtain a warrant and spent four days searching Mincey's apartment, leaving each night and returning the next morning.

Mincey was convicted for murder, assault, and three counts of narcotics offenses. Mincey appealed on the grounds that the evidence used against him had been seized without a search warrant. Ultimately, the United States Supreme Court overturned Mincey's conviction. The Supreme court held that when the police come upon the scene of a homicide they may make a prompt warrantless search of the area to see if there are other victims or if a killer is still on the premises, and the police may seize any evidence that is in plain view during the course of their legitimate emergency activities. However, in the absence of such legitimate emergency activities or consent, the police are required to secure a search warrant in order to continue their search on premises belonging to the defendant.

One of the most important cases regarding seizure of communications was Katz v. US (389 US 347, 1967). Katz used a public telephone to transmit wagering information from Los Angeles to Miami. The FBI attached a recording device to the outside of the public telephone booth, thus capturing his conversation. Katz was convicted but appealed, and the court overturned his conviction, holding that the FBI had violated the Fourth Amendment when they recorded Katz's conversation. The Court justified its ruling as follows:

> For the Fourth Amendment protects people, not places. What a person knowingly exposes to the public, even in his own home or office, is not a subject of Fourth Amendment protection. But what he seeks to preserve as private, even in an area accessible to the public, may be constitutionally protected ... The Government stresses the fact that the telephone booth from which the petitioner made his calls was constructed partly of glass, so that he was as visible after he entered it as he would have been if he had remained outside. But what he sought to exclude when he entered the booth was not the intruding eye – it was the uninvited ear. (Katz v. US, 389 US 347, 1967)

The ECPA extends this reasoning into the computer realm (with some modifications) and should be considered carefully when searching computers and networks and seizing digital evidence.

Naturally, the enactment of laws protecting people's privacy makes it more difficult to investigate criminal activity. Because cybercrime is becoming more of a problem and investigators' need for digital evidence is increasing, law enforcement agencies around the world are attempting to increase their access to information. In 1999, Australia granted the ASIO additional powers to make it easier for them to obtain digital evidence. In the US, the Communication Assistance for Law Enforcement Act (CALEA) was enacted (and funded at phenomenal cost to the taxpayer), giving the FBI remarkable power and freedom to monitor transmissions and obtain a wide range of additional information from telecommunications providers.

The European Union seems to be leaning in the opposite direction, enacting laws to increase the privacy of its citizens. However, the FBI is making a concerted effort to persuade EU Justice and Home Affairs ministers to adopt a plan similar to the US Communication Assistance for

Law Enforcement Act (CALEA). In 1993, the FBI brought together police and security agents from around the world to form the International Law Enforcement Telecommunications Seminar (Ilets). This group has been instrumental in developing communications interception policies in several countries and seems determined to implement wiretapping policies and equipment throughout Europe.

Additional reading on the subject of privacy and intercepted transmissions can be found in *Privacy on the Line: The Politics of Wiretapping and Encryption* (Diffie and Landau 1998).

JURISDICTION

One of the first things to be litigated is where a case will be tried. In the simplest scenario, a case can be tried in the place where the criminal act occurred or where the result occurred. The plaintiff might want the case to be tried in a convenient location by a favorable court (i.e. close to home) but an out-of-state defendant might object to this home field advantage. If there is some contention over where the case should be tried, the jurisdiction of the court must be examined and the alternatives must be considered.

Jurisdiction is the right of a court to make decisions regarding a specific person (personal jurisdiction) or a certain matter (subject matter jurisdiction). In the United States, a case must be tried in a court that has both personal jurisdiction and subject matter jurisdiction. To have personal jurisdiction over a case, state courts must be able to enforce rulings on the parties involved. State courts are only permitted to enforce rulings over residents of the state and over non-residents who submit to the state's jurisdiction as defined in the long arm statute of the state. According to some long arm statutes, an individual who does business with residents of the state has automatically submitted to the state's jurisdiction, even if the individual was never physically present in the state. Two cases involving online gambling have relied on long arm statutes to resolve jurisdiction.

CASE EXAMPLE (Thompson v. Handa-Lopez, Inc.)
Handa-Lopez, Inc., a California-based company, ran an online gambling operation called "Funscape's Casino Royale," where individuals could play blackjack, poker, keno, slots, craps, easy lotto, and roulette. In June of 1997, Tom Thompson was in Texas, using the Internet to play games on Funscape's Casino Royale when he claimed to have won $193,728.40. However, the online casino refused to pay and Thompson brought charges against them.

Thompson wanted the case to be heard in Texas but the defendant contended, pointing out a clause in their online contract stating that all disputes would be resolved in California. The US District Court Western District of Texas noted the following about the disclaimer:

Buried within the contract was an inconspicuous provision which provided that any disputes: shall be governed by the laws of the State of California, excluding choice of law principles, and shall be resolved exclusively by final and binding arbitration in the City of San Jose, County of Santa Clara, State of California, USA under the rules of the American Arbitration Association, and, in the event of such arbitration, no punitive, special, incidental, or consequential damages may be recovered by any party and the arbitrator shall not have the power to award any such damages ... (Thompson v. Handa-Lopez, Inc.)

The judge also noted the following about the Internet and jurisdiction:

In a recent opinion from the Western District of Pennsylvania, the Court discussed the "sliding scale" that courts have used to measure jurisdiction (Zippo, 952 F. Supp. at 1124). This sliding scale is consistent with well developed personal jurisdiction principles. At one end are situations where a defendant clearly does business over the Internet by entering into contracts with residents of other states which involve the knowing and repeated transmission of computer files over the Internet (CompuServe, Inc. v. Patterson, 89 F.3d 1257 [6th Cir.1996]). At the other end are passive Web site situations. A passive Web site that solely makes information available to interested parties is not grounds for the exercise of personal jurisdiction (Bensusan Restaurant Corp. v. King, 937 F. Supp. 295 [S.D.N.Y.1996], aff'd, 126 F.3d 25 [2nd Cir.1997]). Interactive Web sites, where a user can exchange information with the host computer, represent the middle ground.

The court noted that Handa-Lopez, Inc. was marketing to all states by advertising their casino as the "World's Largest" Internet Casino and that their interactive Web site and online contracts created more than enough contact with Thompson to constitute minimum contact with Texas. Furthermore, the court determined that the disclaimer stating that all legal issues would be resolved in California was not sufficient justification for changing the venue of the trail. In short, Texas had jurisdiction.

CASE EXAMPLE (568 N. W.2d 715, 1997 Minn. App.)
In a less clear-cut online gambling case the attorney general of Minnesota filed a complaint against an online sports wagering site called WagerNet (owned by a company in Belize). The attorney general allege that WagerNet had engaged in false advertising and consumer fraud by advertising in Minnesota that gambling on the Internet was lawful. The allegation was based on the fact that an employee of the Minnesota Attorney General's office had called WagerNet, identified himself as a Minnesota resident and asked how to place bets through WagerNet. The court ruled that WagerNet had exhibited a clear intent to solicit business from states including Minnesota and had sufficient contact with Minnesota to give the court personal jurisdiction.

Subject matter jurisdiction refers to the types of disputes a court is empowered to hear. State courts have the power to hear and decide cases that occur in that state unless:

1 There is a *federal question* – the plaintiff's question depends on or is based on a Federal law;

2 There is *diversity* – the plaintiff and defendant are from different states or countries and there is a claim of more than $50,000;

3 The suit is between two states;

4 The Federal government is one of the parties.

If any of these criteria are met, the Federal Court has jurisdiction regardless of the citizenship of the parties or the subject in question[6].

[6]*All Federal courts have limited jurisdiction as defined in article 3 section 2 of the Constitution.*

For example, the owners of a California-based bulletin board were tried and convicted in a Federal court in Memphis, Tennessee for distributing obscene materials across state lines that were beyond the protection of the First Amendment.

> CASE EXAMPLE (US v. Thomas, 74F.3d 701 [6th Cir. 1996])
> In 1993 the "Amateur Action" Bulletin Board System (BBS) was the target in one of the first obscenity cases involving computer-enabled communication between two states. The Amateur Action BBS was owned and run by Robert and Carleen Thomas, a husband and wife in California. The Thomases carefully controlled access to their BBS, only allowing approved members to connect and download pornographic images. Additionally, after being investigated and cleared by the San Jose police, the Thomases were confident that they were not violating any laws. However, to attract attention to the Amateur Action BBS, the Thomases used very strong language that suggested the BBS contained pedophilic materials. These advertisements were reported to a postal inspector in Tennessee named David Dirmeyer by a member of his community.
>
> Believing that he would find child pornography, Dirmeyer became a member of the BBS under a false identity, engaged Robert Thomas in on-line conversations, downloaded some pornographic images, ordered some video cassettes, and entrapped Robert Thomas by offering him (and ultimately delivering) magazines containing child pornography. Dirmeyer's investigation of the Amateur Action BBS culminated in the Thomases being brought to trial in Tennessee on twelve counts, mostly relating to interstate transport of obscene materials. The Thomases argued that they should be tried in California since the BBS was located in California and that the Thomases had not sent the materials to Tennessee – Dirmeyer had downloaded the materials into Tennessee. The Tennessee judge denied this motion, reasoning that the obscene materials had been transported between two states giving both states personal jurisdiction.
>
> Although no child pornography was found, the Thomases were found guilty of transporting obscene materials into Tennessee. Robert Thomas was sentenced to three years in a federal prison in Tennessee and Carleen Thomas was given a sentence of thirty months. Despite the fact that dial-up Bulletin Board Systems are not part of the Internet, this case raises complex questions regarding jurisdiction, community standards, and obscenity that arise when dealing with pornography on the Internet.

Although computer networks add some complexity to jurisdictional questions, the fundamental issues remain the same – does the court have personal jurisdiction and subject matter jurisdiction. For the most part, courts are becoming more familiar with computer networks and are making informed decisions about which courts have jurisdiction.

SUMMARY

Cybercrime has becoming an increasing problem all around the world. Until recently only a few countries had laws that specifically addressed cybercrime. However, more countries are enacting legislation and developing programs to deal with cybercrime. In 1999, the United Kingdom government began working with information technology companies to develop more effective methods for combating cybercrime. The Indian government took its first steps towards enacting cybercrime legislation with their Information Technology Bill. New Zealand took steps to extend its Crimes Act to include cybercrime. Japan also announced an aggressive program to deal with an increase in cybercrime. Additionally, the Chinese and Korean governments have acknowledged cybercrime as a problem.

As more countries develop methods for dealing with cybercrime, we might see an increasing number of prosecutions. However, the fact that the computer crime statutes are rarely used has led lawmakers to seek different approaches to dealing with the problem. For instance, in the US, educational programs are being developed to teach young people that breaking into computers is as illegal as breaking into someone's home. Also, software developers are creating new programs to automate intrusion detection and response. Additionally, a contract law approach has been proposed as an alternative to the use of criminal law in controlling certain types of low-level, high-volume cybercrimes:

> Contract as a means of behavioral control in cyberspace has important advantages over criminal law. Contract's traditional reliance on agreement by the individuals to be bound retains the element of individual responsibility which is such an integral part of cyberian culture. Contract law permits localized enforcement mechanisms, dispensing with the need for a massive and complex central enforcement scheme. Furthermore, contract law, since it is enforced by agreement, transcends the problem of national borders. Contract, in short, is a form of self-enforced law very much in keeping with the traditions and expectations of cyberians. It is far more likely to generate compliance than an externally imposed and administered statutory system of laws. (Dunne 1994)

In any event, computers are here to stay and will continue to be a source of digital evidence in a wide range of crimes. Additionally, given the increase in crime on networks and new legislation, attorneys and law enforcement have a challenging job ahead of them.

REFERENCES

Casey, E. and Garrity, J. (1998) "Internet Misuse in the Workplace: A Lawyer's Primer," *The Florida Bar Journal*, LXXII (10): 22–33.

Diffie, W. and Landau, S. (1998) *Privacy on the Line: The Politics of Wiretapping and Encryption*, Cambridge, MA: The MIT Press.

Dunne, R. (1994) "Deterring Unauthorized Access to Computers: Controlling Behavior in Cyberspace through a Contract Law Paradigm" [http://www.cs.yale.edu/pub/dunne/jurimetrics/jurimetrics.html].

Hollinger, R. C. (1997) *Crime, Deviance and the Computer*, Brookfield, VT: Dartmouth Publishing Company.

Rosenblatt, K. S. (1995) *High-Technology Crime: Investigating Cases Involving Computers*, San Jose, CA: KSK Publications.

Spafford, G. H. (1989) "The Internet Worm: Crisis and Aftermath," *Communications of the ACM*, 32 (6): 678–87.

RESOURCES

Cornell Law Archive [http://www.law.cornell.edu/]

Findlaw [http://www.findlaw.com]

Cyberspace Law Subject Index John Marshall Law School [http://www.jmls.edu/cyber/index/index.html]

Cyberspace Law Encyclopedia [http://www.gahtan.com/techlaw/]

Law Crawler [http://www.lawcrawler.com]

Internet Law Library [http://law.house.gov/]

## CHAPTER 14

THOUGHTS FOR THE FUTURE

We are only seeing the beginning of computer networking. Wireless networks are on the rise and computer hardware and software continues to become more portable and sophisticated. Technology that enables any appliance to be attached to a wireless network is becoming more popular. For instance, Jini (http://www.sun.com/jini/), a flexible technology created by Sun Microsystems, enables a single hand-held device to connect to several wireless networks simultaneously, providing individuals with a wide range of services including cellular phone service, Internet service, and proximity networks (impromptu communities)[1].

Proximity networks can be established when devices come into range of each other and automatically create a temporary, federated network e.g. using IBM's Bluetooth technology (http://www.bluetooth.com/).

These developments in wireless communication promise to change the way we do business and socialize. Additionally, these new technologies will enable new forms of cybercrime, creating new challenges for lawmakers and law enforcers. This chapter describes some educational opportunities and suggests some immediate actions that individuals and organizations can take to prepare for cybercrime investigations, i.e. developing Digital Evidence Recovery Teams (DERT), creating policies and procedures, and sharing information and expertise.

[1]Jini operates on top of existing network and transport layers enabling it to fit into existing systems (e.g. TCP/IP, CNLP, Bluetooth).

EDUCATION AND TRAINING

With the proliferation of computer networks, there is an increasing need for investigators, attorneys, and forensic scientists that are qualified to deal with cybercrime. As a result a growing number of consulting firms that specialize in helping organizations investigate cybercrime and process digital evidence. Additionally, many organizations are hiring full-time investigators to deal with computer intrusions, e-mail harassment, and inappropriate use of computer systems. Law enforcement is also making efforts to cope with cybercrime. Police departments in larger cities are setting up internal computer crime divisions, crime labs are beginning to offer digital evidence processing services, and the FBI is spearheading an ambitious initiative called the National Infrastructure Protection Center (NIPC) to combat cybercrime on a grand scale.

The need for qualified investigators has created a number of private organizations that offer excellent training in specialized areas. Some of these organizations are for law enforcement, some are for attorneys, and others are primarily concerned with computer security and investigating computer intrusions. Also, universities are developing programs to educate individuals about specific aspects of cybercrime. A few recommended training providers are described here and additional resources are listed in Appendix I.

COMPUTER SECURITY INSTITUTE (CSI) (http://www.gocsi.com)

The Computer Security Institute releases annual reports about computer crime and offers training and conferences. The CSI focuses on computer security, and they have several courses that teach individuals how to investigate computer intrusions. A number of these courses incorporate forensic science.

KNOWLEDGE SOLUTIONS (http://www.corpus-delicti.com)

Knowledge Solutions provides online training on a variety of subjects, including criminal profiling and investigating cybercrime. Most of their courses run for ten weeks and are delivered entirely over the Internet enabling students to participate from anywhere in the world. These courses use cases to demonstrate key concepts and to give investigators a practical knowledge of the subjects that can be incorporated easily into their own investigations.

NEW TECHNOLOGIES, INC. (NTI) (http://www.forensics-intl.com)

New Technologies, Inc. (NTI) is an excellent source of tools and training. Their primary expertise lies in the recovering of data from Microsoft operating systems. Some of their tools and training take the Internet into account. NTI also consults on civil cases, helping organizations collect and process digital evidence and testifying in court when necessary.

SEARCH (http://www.search.org)

SEARCH, the National Consortium for Justice Information and Statistics, offers several courses, including:

- The Seizure and Examination of Microcomputers

- The Investigation of Computer Crime
- Advanced Internet Investigations
- Investigation of Internet Crimes Against Children

DIGITAL EVIDENCE RECOVERY TEAM (DERT)

To address the increasing amount of cybercrime larger organizations have created Computer Emergency Response Teams (CERTs) with the specific aim of responding to crimes that involve the organization's computers. As the name suggests, Computer Emergency Response Teams are primarily responsible for containing crisis situations. Collecting evidence and prosecuting criminals is a secondary concern at best.

Possibly because few cybercriminals are being prosecuted, cybercrime is on the rise and organizations are experiencing a corresponding increase of losses. As the losses increase, prosecution becomes more desirable – either to recover damages or simply discourage criminals from targeting the organization in the future. If organizations hope to prosecute cybercriminals they will have to assign an individual or group with the following responsibilities:

- investigate crimes that involve computers, networks, and the Internet;
- recognize, document, collect, preserve, classify, compare, individualize and reconstruct digital evidence;
- know when to call in experts or law enforcement;
- coordinate with other agencies and organizations that become involved in an investigation;
- create and update policies and procedures for computer-related crimes that take into account advances in technology, law and organizational policy;
- manage investigations and prepare cases for trial;
- testify in court when required;
- remain informed about new developments in technology and cybercrime.

These responsibilities do not conform well to the emergency response model that is currently used to deal with cybercrime. Analyzing evidence and preparing a case for trial requires time and meticulous attention to detail. Therefore, it is sensible to create a specialized Digital Evidence Recovery Team (DERT) that picks up where Computer Emergency Response Teams leave off. For example, when an incident is reported, a member of the CERT could respond, contain the damage and then call in a member of the DERT to salvage the remaining digital evidence. The member of the DERT could then analyze the evidence, reconstruct the crime, and determine if it is worth pursuing the perpetrator(s).

This division of responsibility occurs when a person is injured in a crime. Paramedics tend to the injured person's needs while investigators examine the crime scene. Since paramedics are often the first people on the scene, investigators depend on them for information about the crime scene and victims in their original state. If paramedics have changed anything at a crime scene, investigators need to know this before reconstructing the crime. The same situation arises when a crime involves a computer or network and a similar division of responsibility can be useful. A CERT is responsible for responding to incidents and tends to any immediate needs while a DERT is responsible for collecting evidence properly and performing a full investigation of the crime.

POLICIES AND PROCEDURES

Every organization has slightly different policies that will influence the way that they investigate cybercrime and collect digital evidence. This text provides guidelines to help develop policies and procedures for collecting and analyzing digital evidence. Using these guidelines, organizations can create general search and seizure procedures that conform to laws, evidentiary requirements and organizational policy.

Some additional effort is required to create procedures to address specific types of cybercrime because there are so many variations – every criminal and every computer system is different. Chapters 10, 11 and 12 provide some general tips for dealing with specific situations and types of cybercrime. However, these procedures must be adapted to accommodate new technologies and new types of cybercrime.

DIGITAL EVIDENCE MAPS

One of the most useful tools that investigators can have is a map indicating where evidence is located on a network – a digital evidence map. Such a map is even more useful when it specifies how long digital evidence remains on the network and references procedures for collecting the evidence.

When faced with a cybercrime, it can be frustrating to learn about a source of digital evidence after the evidence has been destroyed. Without a digital evidence map, investigators have to track down busy system administrators for information about the network. When large networks are involved, it can take weeks to find all of the sources of digital evidence. Even when these sources contain relevant digital evidence when they are found, investigators have to figure out how to collect the evidence in a way that maintains its authenticity and integrity and conforms with applicable privacy policies and laws. A digital evidence map addresses all of these issues, making it easier for investigators to find and collect relevant digital evidence quickly and safely[2].

[2]Organizations can also use a digital evidence map to assess their liability. After determining the kinds of evidence contained on their networks, organizations might decide that certain sources are a liability and should not be maintained or should be cleansed on a regular basis.

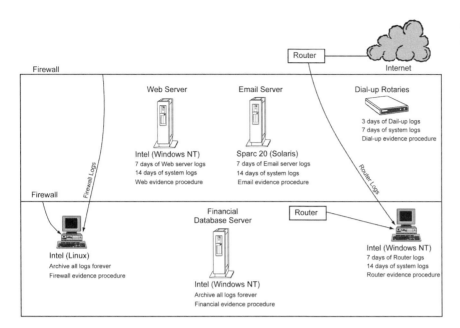

Figure 14.1
Sample digital evidence map.

RESEARCH, DEVELOPMENT AND INFORMATION SHARING

Investigators require detailed information about digital evidence to help them recognize, collect, document, preserve, classify, compare and individualize it. Also, investigators sometimes require assistance in determining the significance of certain kinds of digital evidence. To address these needs, law enforcement, computer security professionals, attorneys and forensic scientists can use computer networks to share information about cybercrime and digital evidence.

There are a multitude of mailing lists, Web pages and publications that deal with various aspects of cybercrime (see Appendix I). Although these resources are useful they are limited to general problems and issues. There is a need for databases that are designed specifically to help investigators identify criminals, link cases, and understand motives. For example, when investigators find an unfamiliar piece of digital evidence, a database of known samples could help them classify their evidence and even find individualizing characteristics. Furthermore, online databases could be used as a foundation for forensic science research in the area of digital evidence.

> A major thrust of forensic science research must concentrate on defining the most distinctive properties of evidence and relating these properties to statistics that measure their frequency of occurrence. (Saferstien 1998)

This kind of research can give forensic scientists a clearer idea of what to look for and could help them develop more effective tools for analyzing digital evidence.

Unfortunately, most victims of cybercrime are reluctant to disclose information about themselves unless they are certain it will not have an adverse effect on their reputation or business. Therefore, a trusted entity must take responsibility for this kind of databasing project – keeping private information private while providing information to investigators that can help them perform their investigations. CERT (http://www.cert.org) has made advances in this area to do this but can only offer general reports, not a database of class evidence.

In the meantime, it is important for investigators to make individual efforts to share information, resources, samples of evidence, research findings, etc. The infrastructure is in place to create a federated network of evidence databases (e.g. on the Web) in which individuals provide detailed information about cases that they have investigated and digital evidence that they have collected. However, organizations must make the decision to invest in this type of resource and must determine what level of detail can be provided to outside organizations and individuals.

SUMMARY

In general, there is a growing awareness that cybercrime can have serious implications in the physical world. In addition to the large sums of money that organizations are losing as a result of cybercrime, individuals are being affected by crimes committed over networks. Individuals are being defrauded through e-mail, harassed in chat rooms, are losing the contents of their hard drives as a result of viruses, and are finding that their children are being solicited in their homes. Additionally, private citizens are beginning to realize that a computer cracker can break into their personal computer, accessing everything on it.

There is no panacea for dealing with cybercrime, but individuals and organizations can ameliorate the situation by being informed and prepared. The more prepared an organization is to deal with cybercrime, the less traumatic and costly each incident and investigation will be. Having clear policies, carefully thought-out procedures and well-trained personnel will make most investigations go more smoothly. Every investigation brings new challenges but well-prepared individuals and organizations will be able to focus on these unforeseeable aspects of investigations, having already primed themselves for the many routine procedures described in this text.

With organizations becoming more interested in prosecuting computer criminals, there is an increasing demand on law enforcement and attorneys to deal with cybercrime. Additionally, law enforcement and attorneys are finding that homicides and rapes have related digital evidence. When confronted with this new and unfamiliar form of evidence law enforcement and attorneys turn to forensic scientists for assistance with this new form of evidence. Therefore, with the rapid advances in networking technology it is incumbent upon law enforcement, attorneys and forensic scientists to rise to the challenge of cybercrime by equipping themselves with the necessary investigative tools and continually updating their training.

As investigators learn to deal with digital evidence and cybercrime, they are bound to make mistakes. Computer security professionals might seize digital evidence that they are not legally permitted to collect or law enforcement might process digital evidence incorrectly, making it inadmissible. Attorneys might overlook digital evidence or legal arguments that could benefit their clients. Forensic scientists might fail to discern a key characteristic of digital evidence or might incorrectly reconstruct a crime. Whenever possible, investigators should help each other understand mistakes and thus improve the overall knowledge in the field. Even if they are on opposing sides of a case, it is important for investigators to realize that they have at least one common goal, to deal with a new and complicated form of evidence (digital evidence) and a growing problem (cybercrime).

SUMMARY OF RESOURCES

COMPUTER CRIME AND FORENSIC SCIENCE RESOURCES

AMERICAN ACADEMY OF FORENSIC SCIENCES (AAFS)

The American Academy of Forensic Sciences is a professional society with members from around the world. The AAFS does not have a section devoted to computers but many of its members have an awareness of technology and are making an effort to develop computer-related research and resources.

Mailing address:

PO Box 669

Colorado Springs, CO 80901-0669

Street address:

410 North 21st Street, Suite 203

Colorado Springs, CO 80904-2798

Phone: (719) 636-1100

Fax: (719) 636-1993

E-mail: Membership@aafs.org

Web: http://www.aafs.org

COMPUTER EMERGENCY RESPONSE TEAM (CERT)

The Computer Emergency Response Team gathers information about computer crime and provides excellent computer security resources and alerts. Also, when appropriate, CERT informs organizations and agencies of specific incidents that might concern them – acting as a coordination center when many disparate groups are involved.

CERT Coordination Center

Software Engineering Institute

Carnegie Mellon University

Pittsburgh, PA 15213-3890

Phone: (412) 268-7090

Fax: (412) 268-6989

E-mail: cert@cert.org

Web: http://www.cert.org

COMPUTER FORENSICS, INC.

In addition to assisting investigators with computer-related evidence, Computer Forensics, Inc. offers planning, training and auditing services to help organizations understand and limit their liability.

501 East Pine Street

Suite 200

Seattle, WA 98122

Phone: (206) 324-6232

Fax: (206) 322-7318

E-mail: cfi@forensics.com

Web: http://www.forensics.com

COMPUTER FORENSICS LTD

[http://www.computer-forensics.com]

Based in the United Kingdom, Computer Forensics Ltd has a variety of offerings including training, toolkits, consulting and laboratory services.

Colonnade House

High Street, Worthing

West Sussex BN11 1NZ

Phone: 44 (0) 1903 823181

Fax: 44 (0) 1903 233545

E-mail: info@computer-forensics.com

Web: http://www.computer-forensics.com

CYBERCRIME-L MAILING LIST

A discussion forum for individuals who are interested in the broad topic of cybercrime.

To subscribe to Profiling-L, go to

http://www.corpus-delicti.com/cybercrime-l.html

ELECTRONIC EVIDENCE DISCOVERY, INC.

A large organization that works with corporations on computer-related cases. EED, Inc also helps organizations identify and reduce risks that are associated with digital information.

The Financial Center

1215 Fourth Ave, Suite 1420

Seattle, WA 98161

Phone: (206) 343-0131

Fax: (206) 343-0172

E-mail: eed@eedinc.com

Web: http://www.eedinc.com

FORENS-L MAILING LIST

Forens-L is an unmoderated discussion list dealing with forensic aspects of anthropology, biology, chemistry, odontology, pathology, psychology, serology, toxicology, criminalistics and expert witnessing and presentation of evidence in court.

To subscribe to Forens-L, send an e-mail message to

MAILSERV@ACC.FAU.EDU with the line

SUBSCRIBE FORENS-L Firstname Lastname

in the body of the message.

FORUM OF INCIDENT RESPONSE AND SECURITY TEAMS (FIRST)

FIRST is a collaborative effort to deal with computer security problems in general and computer crime in specific. FIRST is comprised of government and private sector organizations around the globe.

E-mail: first-sec@first.org

Web: http://www.first.org

GUIDANCE SOFTWARE, INC.

Guidance Software Inc, provides software, training, and technical support for investigators of computer-related crime. Guidance Software's Encase software is a very effective digital evidence collection, documentation and analysis tool.

729 Mission Street, Suite 170

South Pasadena, CA 91030

Phone: (626) 441-3915

Fax: (626) 799-4364

E-mail: info@guidancesoftware.com

Web: http://www.guidancesoftware.com

HIGH TECHNOLOGY CRIME INVESTIGATION ASSOCIATION (HTCIA)

An organization of computer security professionals, law enforcement officers, prosecuting attorneys that are devoted to investigating high-technology crime. Although all of the HTCIA chapters are currently located in the United States, an effort is being made to reach out to other nations.

3567 Benton St, Ste 370

Santa Clara, CA 95051

Phone: (408) 861-0833

Fax: (408) 861-0833

E-mail: admin@htcia.org

Web: http://www.htcia.org

INTERNATIONAL ASSOCIATION OF COMPUTER INVESTIGATIVE SPECIALISTS (IACIS)

The IACIS is an organization of law enforcement professionals dedicated to education in the field of forensic computer science.

PO Box 21688, Keizer, Oregon 97307-1688

Phone: (503) 557-1506

Fax: (503) 557-1506

E-mail: admin@cops.org

Web: http://www.cops.org

KNOWLEDGE SOLUTIONS

Knowledge Solutions provides online training on a variety of subjects, including criminal profiling and investigating cybercrime. Most of their courses run for ten weeks and are delivered entirely over the Internet enabling students to participate from anywhere in the world. These courses use cases to demonstrate key concepts and to give investigators a practical knowledge of the subjects that can be incorporated easily into their own investigations.

1961 Main Street #221

Watsonville, CA 95076

Phone: (831) 786-9238

Fax: (415) 840-0012

E-mail: info@corpus-delicti.com

Web: http://www.corpus-delicti.com

NATIONAL INFRASTRUCTURE PROTECTION CENTRE (NIPC)

The US government created NICP to address the growing threat that cybercrime poses to critical systems like telecommunications, emergency services, government operations, banking, transportation, electric power, gas and oil storage. The NICP mission is "to detect, deter, warn of, respond to, and investigate malicious acts, both physical and cyber, that threaten or target the Nation's critical infrastructures." This initiative combines expertise from the FBI; Departments of Defense, Treasury, and Energy; the Intelligence Community; other federal agencies; state and local governments; and the private sector.

E-mail: NIPC@fbi.gov

Web: http://www.nipc.gov

NEW TECHNOLOGIES, INC. (NTI)

New Technologies, Inc. (NTI) is an excellent source of tools and training. Their primary expertise lies in the recovering of data from Microsoft operating systems. Some of their tools and training take the Internet into account. NTI also consults on civil cases, helping organizations collect and process digital evidence and testifying in court when necessary.

> 2075 Northeast Division Street
>
> Gresham, OR 97030
>
> Phone: (503) 661-6912
>
> E-mail: info@forensics-intl.com
>
> Web: http://www.forensics-intl.com

ONTRACK

Ontrack is an international company that specializes in data recovery. In addition to general data recovery, Ontrack offers specialized evidence recovery and reporting services to assist investigators.

> 6321 Bury Drive
>
> Eden Prairie, MN 55346
>
> Toll Free: (800) 872-2599
>
> Phone: (612) 937-5161
>
> Fax: (612) 937-5750
>
> Web: http://www.ontrack.com

PROFILING-L MAILING LIST

An open forum for anyone who has an interest in discussing methods, standards, practices and issues related to any part of the criminal profiling process. Discussions are geared towards the investigative and courtroom aspects of understanding crime scene behavior of both victim and offender. To subscribe to Profiling-L, go to

> http://www.corpus-delicti.com/profiling-l.html

SEARCH

SEARCH, the National Consortium for Justice Information and Statistics, offers several courses, including: The Seizure and Examination of Microcomputers; The Investigation of Computer Crime; Advanced Internet Investigations; Investigation of Internet Crimes Against Children.

7311 Greenhaven Drive, Suite 145

Sacramento, CA 95831

Phone: (916) 392-2550

Fax: (916) 392-8440

Web: http://www.search.org

VOGON INTERNATIONAL LIMITED

Talisman Business Centre,

Talisman Road, Bicester OX6 0JX, England

Tel: +44 (0) 1869 355255

Fax: +44 (0) 1869 355256

E-mail: data.recovery@vogon.co.uk

http://www.vogon.co.uk/

LEGAL RESOURCES

AMERICAN CIVIL LIBERTIES UNION (ACLU)

Protecting civil liberties, including in cyberspace. The ACLU Web site contains feature articles and useful resources and their Constitution Hall America Online (AOL) site has special events.

125 Broad Street, 18th Floor

New York, New York 10004-2400

E-mail: aclu@aclu.org

Web: http://www.aclu.org

CORNELL LAW ARCHIVE

A useful legal resource that includes information about computer-related law and evidence.

[http://www.law.cornell.edu/]

CYBERIA-L MAILING LIST

An e-mail discussion list that resolves around legal issues regarding computer communications. Many topics are covered in this enthusiastic group of individuals from around the world.

To subscribe to Cyberia-L, send e-mail to LISTSERV@LISTSERV.AOL.COM with the line

SUBSCRIBE CYBERIA-L Firstname Lastname

in the body of the message.

CYBERSPACE LAW SUBJECT INDEX JOHN MARSHALL LAW SCHOOL

A helpful catalog of certain cybercrimes with related information, case citations, and resources.

[http://www.jmls.edu/cyber/index/index.html]

CYBERSPACE LAW ENCYCLOPEDIA

A helpful catalog of certain cybercrimes with related information, case citations and resources.

[http://www.gahtan.com/techlaw]

ELECTRONIC FRONTIER FOUNDATION (EFF)

Protecting civil liberties in cyberspace. The EFF Web site contains many useful legal resources and information about ongoing issues.

1550 Bryant Street, Suite 725

San Francisco, CA 94103

Phone: (415) 436-9333

Fax: (415) 436-9993

E-mail: ask@eff.org

Web: http://www.eff.org

ELECTRONIC PRIVACY INFORMATION CENTER (EPIC)

A research organization that aims "to focus public attention on emerging civil liberties issues and to protect privacy, the First Amendment, and constitutional values." The EPIC Web site is an excellent place to stay informed of recent and emerging legislation.

666 Pennsylvania Ave SE, Suite 301

Washington, DC 20003

Phone: (202) 544-9240

Fax: (202) 547-5482

E-mail: info@epic.org

Web: http://www.epic.org

FINDLAW

A search engine dedicated to legal resources and topics.

[http://www.findlaw.com]

LAW CRAWLER

A search engine dedicated to legal resources and topics.

[http://www.lawcrawler.com]

TECHNICAL RESOURCES

ANTIONLINE

Antionline is a collection of online resources that contain current information about recent security vulnerabilities, computer intrusions, Web graffiti, and more.

395 State Street Suite B

Beaver, PA 15009

E-mail: comments@antionline.com

Phone: (724) 773-0940

Fax: (724) 773-0941

Web: http://www.antionline.com

Web: http://www.anticode.com

CENTER FOR EDUCATION AND RESEARCH IN INFORMATION ASSURANCE AND SECURITY (CERIAS)

(CERIAS) was created to develop expertise in information security and provide related resources. The widely known Computer Operations, Audit and Security Technology (COAST) group is a part of CERIAS.

E-mail: cerias-info@cs.purdue.edu

Web: http://www.cerias.purdue.edu

COAST E-mail: coast-request@cs.purdue.edu

COAST Web: http://www.cs.purdue.edu/coast/coast.html

COMPUTER SECURITY INSTITUTE (CSI)

The Computer Security Institute releases annual reports about computer crime and offers training and conferences. The CSI focuses on computer security, and they have several courses that teach individuals how to investigate computer intrusions. A number of these courses incorporate forensic science.

600 Harrison Street

San Francisco, CA 94107

Phone: (415) 905-2626

Fax: (415) 905-2218

E-mail: csi@mfi.com.

Web: http://www.gocsi.com

COMPUTER SECURITY MAILING LISTS

In addition to hosting several computer security mailing lists, Internet Security Systems, provides a comprehensive catalog of mailing lists at

http://www.iss.net/vd/mail.html

INTERNET SECURITY SYSTEMS (ISS)

Internet Security Systems has a searchable database of vulnerabilities. Portions of this database are also included in their ISS security products. ISS also provides free seminars over the Web (called Webinars) that provide an overview of many topics.

6600 Peachtree-Dunwoody Rd, Bldg 300

Atlanta, GA 30328

Phone: (678) 443-6000

Fax: (678) 443-6477

Web: http://www.iss.net/xforce

Webinars: http://www.iss.net/webinars

L0PHT

A group of hackers that provides exploits, computer security software and a variety of other resources. USENIX publishes a magazine called ;login: and holds regular conferences that are renowned for their high quality.

PO Box 990857

Boston, MA 02199

E-mail: admin@10pht.com

Web: http://www.10pht.com

SYSINTERNALS

A Web site that provides detailed technical information about Microsoft windows products and software that can be very useful in an investigation (e.g. disk editors, undelete utilities, boot disks, data copying programs).

[http://www.sysinternals.com]

SYSTEM ADMINISTRATION, NETWORKING, AND SECURITY (SANS)

SANS is a cooperative research and education organization through which many system administrators, computer security professionals and network administrators share information. SANS offers training, courses and newsletters on a variety of topics related to computer security.

15235 Roller Coaster Rd

Colorado Springs, CO 80921

USA

Phone: +1 (301) 951 0102

Fax: +1 (301) 951 0140

E-mail: sans@sans.org

Web: http://www.sans.org

ROOTSHELL

A Web site that is renowned for providing exploits to known vulnerabilities at. Rootshell also contains news and documents regarding computer security and computer crime.

[http://www.rootshell.com]

USENIX, Advanced Computing Systems Association

Although USENIX is not dedicated to computer security it remains current with technology and the associated problems that arise.

USENIX Association

2560 Ninth Street, Suite 215

Berkeley, CA 94710

Phone: (510) 528-8649

Fax: (510) 548-5738

E-mail: office@usenix.org

Web: http://www.usenix.org

MULTIMEDIA SUPPLEMENT

The primary goal of this multimedia supplement is to create a resource that teaches individuals the fundamentals of processing digital evidence and using it in an investigation. To achieve this goal, an authentic learning environment is created that individuals can use at their convenience, whenever they have time. In this learning environment, individuals are cast in the role of an investigator and are presented with cases that depend heavily on digital evidence. In their role as the investigator, learners are required to use the digital evidence to solve each crime. A variety of cases that involve digital evidence are presented to demonstrate that any crime can involve digital evidence. Individuals will emerge from this experience with a knowledge of computer networks, cybercrime and digital evidence and will be comfortable including digital evidence in any investigation.

The main challenges in teaching a complex domain like digital evidence are not to paralyze the individuals with too much information and to enable them to take what they learn and apply it independently of the educational tool. An educational model called the Investigate and Decide Learning Environment (IDLE) is used to address these challenges. The general idea underlying the IDLE model is to use realistic scenarios to create an engaging learning environment in which learners can develop their investigative skills with the help of experts (see Figure A.1 on page 244).

There are five phases in the IDLE model: Problem; Do; Decide; Communicate; and Wrap-up. Each case in this learning environment is broken up into these five phases as shown in Figure A.1. This design depends heavily on expert guidance, so expert modeling and answers to common questions are provided throughout this learning environment.

The primary audience comprises professionals and university students in the computer security, law enforcement, legal, and forensic science communities. These individuals have an interest in investigation but are not necessarily experienced with computers or evidence collection. Therefore, this work is designed to be accessible to beginners but quickly progresses to an intermediate skill level. Learners are assumed to have little or no

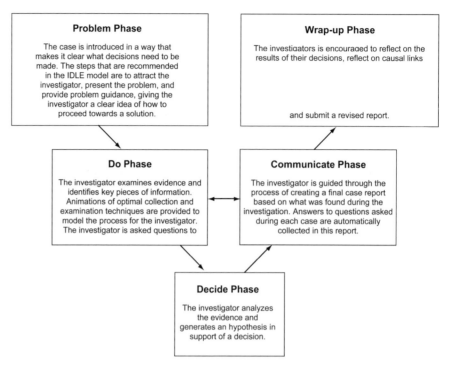

knowledge of the technical, evidentiary and legal issues relevant to digital evidence. Provided they have access to a computer, learners will be able to immerse themselves in an environment that enables them to learn about computers, evidence and the law as they might while investigating cases in the real world.

This appendix describes the rationale behind the design of the multimedia supplement in detail and explains why the IDLE model was chosen. The IDLE model is a specialized implementation of a theory called *goal based scenarios* which is built upon two other learning theories (cognitive apprenticeship, case-based reasoning). An overview of these foundational theories is provided to show the strengths and weaknesses of the IDLE model. Several shortcomings of the IDLE model are noted and the methods used to address the weaknesses of the model are described.

KIND OF LEARNING AND INSTRUCTION IN THIS CONTEXT

Extensive research shows that we learn best through a combination of theory and practice in a realistic context.

> Activity, concept, and culture are interdependent. No one can be totally understood without the other two. Teaching methods often try to impart abstracted concepts as fixed, well-defined, independent entities that can be explored in prototypical examples

and textbook exercises. But such exemplification cannot provide the important insights into either the culture or the authentic activities of members of that culture that learners need. (Brown *et al.* 1989)

A clear example is the training of modern pilots. Attending lectures and reading books are necessary, but not sufficient, training for a pilot. There is an obvious need for practical experience. Millions of dollars have been spent on flight simulators to provide a safe, realistic environment to practice skills and learn from inevitable mistakes. Similarly, in the investigation of crimes that involve digital evidence, students learn best by applying theory and skills to realistic cases in an environment where they can make mistakes without the real-world consequences of failure.

So, though there is a large amount of technical and legal information to be conveyed when teaching individuals about digital evidence and cybercrime, it should not be the sole focus. Learners will absorb this declarative information with relative ease provided it is presented in context and is clearly relevant to their personal interests and goals – solving crimes. Therefore the primary challenge in teaching these subjects is to create an authentic environment that helps individuals develop skills and problem-solving strategies that they can apply to real-world investigations.

AUTHENTIC ENVIRONMENT

This multimedia supplement uses computers and computer networks to create an authentic learning environment that helps individuals learn about digital evidence and cybercrime. A CD-ROM presents learners with cases to solve and directs them to external resources that contain related declarative information (such as Web sites and the accompanying text). As learners progress, they are encouraged to move out of the confines of the CD-ROM to explore their own computers and the networks around them (e.g. the Internet). The CD-ROM also provides links to an online discussion forum where individuals can share ideas and ask each other questions.

When teaching adults about digital evidence and cybercrime, it is not necessary to create an expensive three-dimensional simulation. Adults require less visual stimulus to hold their attention than younger audiences do. Also, adult learners are more impressed by the realism and relevance of the cases they encounter than by immaterial frills. Therefore, this CD-ROM creates a simple form of simulation by presenting realistic case materials, casting learners as the investigator in the case and giving learners dynamic and continuous feedback.

In an effort to make the learning experience even more authentic, the graphical user interface in this CD-ROM consistently resembles a case file. Learners are presented with the computer equivalent of a set of manila folders containing relevant materials. This case file metaphor will be immediately recognizable and familiar to the learners.

CASE-BASED INSTRUCTION

The decision to use cases to teach individuals about the digital evidence and cybercrime is a straightforward one. After all, the theory and skills being taught are inextricably bound to cases – they were developed from past cases and are used to investigate new ones. So, to situate the learning fully, cases must be used. However, there are some subtleties in the implementation of case-based instruction that deserve serious consideration. It is not enough to teach using a single case, or to string cases together in an arbitrary manner and expect students to flourish.

A theory called *case-based reasoning* (CBR) (Kolodner 1994; Schank and Abelson 1977; Schank 1990) indicates that when we are presented with a new case, we automatically remember past cases that are similar to the current one and draw comparisons. For example, after examining evidence in a new case, an investigator is reminded of several similar cases that he solved a year ago. The investigator then uses the solutions in the previous cases to help him solve the new case. Similarly, when a forensic scientist is presented with a potential source of digital evidence, she is reminded of a mistake that she made when examining similar evidence in the past. She uses the memory of the mistake to avoid repeating it again. If we cannot remember a similar case, we try to remember a contradictory one and juxtapose the new with the old. For instance, when a computer security expert discovers a break-in, he first contrasts it with known vulnerabilities and looks for familiar clues. When no obvious clues are found, the computer security expert makes inferences by contrasting the new break-in with old, familiar ones.

> I browsed around [my computer] for awhile, looking through endlessly scrolling directories of files to see if anything was obviously amiss. On the surface, everything appeared normal, so it was unlikely this was a mere prankster's break-in. As the altering of our log files had indicated, somebody was trying to cover his tracks. (Shimomura and Markoff 1996)

In short, we use similarities and differences between cases to draw generalizations and these generalizations lead to understanding.

Learning to reason in this case-based manner requires that we solve some cases.

> Learning in CBR occurs as a natural by-product of problem solving. When a problem is successfully solved, the experience is retained in order to solve similar problems in the future. When an attempt to solve a problem fails, the reason for the failure is identified and remembered in order to avoid the same mistake in the future. (Aamodt and Plaza 1994)

Additionally, cased-based reasoning proposes a method of choosing and arranging instructional cases in a way that helps individuals make generalizations and thus understand important aspects of what is being taught. In simple terms, the theory suggests that people arrange cases in categories and themes and that educators can arrange instructional cases in a way that roughly mirrors how learners might organize the cases in their minds. For example, all cases that involve e-mail as evidence would be grouped together in one category and all cases that involve breaking into computer systems would be grouped together in another category. Cases that involve similar themes like "neglecting to look through all of the available evidence can result in missing key evidence" will be linked together in a theme. This case organization is shown in Table A.1.

	CATEGORY 1 E-mail evidence	**CATEGORY 2** Computer intrusions
Theme 1 Neglecting to look through all of the available information in a case can result in missing key evidence	*E-mail rape case* Did not search through all of suspect's e-mail initially and therefore missed messages to other victims	*Boastful hacker case* Did not search the Internet initially and therefore missed IRC boastful messages posted by the hacker
Theme 2 A single perpetrator can be linked to two or more seemingly unrelated cases using the perpetrator's behavior	*E-mail harassment case* E-mail in a stalking case contained verbal behavior that linked it to another, seemingly unrelated harassment case	*Habitual hacker* A hacker who breaks into completely unrelated computers exhibits the same behavior in all instances

Table A.1

A tabular interpretation of the relationship between categories and themes as described in case-based reasoning.

Cases in this work are chosen and arranged to emphasize important categories and themes. The hope is that this will help students build and reinforce important categories and themes, ultimately leading to a good understanding of digital evidence and cybercrime.

PRACTICE MAKES PERFECT

The ultimate goal of this work is to have learners transfer their newly acquired knowledge from an instructional context into their lives and work. Research indicates that practicing skills in a variety of contexts is the key to knowledge transfer.

> as students learn to apply skills to more diverse problems and problem situations, their strategies become freed from their contextual bindings (or perhaps more accurately, acquire a richer net of contextual associations) and thus are more readily available for use with unfamiliar or novel problems. (Collins *et al.* 1989)

In other words, practicing the same skills in a variety of cases helps students to abstract or generalize what they have learned, and apply the skills in new and innovative ways. Therefore, this work chooses cases that build on one another, giving students the opportunity to reuse skills they have acquired in previous cases. The hope here is that individuals will eventually be able to take the skills that they learn here and apply them to actual cases they encounter.

EXPERT GUIDANCE

Careful choice and arrangement of cases is necessary, but not sufficient, for teaching students to make appropriate case comparisons and generalizations. Improper case comparisons often arise when individuals are given too little information and guidance. For example, investigators in Arkansas encountered an horrific homicide and incorrectly concluded that it was a satanic ritual killing. Apparently, when investigators encountered the crime scene, the only similar experience that they could recall was satanic ritual killing, and because they did not rely on evidence or expert guidance, they made an incorrect case comparison.

So, it is crucial to provide learners with useful information and expert guidance to help them make appropriate case comparisons. This is especially true in a complex domain like digital evidence and cybercrime, when acquisition of relevant knowledge and skills is not a simple matter. In the words of the pioneers in situated cognition (Brown *et al.* 1989), we learn best when we learn "to use the tools as practitioners use them." This is where the teaching strategy called *cognitive apprenticeship* (Collins *et al.* 1989) becomes useful.

In cognitive apprenticeship the expert first gives students an overview of what they will be learning. Ideally, this overview will give students a mental model of the domain they can use to piece together information as they learn. The expert then demonstrates how to perform certain tasks, giving students a conceptual model of the task. As the instruction progresses, the tasks become increasingly demanding, leading the student into the culture of expert practice. Students try each task themselves with some coaching from the expert. The expert gradually reduces the coaching, ultimately leaving the students to perform the tasks on their own. Students are encouraged to share understanding with each other and to explore, reflect upon, and articulate ideas throughout the learning process.

Although this is not the place to describe the cognitive apprenticeship framework in full, no description of cognitive apprenticeship would be complete without a mention of scaffolding. Scaffolding is a catch-all term for anything that supports learning – like directing a student's focus, or hiding complexity. One of the strongest examples of scaffolding is to provide students with a partially completed problem so that they do not have to perform every step in the solution. Over time, scaffolding is removed so students learn to perform all of the tasks necessary to solve a given problem.

Choosing cases and presenting them in a way that takes into consideration all of the CBR research is a major undertaking. Fortunately, a powerful instructional model called *goal-based scenarios* (GBS) (Schank *et al.* 1994; Schank 1994a; 1994b) cleverly combines cognitive apprenticeship with what is known about case-based instruction to make it easier to create effective, case-based, learning environments.

INVESTIGATE AND DECIDE LEARNING ENVIRONMENT

The *Investigate and Decide Learning Environment* (IDLE) (Bell 1996; 1998) is an implementation of the goal-based scenarios model that was specifically developed for teaching investigative domains. The relationship between cognitive apprenticeship, case-based reasoning, goal-based scenarios and IDLE is roughly depicted in Figure A.2.

One powerful aspect of the IDLE model that is easy to overlook is the use of expert questioning. Throughout any implementation of the IDLE model, the investigator should be given a set of questions to ask an expert about the current situation. For example, an evidence screen containing an e-mail header might allow the investigator to ask three questions: What is an e-mail header? How do I read an e-mail header? How do I view my own e-mail headers? Responses to these questions can be in any form (e.g. a video clip of talking head; an animated demonstration; direct communication with an expert) but should be appropriate to the message being conveyed.

By providing the investigator with pre-specified questions to ask experts, three things are achieved. First, the question itself gives the investigator an example or model of what sorts of questions to ask at a given point, giving a

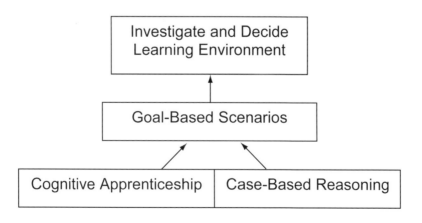

Figure A.2

The relationship between cognitive apprenticeship, case-based reasoning, goal-based scenarios and IDLE.

simplified model of expert problem-solving strategies. Secondly, the questions act as scaffolding by constraining the complexity of the situation and thus making it easier for the student to make decisions and achieve goals. Thirdly, the questions lead to expert modeling that will help the student learn necessary skills.

In this work, directed questions lead to expert modeling – demonstrations of skills that are related to the situation at hand. This expert modeling is one of the most important parts of the learning environment because it helps the investigator understand and develop expert practices. To encourage the investigator to utilize this expert advice they are asked questions about the evidence on each screen. These evaluation questions also help the investigator make decisions during the investigations and enable this learning environment to address any misunderstandings immediately. Answers to these incremental questions are collated in a final report that the investigator must complete in the Communication phase of each case.

The part of the IDLE model that is not well suited to computer automation is the final Wrap-up phase. Evaluating comprehension and addressing misunderstandings in complicated domains like digital evidence and cybercrime is complex and depends on the individual – different individuals have different needs and questions. However, computers can play a role in the Wrap-up phase. When used strategically, online discussion forums are excellent educational aides, enabling instructors to evaluate their students' comprehension of a subject and address problems and questions. Also, in an online discussion forum, students can collaborate to solve a case, sharing ideas and information, ultimately learning from each other.

SHORTCOMINGS OF THE IDLE MODEL

The IDLE model has several shortcomings that are important to mention and address. Firstly, the model does not consider the importance of choosing and structuring multiple case scenarios in a way that helps students develop appropriate categories and themes. Secondly, the IDLE model does not take into account the importance of arranging cases in a way that enables learners to practice skills in a variety of contexts, thus abstracting the knowledge and transferring it to new situations. Thirdly, the IDLE model does not acknowledge the importance of students learning from each other. This work compensates for these shortcomings by implementing aspects of cognitive apprenticeship and case-based reasoning that are not included in the IDLE model such as collaborative learning, case categories and themes, and practicing skills in diverse contexts.

DESIGN DETAILS

Initially, a student chooses between the Introduction, Cases and Reference modes (Norman 1993) as shown in Figure A.3.

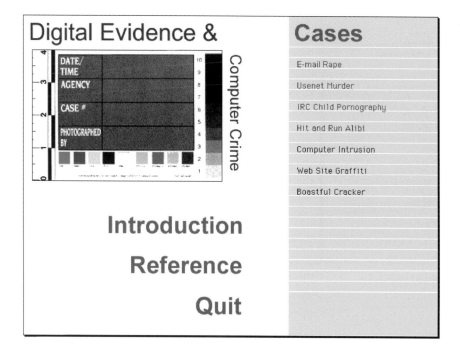

Figure A.3

The Main screen gives the investigator the initial choice of what part of the environment to access.

The Introduction orients the student by describing the main topics, giving some examples of cases and providing definitions of key terms. The Reference mode provides an index of topics to enable the student to jump to a specific topic of interest without going through an entire case. The Cases mode launches directly into the cases, casting the student as the investigator. In Cases mode, the investigator can choose from a list of cases.

When the investigator chooses a case, the Mission screen appears (see Figure A.4 on page 252 for example). The Mission screen performs the actions described in the Problem phase of the IDLE model. For each case, the problem is defined and the direction and goal(s) are set using a combination of text, audio and video or animation.

The other folders available from the Mission screen are: Crime Scene, Victim, Suspect and Report. The Crime Scene, Victim and Suspect screens implement the Do phase of the IDLE model, making up the body of each case and mirroring Locard's Exchange Principle described in Chapter 1. The contents of the Crime Scene, Victim and Suspect screens will be determined on a case-by-case basis. Together, these screens will show all evidence related to the crime scene, victim and suspect. In most cases the

Figure A.4

The Mission screen presents the case to be solved and helps the investigator get started.

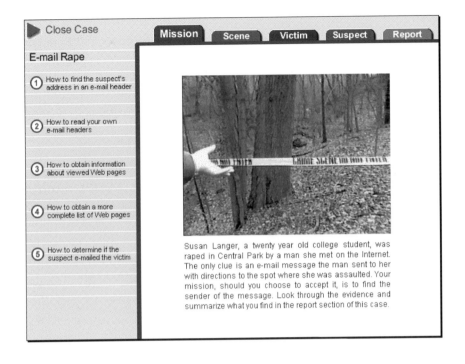

Figure A.5

In the Do phase, the investigator is presented with evidence related to the crime scene, victim, and suspect.

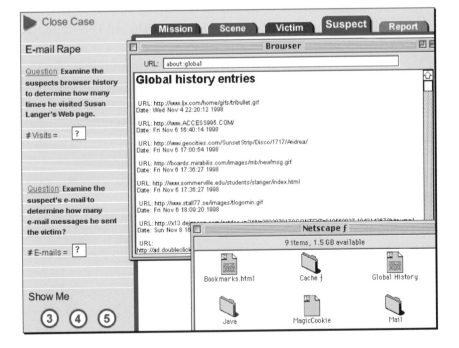

investigator will be expected to collect, examine and obtain some meaningful results from the evidence. Expert advice is presented at key points in the form of leading questions. For example, if the evidence is an e-mail header, clicking the "How do I read an e-mail header?" button leads to a demonstration of how an e-mail header is created and how it can be deciphered.

On each Crime Scene, Victim and Suspect screen, the investigator is required to provide information about the evidence found on that screen. This acts as an evaluation stage for each type of evidence. Although more advanced stages of the investigation can be accessed even with incorrect information, the investigator is notified immediately when the information is incorrect (see Figure A.5).

The Report screen implements the Communication phase of the IDLE model by summarizing all of the findings in a given case (see Figure A.6 for example). If the investigator answers the questions related to each piece of evidence, the information is automatically entered in the report. It is possible for the investigator to go directly to the Report screen without examining evidence but it is unlikely that the investigator will be able to complete the report correctly. Once the report is complete, expert advice is available to help the investigator interpret the results, reach conclusions and develop important categories and themes for each case.

If the conclusions are uninformed, the flaws are presented to the

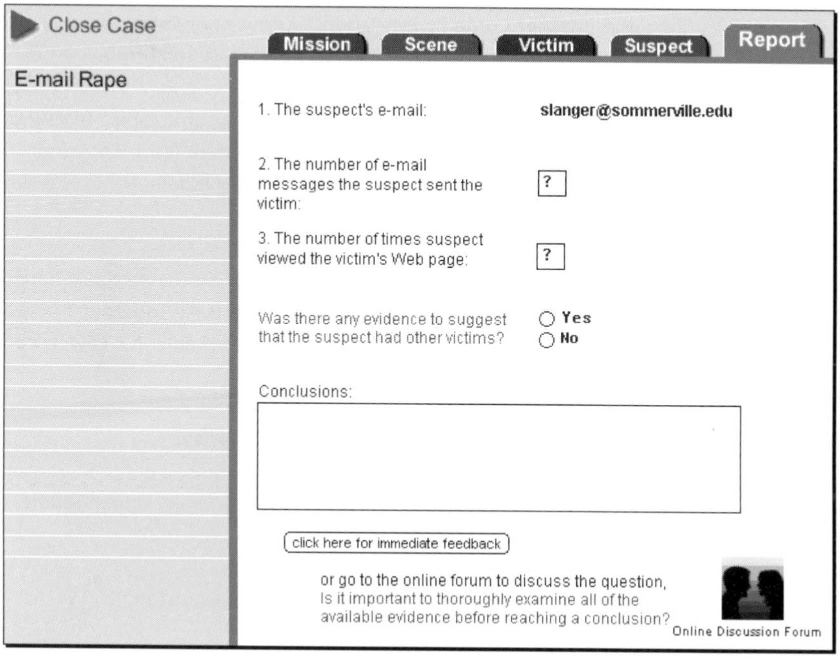

Figure A.6

Evidence is collated on the Report screen and the investigator is encouraged to make some conclusions about the case.

investigator. When the investigator is satisfied with his/her conclusions, or has questions about the case, he/she can log into an online discussion forum (from anywhere in the world) to convene with other investigators. This collaboration helps investigators Wrap-up and reflect upon their findings.

REFERENCES

Aamodt, A. and Plaza, E. (1994) "Case-Based Reasoning: Foundational Issues, Methodological Variations, and System Approaches," *AICom – Artificial Intelligence Communications*, 7 (1).

Bell, B. L. (1996) *A Special-purpose Architecture for the Design of Educational Software*, Tech. Rep. No. 70, Evanston, IL: Northwestern University, The Institute for the Learning Sciences.

Bell, B. L. (1998) *Investigate and Decide Learning Environments: Specializing Task Models for Authoring Tool Design.*

Brown, J. S., Collins, A. and Duguid, P. (1989) "Situated Cognition and the Culture of Learning," *Educational Researcher* 18(1): 32–42.

Carter, D. L. and Katz, A. J. (1996) "Cybercrime: An Emerging Challenge for Law Enforcement," *FBI Law Enforcement Bulletin*, available on the World Wide Web (http://www.fbi.gov/leb/dec961.txt).

Casey, E. (1997) "Using Case-Based Reasoning and Cognitive Apprenticeship to Teach Criminal Profiling and Internet Crime Investigation," *Knowledge Solutions*, available on the World Wide Web (http://www.corpus-delicti.com/case_based.html).

Collins, A., Brown, J. S. and Newman, S. E. (1989) "Cognitive Apprenticeship: Teaching the Crafts of Reading Writing and Mathematics," in L. B. Resnick (ed.), *Knowing, Learning, and Instruction: Essays in Honor of Robert Glaser*, Hillsdale, NJ: Lawrence Erlbaum Associates, pp. 140–85.

Kolodner, J. (1994) "From Natural Language Understanding to Case-Based Reasoning and Beyond: A Perspective on the Cognitive Model That Ties It All Together," in R. C. Schank (ed.), *Beliefs, Reasoning and Decision Making*, Hillsdale, NJ: Lawrence Erlbaum Associates, pp. 55–110.

Norman, Donald (1993) *Things that Make Us Smart*, Addison-Wesley.

Saferstein, R. (1998) *Criminalistics: An Introduction to Forensic Science*, Upper Saddle River, NJ: Prentice-Hall, Inc.

Schank, R. C. (1990). *Tell Me a Story: Narrative and Intelligence*, Evanston, IL: Northwestern University Press.

Schank, R. C. (1994a) "Goal-Based Scenarios: A Radical Look at Education," *The Journal of Learning Sciences*, 3: 429–53.

Schank, R. C. (1994b) "Goal-Based Scenarios," in R. C. Schank (ed.), *Beliefs, Reasoning and Decision Making*, Hillsdale, NJ: Lawrence Erlbaum Associates, pp. 55–110.

Schank, R. C. and Abelson, R. (1977) *Scripts, Plans, Goals and Understanding*, Hillsdale, NJ: Lawrence Erlbaum Associates.

Schank, R. C., Fano, A., Bell, B. and Jona, M. (1994) "The Design of Goal-Based Scenarios," *The Journal of Learning Sciences*, 3: 305–45.

Shimomura, T. and Markoff, J. (1996) *Takedown*, New York: Hyperion.

Anger excitation (AKA sadistic) behaviors: These include behaviors that evidence offender sexual gratification from victim pain and suffering. The primary motivation for the behavior is sexual, however the sexual expression for the offender is manifested in physical aggression, or torture behavior, toward the victim.

Anger retaliatory (AKA anger or displaced) behaviors: These include offender behaviors that are expressions of rage, either towards a specific person, group, institution, or a symbol of either. The primary motivation for the behavior is the perception that one has been wronged or injured somehow.

Application: Software that performs a specific function or gives individuals access to Internet/network services.

Application layer: Provides the interface between people and networks, allowing us to exchange e-mail, view Web pages, and utilize many other network services.

ARCNET (Attached Resource Computer Network): One of the earliest local area networking technologies initially developed by Datapoint Corporation in 1977. Uses 93-ohm RG62 coaxial cable to connect computers. Early versions enabled computers to communicate at 2.5 Mbps. A newer, more versatile version called ARCNET Plus, supports 20 Mbps throughput.

ARP (Address Resolution Protocol): A protocol in the TCP/IP suite that is used to dynamically associate network layer IP addresses with data-link layer MAC addresses.

ATM (Asynchronous Transfer Mode): A connection-oriented network technology that provides gigabit-per-second throughput. This high-performance network technology can transport high-quality video, voice and data.

Behavioral evidence: Any type of forensic evidence that is representative or suggestive of behavior.

Behavioral evidence analysis: The process of examining forensic evidence, victimology, and crime scene characteristics for behavioral convergences before rendering a deductive criminal profile.

Behavior-motivational typology: A motivational typology that infers the motivation (i.e. anger-retaliatory, assertive, reassurance, sadistic, profit, and precautionary) of behavior from the convergence of other concurrent behaviors. Single behaviors can be described by more than one motivational category, as they are by no means exclusive of each other.

Broad targeting: Any fire or an explosive that is designed to inflict damage in a wide-reaching fashion. In cases involving broad targeting, there may be an intended target near the point of origin, but it may also be designed to reach beyond that primary target for other victims in the environment.

Bulletin board system (BBS): An application that can run on a personal computer enabling people to connect to the computer using a modem and participate in discussions, exchange e-mail and transfer files. These are not part of the Internet.

Collateral victims: Those victims that an offender causes to suffer loss, harm, injury or death (usually by virtue of proximity), in the pursuit of another victim.

Computer cracker: Individuals who break into computers much like safe crackers break into safes. They find weak points and exploit them using specialized tools and techniques.

Computer crime: As defined in Federal and State Statutes. Includes theft of computer services; unauthorized access to protected computers; software piracy and the alteration or theft of electronically stored information; extortion committed with the assistance of computers; obtaining unauthorized access to records from banks, credit card issuers or customer reporting agencies; traffic in stolen passwords and transmission of destructive viruses or commands.

Corpus delicti: Literally interpreted as meaning the "body of the crime;" refers to those essential facts that show a crime has taken place.

Crime reconstruction: The determination of the actions surrounding the commission of a crime. This may be done by using the statements of witnesses, the confession of the suspect, the statement of the living victim, or by the examination and interpretation of the physical evidence. Some refer to this process as crime scene reconstruction, however the scene is not being put back together in a rebuilding process, it is only the actions that are being reconstructed.

Crime scene: A location where a criminal act has taken place.

Crime scene characteristics: The discrete physical and behavioral features of a crime scene.

Crime scene type: The nature of the relationship between offender behavior and the crime scene in the context of an entire criminal event (i.e. point of contact, primary scene, secondary scene, intermediate scene, or disposal site).

Cybercrime: Any offense where the *modus operandi* or signature involves the use of a computer network in any way.

Cyberspace: William Gibson coined this term in his 1984 novel *Neuromancer*. It refers to the connections and conceptual locations created using computer networks. It has become synonymous with the Internet in everyday usage.

Cyberstalking: The use of computer networks for stalking and harassment behaviors. Many offenders combine their online activities with more traditional forms of stalking and harassment such as telephoning the victim and going to the victim's home.

Cybertrail: Any convergence of digital evidence that is left behind by a victim or an offender. Used to infer behavioral patterns.

Data-link layer: Provides reliable transit of data across a physical link using a network technology such as Ethernet. Encapsulates data into frames or cells before sending it and enables multiple computers to share a single physical medium using a media access control method like CSMA/CD.

Digital evidence: Encompasses any and all digital data that can establish that a crime has been committed or can provide a link between a crime and its victim or a crime and its perpetrator.

E-mail, or email: A service that enables people to send electronic messages to each other.

Equivocal forensic analysis: A review of the entire body of physical evidence in a given case that questions all related assumptions and conclusions. The purpose of the equivocal forensic analysis is to maximize the exploitation of physical evidence to accurately inform the reconstruction of specific crime scene behaviors.

Ethernet: A local area networking technology initially developed at the Xerox Corporation in the late 1970s. In 1980, Xerox, Digital Equipment Corporation, and Intel Corporation published the original 10 Mbps Ethernet specifications that were later developed by the Institute of Electrical and Electronic Engineers (IEEE) into the IEEE 802.3 Ethernet Standard that is widely used today. Ethernet uses CSMA/CD technology to control access to the physical medium (Ethernet cables).

FDDI (Fiber Distribution Data Interface): A token ring network technology that uses fiber optic cables to transmit data by encoding it in pulses of light. FDDI supports a data rate of 100 Mbps and uses a backup fiber optic ring that enables hosts to communicate even if a host on the network goes down.

Hardware: The physical components of a computer.

High risk victim: An individual whose personal, professional and social life continuously exposes them to the danger of suffering harm or loss.

Host: A computer connected to a network.

ICQ ("I Seek You"): An Internet service that enables individuals to convene online in a variety of ways (text chat, voice, message boards). This service also enables file transfer and e-mail exchanges.

Internet: A global computer network linking smaller computer networks, that enable information sharing via common communication protocols. Information may be shared using electronic mail, newsgroups, the WWW, and synchronous chat. The Internet is not controlled or owned by a single country, group, organization or individual. Many privately owned networks are not a part of the Internet.

Internet/network service: A useful function supported by the Internet/network such as e-mail, the Web, Usenet, or IRC. Applications give individuals access to these useful functions.

Internet Service Provider, or ISP: Any company or organization that provides individuals with access to, or data storage on, the Internet.

Internet Relay Chat (IRC): An Internet service that enable individuals from around the world to convene and have synchronous (live) discussions. This service also enables individuals to exchange files and have private conversations. The primary networks that support this service are EFNet, Undernet, IRCnet, DALnet, SuperChat and NewNet.

Jurisdiction: The right of a court to make decisions regarding a specific person (personal jurisdiction) or a certain matter (subject matter jurisdiction).

Locard's Exchange Principle: The theory that anyone, or anything, entering a crime scene both takes something of the scene with them, and leaves something of themselves behind when they leave.

Low risk victim: An individual whose personal, professional and social life does not normally expose them to a possibility of suffering harm or loss.

Media Access Control (MAC) address: A unique number that is assigned to a Network Interface Card and is used to address data at the data-link layer of a network.

Message digest: A combination of letters and numbers generated by special algorithms that take as input a digital object of any size. A file is input into a special algorithm to produce a sequence of letters and numbers that is like a digital fingerprint for that file. A good algorithm will produce a unique number for every unique file (two copies of the same file have the same message digest).

Method of approach: A term that refers to the offender's strategy for getting close to a victim.

Modem (see Modulator/demodulator): A piece of equipment that is used to connect computers together using a serial line (usually a telephone line). This piece of equipment converts digital data into an analog signal (modulation) and demodulates an analog signal into digits that a computer can process.

Modus operandi: *Modus operandi* (MO) is a Latin term that means, "a method of operating." It refers to the behaviors that are committed by an offender for the purpose of successfully completing an offense. An offender's *modus operandi* reflects how an offender committed their crimes. It is separate from the offender's motives, or signature aspects.

Motive: The emotional, psychological or material need that impels, and is satisfied by, a behavior.

Motivational typology: Any classification system based on the general emotional, psychological or material need that is satisfied by an offense or act.

Narrow targeting: Any fire or explosive that is designed to inflict specific, focused, calculated amounts of damage to a specific target.

Network Interface Card (NIC): A piece of hardware used to connect a host to the network. Every host must have at least one network interface card. Every NIC is assigned a number called a Media Access Control (MAC) address.

Network layer: Addresses and routes information to its destination using addresses, much like a postal service that delivers letters based on the address on the envelope.

Newsgroups: The online equivalent of public bulletin boards, enabling asynchronous communication that often resembles a discussion.

Physical Evidence: Any physical object that can establish that a crime has been committed or can provide a link between a crime and its victim or a crime and its perpetrator.

Physical layer: The actual media that carries data (e.g. telephone wires, fiber optic cables, satellite transmissions). This layer is not concerned with what is being transported but without it, there would be no connection between computers.

Point of contact: The location where the offender first approaches or acquires a victim.

Point of origin: The specific location at which a fire is ignited, or the specific location where a device is placed and subsequently detonated.

Port: A number that TCP/IP uses to identify Internet services/application. For example, TCP/IP e-mail applications use port 25 and Usenet applications use port 119.

Power assertive (AKA entitlement) behaviors: These include offender behaviors that are intended to restore the offender's self-confidence or self-worth through the use of moderate to high aggression means. These behaviors suggest an underlying lack of confidence and a sense of personal inadequacy, that are expressed through control, mastery and humiliation of the victim, while demonstrating the offender's sense of authority.

Power reassurance (AKA compensatory) behaviors: These include offender behaviors that are intended to restore the offender's self-confidence or self-worth through the use of low aggression or even passive and self-deprecating means. These behaviors suggest an underlying lack of confidence and a sense of personal inadequacy.

Presentation layer: Formats and converts data to meet the conventions of the specific computer being used.

Primary scene: The location where the offender engaged in the majority of their attack or assault upon their victim or victims.

Router: A host connected to two or more networks that can send network messages from one network (e.g. an Ethernet network) to another (e.g. an ATM network) provided the networks are using the same network protocol (e.g. TCP/IP).

Search engine: A database of Internet resources that can be explored using key words and phrases. Search results provide direct links to information.

Secondary scene: Any location where there may be evidence of criminal activity outside of the primary scene.

Session layer: Coordinates dialog between computers, establishing, maintaining, managing and terminating communications.

Signature aspects: The emotional or psychological themes or needs that an offender satisfies when they commit offense behaviors.

Signature behaviors: Signature behaviors are those acts committed by an offender that are not necessary to complete the offense. Their convergence can be used to suggest an offender's psychological or emotional needs (signature aspect). They are best understood as a reflection of the underlying personality, lifestyle and developmental experiences of an offender.

Software: Computer programs that perform some function.

Souvenir: A souvenir is a personal item taken from a victim or a crime scene by an offender that serves as a reminder or token of remembrance, representing a pleasant experience. Taking souvenirs is associated with reassurance oriented behavior and needs.

Symbol: Any item, person or group that represents something else such as an idea, a belief, a group or even another person.

Synchronous chat networks: By connecting to a synchronous chat network via the Internet, individuals can interact in real-time using text, audio, video and more. Most synchronous chat networks are comprised of chat rooms, sometimes called channels, where people with similar interests gather.

Target: The object of an attack from the offender's point of view.

TCP/IP: A collection of internetworking protocols including the Transport Control Protocol (TCP), the User Datagram Protocol (UDP), the Internet Protocol (IP), and the Address Resolution Protocol (ARP).

Transport layer: Responsible for managing the delivery of data over a network.

Trophy: A personal item taken from a victim or crime scene by an offender that is a symbol of victory, achievement or conquest. Often associated with assertive-oriented behavior.

Usenet (User's Network): A global system of newsgroups that enables people around the world to post messages to the equivalent of an online bulletin board.

Victimology: A thorough study of all available victim information. This includes items such as sex, age, height, weight, family, friends, acquaintances, education, employment, residence and neighborhood. This also includes background information on the lifestyle of the victim such as personal habits, hobbies and medical histories.

World Wide Web (WWW or Web): A service on the Internet providing individual users with access to a broad range of resources, including e-mail, newsgroups and multimedia (images, text, sound, etc.).

ForensiX

ForensiX is a new digital forensics examination system from *Fred Cohen & Associates. ForensiX* is a Linux-based graphical interface and software system designed to facilitate efficient and properly documented imaging, examination, and analysis of digital forensic data, including:

> IP traffic and Internet site analysis
> Floppy Disks
> Hard Disks (IDE, SCSI)
> CD-ROMs
> PCMCIA cards
> Many other devices

ForensiX works on raw images as well as mounted file systems:

> Windows, NT, and DOS
> Unix, Linux, and related environments
> MacIntosh
> PalmOS and other PDAs
> Images up to 16 Tera bytes

Other features include:

- Automatic documentation of actions
- Replay of the forensic analysis process
- "Just Don't Look Right" analysis
- File type identification by content
- "Hashkeeper" searches
- Automatic display of graphical images
- Known but deleted file searches
- Tracing IP connections
- IP analysis and session extraction
- Decoding proxy UIDs and passwords
- Forensic system integrity checking
- MD5 checksums of images and files
- Easy to use graphical interface
- Audio/visual training on the CD
- Sample analysis files included
- Image to tape, CD-W, Disk, and file

And many other features too extensive to list here.
Read the *ForensiX* manual on-line at all.net
For further information, visit *http://all.net*
Or email to fc@all.net